"A wonderful story of love, forgiveness, and stewardship over the world God has given us. I'm looking forward to more stories from Karen Ball!"

—FRANCINE RIVERS

"Karen Ball writes with a gifted pen. Reunion is brimming with God's loving spirit, Karen's marvelous zest for life, and a page-turning story of two very special people who discover the meaning of true love. Definitely a keeper!"

—LORI COPELAND

"To paraphrase a proverb: 'There are three things which are too wonderful for me, four which I do not understand: the way of an eagle in the sky, the song of a wolf in the night, the way of a horse on a mountain trail, and the way of a man with a maid.' They're all here, within this book. Experience the wonder for yourself!"

—ANGELA ELWELL HUNT

"Move over, romance writers—there's a new kid on the block! Karen Ball has come up with a barn-burner of a romance!"

—GILBERT MORRIS

Taylor laughed. "I'd be a good case for an angel to cut his wings on, wouldn't I?"

"You'd definitely be a challenge." His eyes twinkled. "But a delightful one."

She was surprised—and a bit disturbed—at how good his comment made her feel.

"Well—" he stepped back—"I'd better get some rest. My boss is a regular slave driver. Believes in starting the day at the most unearthly hour."

She grinned. "Terrible the things a working man has to suffer."

"Indeed. But it's really not all that bad."

"Oh?"

"Nope…" His gaze roamed her face. "It's not bad at all." He reached out a finger to tilt her chin. "Because this particular boss has the most amazing…" He lowered his head, his warm breath fanning her face.

Taylor's breath caught in her throat, and she was sure her heart had stopped beating. He was going to kiss her. She was sure of it.

"…cook," he finished, pressing his lips, with feather softness, to her forehead. Then he stepped back, walked to the door, and left.

Shaking herself free from Connor's spell, she laughed lightly. *I wonder…* She glanced after him. *I wonder if guardian angels are tall and broad shouldered and have smiles that can melt your insides?*

♛♡*Palisades Pure Romance*

$\mathcal{R}$EUNION

$\mathcal{K}$AREN $\mathcal{B}$ALL

Palisades is a division of Multnomah Publishers, Inc.

This is a work of fiction. The characters, incidents, and dialogues are products of the author's imagination and are not to be construed as real. Any resemblance to actual events or persons, living or dead, is entirely coincidental.

REUNION
published by Palisades
a division of Multnomah Publishers, Inc.

© 1996, 1999 by Karen Ball
International Standard Book Number: 1-57673-597-4

Cover illustration by Aleta Jenks
Cover photo of wolf by Photodisc
Cover design by Ann Gjeldum

Scripture quotations are from *The Holy Bible,* New International Version (NIV)
© 1973, 1984 by International Bible Society,
used by permission of Zondervan Publishing House
Also quoted: *New American Standard Bible* (NASB)
© 1960, 1977 by the Lockman Foundation

Palisades is a trademark of Multnomah Publishers, Inc., and is registered in the U.S. Patent and Trademark Office.

Printed in the United States of America

For information:
MULTNOMAH PUBLISHERS, INC.•P.O. BOX 1720•SISTERS, OREGON 97759

Library of Congress Cataloging-in-Publication Data:
Ball, Karen, 1957
  Reunion / Karen M. Ball.
    p. cm.
  ISBN 1-57673-597-4 (alk. paper)
  I. Title.
PS3552.A4553 R4 1999
813'.54—dc21   99-22189
                                                          CIP

99 00 01 02 03 04 05 — 10 9 8 7 6 5 4 3 2 1

To Mom and Dad—
You taught me to love and respect the beautiful world
God gave us—and you endured my owning nearly
every kind of four-legged creature
(and a few feathered ones)
known to man! I love you.

To Angie, Frani, Gil, and Johnnie—
You've been telling me for years to get
out there and write.
So this is all your fault!
I'm grateful to each of you for your encouragement,
guidance, and instruction—
but most of all for your friendship.

*Speak up for those who cannot speak
for themselves....
Speak up and judge fairly.*

PROVERBS 31:8–9 (NIV)

PROLOGUE

November

THE LAST THING ON JOSH'S MIND THAT MORNING WAS DEATH.

He was too in love with life. He had a wife he adored and a life that challenged and delighted him.

So when he stepped out of his tent on that cold autumn day and drew in a deep breath of the clean, cold mountain air he loved, there was only one thing on his mind: having as much fun as possible. After all, this was the last day of his annual week-long camping trip with the boys from church, and he always did his best to end things with a bang.

And nothing livened up a day like a trust walk.

Josh studied his charges as they gathered in the clearing. Varying in age from twelve to eighteen, they'd all piled out of their tents, dressed in flannel shirts, jeans, and hiking boots, ready to take on the wilds of a Wyoming mountain.

"Do we have to be blindfolded?" whined Eric, one of the younger boys, scanning the rough terrain and woods around them. Eric's family had moved to Wyoming less than a year ago, and the boy was still getting used to the rugged wilderness surrounding them.

"'Course you do!" Josh grinned at this quick response from Mike—one of the juniors—who added emphasis by tapping the bill of Eric's baseball cap. "That's what makes this so much fun."

"But—"

"Don't worry, kid." Mike slung his arm around the smaller boy's slender shoulders. "I'll be there to make sure you survive."

Noting the uncertain look on the boy's face, Josh decided it was time to step in. "You'll be okay, Eric." He smiled as he handed the boy one of the strips of cloth they used for blindfolds. "You might even have fun."

Josh was grateful that he had two seniors and a junior to help him oversee the trust walk this year. The younger boys were a good group, but they could be a handful.

As he scanned the eager faces before him, Josh felt a surge of pride. These boys were ready to face the challenges waiting for them. They were all strong, physically and spiritually, and Josh was pleased that he'd had something to do with that.

"Who are you gonna go with, Brad?"

At Eric's question, Josh's sense of satisfaction dimmed a bit. Well, almost all of them.

Tall and athletic, Brad Momadey was the kind of young man who drew attention. There was something about the way he stood and walked, the look in his brooding dark eyes, the remote yet kind way he treated others. Everything about the boy spoke confidence and dignity and gave an impression of underlying strength and intelligence. He was a natural leader and, for the most part, perceptive and considerate. Though Brad always held himself apart, Josh had never seen him treat the other youth group members with condescension or disdain. From all Josh had seen, Brad treated even the youngest or nerdiest kid with respect.

Too bad he can't extend that respect to Jim and me. All Josh or Jim Wilson, the youth pastor, had to do was say white and Brad would respond with a resounding black. The young man had made it abundantly clear he wanted nothing to do with either of them.

Or with their God.

Taylor, Josh's wife, had helped him understand the situation a little better.

"Brad's Native American heritage goes deep." She was part Ojibwa herself. "He knows the importance of honoring his elders"—she grinned at his incredulous look—"his *tribal* elders. He's loyal to those in authority who are of his world"—her cheeky grin peeked out again—"and indifferent to those who aren't."

Watching Brad now as he leaned against the tall trunk of an evergreen, his arms crossed over his chest, that slightly mocking light in his dark eyes, Josh knew Taylor had been right on target. Bradson Momadey respected and loved his parents and did his best to

9

honor them—which was the main reason he came to the youth group at all.

Brad's only response to Eric's question was a casual shrug. Josh sighed and turned his attention to his eager charges.

"Okay, guys, line up and let's count off."

He'd already explained how the hike worked. One person was blindfolded and led by the others for ten minutes. Then the team members would switch places. Rendezvous was in twenty minutes. The idea was to learn both to rely on each other and to take care of each other, making sure everyone stayed out of trouble.

"Okay, remember, we meet back here in twenty minutes, so you older guys keep an eye on your watches. And one final caution: make sure your team sticks to the path. It's been pretty warm lately, and the higher temps have caused some thawing. There are a lot of places that look safe but aren't. Any questions?" When none were forthcoming, Josh inclined his head. "Okay, seniors and juniors, pick a team to follow."

Each of the older boys moved to stand next to one of the pairs—except Brad. He didn't budge. He just stood there, leaning against the tree with casual disinterest.

"We get Brad!" This pronouncement came from Billy, a sturdy sixth-grader, who grabbed his partner, the hesitant Eric, and hauled him over to stand next to the senior.

Josh was pleased he managed to hold back his grin.

Now there's an interesting team. Eric, who's scared of his shadow out here, and Billy, who's not scared of anything. Those two would drive Brad crazy. If that wasn't poetic justice, he didn't know what was.

"All set?" Josh said. "Go to it!"

The group exploded into activity. Each of the teams was off and running—even Eric and Billy, except they didn't exactly explode into action. Rather, they launched into a heated debate over who would wear the blindfold first. From his nearby leaning post, Brad watched the two kids push the cotton cloth back and forth between them.

Of course, Josh hadn't expected Brad to intervene. Not really. He was a law unto himself, though Josh gave him credit that he wasn't blatantly defiant or disobedient. He would simply listen as Jim or Josh talked, wait until everyone else was involved in his or her activity, then go his own way. Quietly. And alone.

Several times Jim had come close to asking Brad to leave the youth group, but Josh always talked him out of it.

"The kid needs someplace to belong. Someplace where he'll hear truth, even if he doesn't seem to respond." Reluctantly, Jim had agreed. But with graduation around the corner, Brad's time with the group was coming to an end.

What's it going to take to reach this kid, Lord? Josh shook his head. He'd asked the question more times than he could count. With a sigh, he walked over to Brad. "Well, looks like you've got quite a job here with these two."

Brad didn't budge. His dark gaze raked Josh with disdain.

There's got to be a way to get through to him, Lord! The memory of the morning he'd left for this trip ran through his mind. He'd held Taylor close and kissed her good-bye.

"Pray for me." He'd rested his chin on the top of her head, inhaling the sweet fragrance of her hair. "I have a feeling something incredible is going to happen on this trip. Something Brad won't be able to resist."

"Something other than your boyish charm and disarming sincerity?"

The image of her laughing eyes and sweet face lifted his sagging spirits. Even after nearly eight years, he could scarcely believe God had blessed him with such a wife. Their parting that morning had been bittersweet. She'd seemed uncertain, worried. So he held her close, kissed her, and promised her, "I'll miss you. I'll see you soon."

He felt a smile lift his lips. Taylor's love and belief in him always made him feel he could do anything, overcome any obstacle—even the solid steel walls Brad seemed to have erected around his heart. He looked at the boy's bored face. "You know it would only take a word from you, and they'd stop fighting."

Josh watched the mocking light deepen in Brad's eyes.

"Hey, they're not *my* responsibility."

"Actually, I'm afraid they are." He met and held Brad's gaze.

Brad's defiance was almost palpable. "I don't *have* to do this."

"True enough. So go ahead. Whatever happens to these two is up to you. But I just want you to know I trust you."

With that Josh turned and headed for the path into the woods. As he reached the edge of the clearing, he tossed one last comment over his shoulder. "By the way, Jim and I have a bet on how long it takes."

Brad snorted. "For what?"

"For those two to drive you totally crazy." He turned and grinned at Brad. "I give them two minutes. Tops."

Brad watched Josh disappear down the path, then looked away. What a jerk. *"I just want you to know I trust you."* Like that mattered—

A loud wail interrupted Brad's thoughts, and he looked to see Billy sitting on top of Eric, trying to tie the blindfold on the smaller kid's head. With a disgusted sigh, Brad stepped forward, grabbed Billy by the back of the shirt, and lifted him off his victim.

"Hey!" Billy complained, and Brad let him go. The boy flopped on the ground in a pile next to his partner.

Both boys looked up at him angrily, but Brad held up his hand. "Just knock it off!"

They fell silent. Eric's lip started to tremble.

Oh no...not tears!

"Here." Brad quickly stepped toward Eric and extended a hand, pulling him up. "You go first, buddy. I'll make sure Billy leads you right. And since you've spent at least five minutes fighting, you'll only have five minutes to be blindfolded instead of ten. And that's no sweat. You'll be done in no time."

Eric took the blindfold, then looked up at Brad doubtfully. "You'll watch him? Close?" He glared at Billy. "Make sure he doesn't send me off a cliff?"

"Oh, right!" Billy shot back. "Like you could walk that far!"

Brad silenced the older boy with a look and put his hand on Eric's shoulder. "I'll watch him."

Eric put the blindfold over his eyes. Brad tied it at the back of his head.

"Okay, Billy. Move it out."

Five minutes later, Brad was bored out of his mind. He watched as Eric whipped off the blindfold with a triumphant grin and tossed it to Billy.

Brad leaned down to Eric, his lips close to the kid's ear. "Tell you what. You go ahead and lead Billy down the path. Do as good a job for him as he did for you. I'll head back to the clearing and let Josh know everything's okay."

A frown creased Eric's brow. "I thought you were supposed to stay with us."

"Just until you got the hang of things. Besides, you know the way back, right?"

Eric gave a slow nod. "Right."

"So no sweat." Brad thumped Eric on the back. "See you there."

Josh stood in the clearing, watching the teams straggle in and checking off names to be sure everyone was back. The boys were whooping and hollering, laughing as they took off their blindfolds, giving each other high fives.

Then he spotted Brad, leaning against a tree.

Alone.

Josh pushed away the sudden apprehension tugging at his gut. "Mike, have you seen Eric or Billy?"

The blue-eyed junior cast a quick glance over the group, then shrugged. "No, come to think of it, I haven't. I thought Brad was with them."

"Yeah, so did I." With a sigh Josh walked over to Brad.

"Where are the boys?" Josh tried to remain calm. Surely Brad hadn't left them alone in the woods.

Brad looked at him, his expression bored. "They're coming."

"What do you mean, 'they're coming'? Why aren't you with them?"

Brad stiffened. "Hey, I *told* you they weren't my responsibility."

"And *I* told you they were."

Before Brad could respond, Eric burst into the clearing, eyes wide, face pale.

"Josh! Josh, you gotta come! Quick!"

Josh pushed past the other boys who had swarmed around Eric. "What's happened? Where's Billy?"

Eric was gasping, as though he'd run for all he was worth to get back as fast as he could. "He—he's in trouble. He's on a ledge. I—I think he's gonna fall! I told him I'd come get you." He grabbed Josh's sleeve and pulled. "You gotta come! Now!"

"Mike, you and Brad stay here—"

"Brad's gone."

A quick look told Josh that Mike was right. "Okay, you stay here until Jim gets back. I'll send Eric back if I need more help." He didn't wait for a response. "Let's go, Eric." He broke into a run.

Brad raced down the path, his eyes narrowed, searching. Five minutes away from the clearing, he spotted two sets of tracks in the snow leading into the woods, away from the path.

"Stupid! Stupid, stupid kids!"

He followed the tracks, jumping brush and dodging low-hanging branches as he ran. He burst out of the woods and slammed to a halt. What he saw made his blood run cold.

He stood at the edge of a steep drop-off. Below was

an icy slope, and at the bottom were huge scattered boulders. To his left was a narrow ledge that followed the mountainside. From what Brad could tell, the ledge, which was barely two feet wide, was primarily made of ice. And there, fifteen feet out on the ledge, was Billy, face pressed to the rocky mountainside, tears running down his red cheeks.

"Oh, man…" Brad breathed. "What have I done?"

Standing just behind Brad, Josh heard the young man's horrified whisper.

"Good question." He knew his voice was low and angry, but he didn't care. Brad spun around to face him. He'd been so focused on Billy, he hadn't heard Josh and Eric come up.

Josh stepped past Brad without giving him a chance to respond. "Billy." He kept his voice calm. "Billy, you hear me?"

The boy didn't answer. He just stood, shaking, plastering himself against the frozen mountain.

"I told him not to go there." Eric's voice was choked with tears. "But he said he could do it. He was just going to go out and come right back. But when he started to turn around, he got scared…"

Josh looked below the ledge, noting the ice and the boulders.

Now that would be a nasty fall. And a deadly one.

"I'm gonna get him." Brad started to move toward

the ledge, but Josh's hand shot out to grasp his sleeve.

"No!"

Brad turned on him. "It's my fault he's there! I'm going after him."

Josh held him fast. "Listen to me. I can't let you go out there, so forget it." When Brad moved to shake his hand off, Josh gripped him more firmly. His blue eyes locked with Brad's dark, angry gaze.

"You want to help?" Josh's voice was low. "Then stay here. Watch Eric and make sure he doesn't do anything stupid. And stay close to the edge."

Brad's eyes narrowed. "Close to the edge?"

Josh looked at Billy, studying the ledge he was perched on. "I'll do what I can to bring him back safely." His gaze swiveled back to Brad's. "But if I can't, if that ledge goes, I'll throw Billy your way. He's small. If we can get close enough, I should be able to get him to you. But I need you there to catch him."

Brad's eyes held Josh's for a moment, then gave a curt nod. "I'll be there."

Josh's grip on the boy's arms slackened. "Okay. Good." He let go and moved toward the ledge.

"What about you?" Brad's question was hoarse, almost desperate.

"I'll be okay."

"Yeah? You Superman or something?" Brad turned a meaningful glance to the boulders below.

If the situation hadn't been so critical, Josh would have laughed. He just shook his head. "No. Not hardly.

But I've got God with me. No matter what happens to me, I'll be with him. I know where I'm spending eternity." He stepped onto the ledge. "That's another reason I'm going out here and not you."

Brad was incredulous. "You're going out there because you don't think I'm going to heaven?"

"Not entirely." Josh moved cautiously along the narrow shelf. *Now* the kid wanted to talk about God? He paused and drew a deep breath. There was barely enough room for him. He had to plaster his back against the mountainside, his arms spread out, his hands flat against the rough, cold stone. *Help me, Lord. Don't let that little boy fall. Please.*

"Not *entirely*?" Brad echoed.

Keeping his eyes on the ledge beneath his feet, Josh inched his way toward the spot where Billy stood in terrified silence. "I'm doing this," he responded, "because Billy needs help. And I won't let you do it because I don't know where you stand with God. I'm not willing to risk losing you for eternity."

He tossed a quick glance back at Brad. The boy was standing in silence, his dark eyes mirroring the tortured dullness of disbelief.

Josh took another step closer. "Brad, God cares about you. Whatever you think, whatever you've been told, the only truth is that God cares about you."

Brad flinched and looked down. "Okay." He spoke so quietly that Josh wasn't sure for a moment if he'd really spoken. "Okay, I hear you." Brad looked up again, his expression one of entreaty. "But I've had enough of this little lesson, you know? So get Billy and get back here."

"Believe me, that's exactly what I intend to do." Now Josh was only a few feet away. He could see the way Billy was trembling, the way his fingers were trying to dig into the dirt and rock of the mountainside.

"Billy, I'm right here." Josh brought his hand down and rested it gently on the slim, trembling shoulder. "We're going to be okay, son."

The boy turned his face to look at Josh. Tears had left streaks across his dirt-smudged cheeks, and his eyes were red and swollen—and filled with fear.

"One step at a time, buddy. Just hold onto my hand and inch your feet along." Josh smiled. "We'll be back on solid ground in no time, okay?"

"O-okay…" He sounded terrified. Josh couldn't blame him.

"That's the spirit." Josh reached out to take the boy's small hand. It was like ice. Josh gave him a smile, doing his best to appear unconcerned. "Ready?"

Billy kept his eyes fixed on Josh. "I—I guess so."

Josh started to take a step toward safety, but he felt Billy stiffen.

"I'm scared!"

"I know. Me, too. But we're going to do this together, okay? You and me and God."

Billy swallowed, then nodded. Together, they started

back toward solid ground. Each step was an exercise in terror and prayer, but soon relieved laughter bubbled from Josh's throat. They were only three feet away. They were going to make it.

"I'll tell you one thing, guys," Josh grinned. "This fresh air is getting to me. I'm so hungry I could—"

He froze. Every ounce of awareness raced to focus on his foot, on the spot where he'd just stepped...the spot that had shifted, sank—and a chill of terrible understanding touched Josh's spine.

"Josh?" Billy's voice was small, terrified.

Josh's eyes flew to meet Brad's disbelieving gaze.

"No!"

Brad's horrified denial washed over Josh, and he surged into action. Jerking Billy into his arms, Josh slid his hands under the boy's armpits and lifted him as he threw his back against the mountainside. The ledge shuddered, and Josh threw Billy as hard as he could.

Billy screamed as he went airborne, his arms and legs windmilling. He landed with a thud in Brad's outstretched arms, and the two of them fell backward in a tangled heap. In the next second, Brad sprang to his feet, scrambling back to the edge, reaching for Josh.

He was too late.

The ledge seemed to dissolve beneath Josh's feet, and in one blazing flash of terrible clarity, Josh knew what was coming. An odd mixture of anticipation and regret flooded him.

He was going home.

He was going to break his promise to Taylor.

Jesus! The prayer bolted from Josh's mind as everything seemed to go into slow motion. *Don't let Brad go! Don't lose him!*

For a second Josh seemed suspended in midair, almost as though he were hovering, and then he fell.

"Noooo!" Brad's scream pierced the air, following Josh as he plummeted toward the boulders.

Father, take care of Taylor. It was Josh's last thought before everything went black.

ONE

TAYLOR SORENSEN COULDN'T REMEMBER A SPRING THIS HOT IN years.

She shifted her weight in the saddle, pulled off her hat, and fanned herself as she squinted against the merciless sun to study the hills in front of her.

What a rotten day.

How appropriate. She shoved her hat back in place and let an angry huff escape. *The hottest May in decades and I'm out here. You'd better appreciate this, Josh.*

Pushing her sunglasses back up her nose, she took up the reins and urged Topaz, her ten-year-old buckskin, forward. The two of them had been together since Topaz was a yearling, and the trust they had in each other was implicit. Taylor knew if any horse could make it to Reunion in this blistering heat, it was Topaz. And he'd do it without a complaint.

Why couldn't men be more like horses?

Choosing his steps with both caution and confidence, the gelding climbed the rocky rise. Taylor breathed a small sigh of relief when they reached the top. Now there was only the descent left. Tricky, but nothing they hadn't done hundreds of times.

Never for this reason, though. The thought came unbidden, unwelcome. As did the tears.

Josh, how could you do this to me? How could you—

A sudden jerk pulled Taylor from her thoughts, and her eyes widened. Topaz whinnied once—a piercing sound—and then Taylor was airborne.

She landed with a thud on the rocky ground, her momentum causing her to roll a few feet until she came to a halt in a breathless pile at the edge of the grass. Taylor lay still, panting, wondering if anything was broken. She moved, one limb at a time. When she was sure her arms and legs were only bruised, she pushed herself into a sitting position, testing her back and shoulders. She'd be sore, no doubt about that, but at least she was in one piece. With a sigh, she leaned back on her elbows and drew in a calming breath, then glanced at Topaz. The buckskin was regarding her with a decidedly sheepish expression.

"Got a little careless those last few steps, did we?"

He tossed his head, then stepped forward to lower his nose and nudge her.

With a moan she sat up, then stood. She brushed herself off, straightened her shoulders, and looked around. The beauty of this valley never failed to stir her. No one would ever imagine it was here, nestled in the rocky outcropping. She'd found it when she was a teen, riding aimlessly, exploring her parents' Wyoming ranch.

The majesty and ruggedness of northwestern Wyoming had always awed her. Her parents' ranch, Galloway Glen, was just east of the Grand Tetons and just south of Yellowstone. Its location was so remote that it was almost wilderness. Here, Taylor had seen nature in all its splendor—and all its power—for as long as she could remember. But discovering the hidden lushness of the valley had been like tripping over a two-pound nugget of solid gold: unexpected and wonderful.

It wasn't large—no more than 150 feet long and about 80 feet wide—but every inch was a feast for the senses. The steep path leading to the valley floor ended at a carpet of emerald grass dotted with wildflowers. Lupine, phlox, and wild iris danced in the breeze. Small stands of lodgepole pine and other conifers bordered a clear, deep, spring-fed pool.

Over the years Taylor had enjoyed every aspect of the pool, from using it to quench her thirst after a long ride to letting it cool her skin with a refreshing swim. Then she'd discovered a treasure within a treasure: a cave, located on the far side of the pool. The entrance had been concealed by brush and trees, which Taylor's unending curiosity had prompted her to push aside.

There was a main chamber, then a narrow corridor branching off to the right. The corridor turned and opened up into another small chamber—a perfect hiding place.

She hadn't told anyone about the valley; it was hers and hers alone.

Until Josh.

They had met in college, in November during her senior year. The first time their gazes met she'd known something monumental had happened. Apparently he'd felt the same, for within six months they were married.

She could recall that day with vivid clarity. They'd come to Galloway Glen during spring break when the colors of spring were exploding everywhere. She remembered the emotions that flooded her as she placed her hand in Josh's and vowed to love, honor, and cherish him. It was the happiest day of her life.

May 6. Eight years ago today.

And with those vows, Taylor's life had suddenly taken on a dimension she'd never imagined was possible. Without even trying, Josh had managed to pull her out of her reclusive shell and help her see how incredible life could be when you opened yourself to someone. He brought her love and laughter and the certainty that life was good.

Or at least it used to be.

All that had changed six months ago on the youth group camping trip.

She remembered the last words he'd spoken to her on the morning he left for the trip. "Pray for me."

She'd done that.

"I'll see you soon."

She'd believed him. She had no reason not to. No solid explanation for the gnawing apprehension that seemed to hover on the edge of her awareness for the next several days. Numerous times she stared at the phone, willing it to ring, willing Josh to be on the other end.

The call never came. But a knock at the door did. Taylor peered out the peephole, and when she saw Jim Wilson standing there with her parents and her brother, Ryan, her heart seemed to freeze in her chest. She'd rested her head against the door for a moment as the niggling apprehension became a wave of dread.

"God…" she whispered, "please." Then she drew a deep breath and pulled open the door to the news that had changed her life forever.

She didn't remember much of what Jim had told her. From the moment he'd said Josh was dead, she'd stopped listening. It wasn't until days later that she'd been able to take in the facts and had learned of Brad Momadey's part in her husband's accident.

Rage washed over her again. Brad hadn't been to church since the accident, but Taylor couldn't find any regret in her heart. She was glad he was gone. *He should have been the one to go out on that ledge, Lord. He should have been the one to die.*

Taylor drew a deep breath, fighting against the fear and anger that threatened to overwhelm her.

She believed in God, believed with her whole heart. And yet belief didn't keep her heart from breaking or from crying out that if God were in control, why would he allow someone so alive, so vibrant and loving, to die? Why would he take away the only person outside of her family who had ever made Taylor feel as though she belonged?

The pain of her memories cut at her heart, and Taylor turned from them, her eyes scanning the sun-kissed valley.

Stop it. Stop thinking. Stop remembering.

She went to Topaz's side, lifted the flap on the saddle-bag, and reached in. Her hand closed around the cool ceramic container she'd slipped into the bag earlier that morning. The container holding Josh's ashes.

She moved through the small stand of conifers that surrounded the water, oblivious for once to their beauty and grace. She stopped at the edge of the pool.

"Well, Josh." Her voice was deep and dusty. "Here we are. At Reunion. I wonder if you knew when you named this place how appropriate that name would be." Tears begged for release, but she pushed them away. "This was supposed to be our retreat, our spot of restoration. Nothing was going to be allowed here that would keep us apart." A humorless laugh escaped her, and she was almost startled by the sound. Shivering, she closed her eyes. The valley had always seemed to hold a remarkable peace, and she stood for a few moments, willing herself to feel it now.

But it wasn't there. All she felt was…empty. Hollow. She brushed at her eyes with the back of her hand.

I trusted you, Josh, gave you my heart...and you risked it all.... Pain shot through her, and she hugged the ceramic container tightly. *You risked it, and I lost. How is that right? How do I live without you?*

Silence answered her, and she felt a wretchedness of mind and spirit that she'd never known before. It was as though icy fingers seeped into every pore and left something deep within her—some part that had been vital and living—brittle, fragile, ready to shatter.

"Get a *grip*, Taylor!" She willed herself to ignore the deep, stubborn pain in her chest.

There was silence all around her, as though even the birds and wind had stilled with regret. Then, almost in dreamlike slow-motion, she removed the lid, lifted the container, and turned it upside down. The ashes spilled out into the water with a slight whoosh, and Taylor chuckled through her tears. Even in death Josh was in a hurry to get where he was going.

She sank to the ground, setting the container beside her and pulling her knees to her chest. Resting her forehead on her knees, she surrendered at last to the grief she'd been wrestling for the last six months.

It was growing dark by the time Taylor lifted her head, her eyes sore from weeping and her cheeks still wet with tears. Her head ached and her throat felt tight and raw. She'd always heard that crying was healthy, cathartic, the beginning of healing—so why didn't she feel better? Maybe some pain went so deep that even tears couldn't touch it.

Listlessly she stared across the pool, her gaze resting, unseeing, on the cave…and then she froze.

She was being watched.

There, at the edge of the rock face, on the rise just above the cave entrance, sat a wolf.

So this is what it's like to go crazy. Taylor stared, her mouth hanging open. There weren't any wolves in Wyoming. Hadn't been for sixty years. There was no possible way she could be seeing one now.

She squeezed her eyes shut, then opened them again.

The wolf was still there, his head held high, his ears perked, his amber gaze fixed on her. Apparently he didn't know he was an impossibility.

Taylor leaned forward, and the animal crouched slightly, as though ready to flee. She stilled, and after a moment he seemed to relax. His haunting, penetrating eyes were intelligent, startlingly compelling.

He was more slender than Taylor had thought a wolf would be, but his demeanor was positively aristocratic; he gave the impression of a sovereign surveying his domain—and one of his subjects. His coat—a study of light grays, browns, and flecks of black—was so thick and luxurious that Taylor's fingers itched to touch him, to bury themselves in what promised to be remarkable softness. The look on his gray face, though watchful, was sweet—disarmingly so—and she had the distinct impression he found her fascinating.

A quick and disturbing thought coursed though her, bringing alarm on its heels. Did wolves attack people? Was this majestic beast looking at her with such interest not out of curiosity but because she was a threat? Or an enemy?

Or, worse yet, an item on his dinner menu?

Her eyes widened at the thought, and she swallowed with difficulty. Frozen in place, loathe to move and precipitate any response, she could only continue the furtive exchange of glances. Then, for a brief, incredible moment, her eyes met the wolf's golden gaze. The contact lasted only a second, but before his eyes flicked away, something clicked in her mind.

She was in no danger.

Her apprehension melted as the assurance resonated within her, filling her with a peaceful certainty that she had nothing to fear. In fact, she had the oddest feeling that the wolf was watching her out of concern and a kind of protectiveness.

They sat in silence for a few moments, regarding each other without ever repeating the eye contact. Taylor was mesmerized. The creature was a barely controlled store of power coiled in a slender frame; he was everything that was wild and graceful and beautiful.

And then, as suddenly as he had appeared, the wolf was gone. It was as though he'd simply melted into thin air.

Taylor blinked twice, then frowned.
Okay, God. What are you doing now?

TWO

One Year Later

IRENE SMITH WATCHED AS CONNOR ALEXANDER STROLLED down the carpeted hallways of the home office of Wildlife Awareness Coalition. She knew Connor was totally oblivious to the ripple of interest that followed in his wake. Had he stopped and glanced behind him, he would have seen several women, standing on tiptoe, watching over their office dividers as he walked by. More than one had an appreciative glimmer in her eyes, and several were rummaging in their desks for mirrors and makeup.

Not that Irene didn't understand their reactions. Their dreamy-eyed fascination was due in part to Connor's rugged good looks, broad shoulders, and lean, muscular build. But as someone who'd worked with the young man for years, she knew those assets, as attractive as they might be, weren't the greatest source of women's response to him. What seemed to draw the most attention were Connor's eyes. Irene had seen many a woman fall speechless when fixed with that penetrating blue gaze—a gaze made even more captivating by its curious blend of sincerity, respect, and audacity.

More often than not, Connor would listen to others, content to take in what they had to say. When asked, however, he didn't hesitate to express his thoughts, beliefs, and values. He spoke what he believed, even when the words were difficult to hear. Irene respected that about him. Oh, he did his best to be kind, but kindness did not always remove the sting of tough truths. Especially when those truths had to do with his feelings toward the women who so often pursued him.

Connor enjoyed women, even enjoyed dating occasionally, or so he'd told her. But he'd made it clear he didn't have time in his well-ordered life for a relationship. He was "married" to his career. Irene shook her head. What a waste. Still, that was Connor's focus. So he made it a rule not to play with anyone's emotions. He kept his distance. He said it was much safer that way.

So it was that he walked along in determined ignorance, unaware of the havoc he was wrecking in several women's hearts.

Irene gave a sigh. She'd love to see Connor married to a woman he adored…someone who would bring a perpetual smile to that kind but far too serious face.

Ah, well, matchmaking wasn't in her job description. What was in her job description, however, was getting Connor to the meeting for which he was already late.

‹VVVVVVVV›

As on most days, WAC—or "Wacky" as some of the politicians in D.C. liked to call the Wildlife Awareness Coalition—was buzzing with activity.

Connor enjoyed listening to the lively discussions emanating from the offices he passed. He'd spent some of his most enjoyable—and infuriating—days caught up in similar meetings. Brainstorming, venting, screaming, cheering.

He was going to miss this place.

The clean white walls were adorned with strikingly beautiful prints of bears, eagles, dolphins, wolves— every sort of endangered or threatened species. One wall was dedicated to plaques and certificates, most of them commending WAC for its work in educating the public regarding wildlife management issues. That was what had first drawn Connor to WAC: their profound dedication to raising the public's awareness and deepening their understanding of wildlife issues. The organization had enjoyed remarkable success through programs that were both educational and entertaining. Information, Not Persuasion was the motto by which they lived. And it was this ideology that had drawn Connor to the organization sixteen years ago when he emerged from college with a degree in wildlife biology and a head full of idealistic goals and passions.

He paused to study a print of an eagle, admiring the beauty of one of God's most magnificent creations, remembering with wry humor the young man he'd been—enthusiastic, fervent, eager to take on a world that seemed all too ready to destroy nature in the name of progress. Ask him to live in the wilds, to stand against any foe, to sacrifice comfort, society, and human relationships—he would have done it all. All that mattered was protecting God's wonderful wild creatures who, despite claws, fangs, or seemingly gargantuan strength, could not protect themselves from mankind and its constant efforts to "subdue the earth."

He turned to continue down the hallway. That young man had been so sure he could change the world. Instead, he'd run head-on into reality, learning some hard facts about the politics of wildlife management. He'd discovered that many of the true battlegrounds for effective wildlife management weren't in the wilderness, but right here in Washington, D.C., in people's offices. And contrary to his idealistic beliefs, human relationships were one of the most vital factors in the battle. With God's help and guidance, he'd learned to deal with all kinds of people—politicians, ranchers, educators, government officials—even others involved in wildlife management, many of whom had their own agendas and prejudices. Talk about being refined by fire!

Fortunately, Connor was blessed with a quick mind, a teachable heart, and a spirit committed to following God's principles. It hadn't taken him long to discover that his most effective tools were tact, respect, and honesty.

"Well, it's about time you showed up."

Connor turned to find Irene Smith walking behind

him, her expression one of tolerant affection. Her salt-and-pepper hair framed her face softly, and her brown eyes glowed with an amiable courtesy. All in all, she had the appearance of a sweet grandmother—but Connor knew WAC's executive secretary could be an iron-willed tyrant when she had to be.

He smiled at her fondly and perched on the edge of her desk. "I suppose he's waiting patiently?" He folded his arms across his chest and angled a look at the office door beside her desk as she sat down. *President* was etched in the decorative frosted glass of the door.

"Oh, of course. And penguins can fly."

He laughed.

"Well, what are you waiting for?" She gave him a push off her desk. "Go forth and conquer."

He was still smiling as he opened the door and entered the cluttered office. His amused gaze roamed the room. One thing he could always count on: Harry Crowley, the founder of and visionary behind WAC, would never change. "Harried Harry" he was called by those who knew him well, but always with a smile and a wink.

"So nice of you to honor me with your presence, Mr. Wonderful."

The dry remark came from behind a large pile of papers, and Connor grinned. "I just hated to interrupt you, Harry, knowing how busy you always are."

"Hmpf!" The man came to clamp a large hand on Connor's shoulder.

Big and bearlike, Crowley presented an imposing figure. His height was well-balanced by his breadth—where he found such stylish tailored suits to fit his bulk, Connor would never know—and his eyes snapped with intelligence and awareness. Harry had been in the capitol city for a lot of years. He knew everyone, and his keen wit, ready laugh, and enviable knack of understanding and being able to relate to opposing sides of any debate had earned him the respect of many—an amazing accomplishment in a city filled with potential enemies and proven adversaries. Connor's boss wasn't timid about taking a stand, but he did so in such a way that people seldom felt disregarded or discounted.

No, not my boss, Connor corrected himself. *My ex-boss. Almost.*

"Sit! Sit!" Harry swept books from one of the leather chairs in front of his desk, then eased himself onto the edge of his desk and regarded Connor with sparkling eyes. "So! How's the world-famous wildlife photographer?"

Connor arched an eyebrow. "Now, Harry, we both know you didn't call me in here to talk about my change in professions. A change, I might add, that you considered…let's see, how did you put it? 'Ludicrous and lunacy,' wasn't it?"

An impenitent grin crossed the big man's face. "Nice alliteration, don't you think? Kind of fits with 'morosely moronic' or 'downright doltish' or—my personal favorite—'clearly and concisely crazy and cockeyed.'"

"So why have you called me here, O great guru of the gazelles?"

"You're learning." There was an appreciative twinkle in Harry's eyes. "And that's exactly why I think you should stay with us."

Connor gave an exaggerated sigh. "Harry, we've talked all this over. You've done too good a job of teaching me. I think you're right on the money when you say the most effective way to get people fired up about supporting wildlife management is to educate them, to let them see for themselves what the issues are and why. Information, Not Persuasion, remember? I just happen to think I can accomplish more through the lens of a camera than by participating in yet another debate with yet another opponent in some bureaucrat's office."

Harry's huff was full of disappointment. "So you intend to go through with this, eh? Just travel around the country, looking for unexplored wilderness and wildlife in all its glory and taking pictures?"

Connor leaned back in his chair with a grin. "Yup. Pretty much. Take pictures, write articles, maybe even put together a showing or exhibit. After all, if my work is good enough to hang on the hallowed walls of WAC—"

"I only bought those prints to placate what I thought was a phase you were going through. You're one of my best field reps. I never figured you'd jump ship on me!"

"Hmmm, of course not. That's why you asked me to

supply you with prints of my work to sell at your fund-raisers—"

"Pure marketing acumen. Wealthy people love to spend money on artsy stuff like your photos."

"—which led to some of my photos being published in a nationally known wildlife magazine—"

"Hey, can I help it if they thought you were some kind of creative genius?"

"—and an offer from one of your pals, who just happens to own a D.C. art gallery, to hold a showing of my work next spring."

Harry crossed his arms over his broad chest. "Well, now that you mention it—" his eyes widened as though just realizing some great truth—"I guess your success is entirely my doing. I just hope you're appropriately grateful!"

Connor grew serious. "You know I am, Harry." All jesting was gone. "You've helped give my dream life and breath, and I'm more grateful than I can say."

"Good!" Crowley boomed, moving to sit in his large, sturdy leather desk chair. "Then you won't mind doing me a little favor."

Connor paused, eyeing his almost ex-boss. "A...favor?"

"Nothing big. By the way, have you decided where you're going first on this photo expedition of yours?"

"Not yet."

"Terrific! Then it shouldn't be a problem to start in Wyoming."

Connor leaned back in his chair. "Okay, Harry, out with it. What's in Wyoming?"

"Nothing, as far as I'm concerned." He tossed a folder on the desk and several papers and photos slid out. "However," he continued as Connor scanned the materials, "there are those who don't agree with me."

Connor looked up. Could what he'd just read be true? "Wolves in Wyoming. Do you think this is for real?"

Harry's shrug was noncommittal. "Normally I wouldn't give reports like these a second thought. But with the wolves that were released in Yellowstone and then in Sawtooth a few years ago, who knows? It's improbable, but…"

Connor knew where he was heading. "Not impossible. A wolf could have made its way that far."

"Right into the backyard of a whole passel of ranchers, none of whom would send the welcome wagon out to greet him."

"More likely the meat wagon."

Harry inclined his head in agreement. "We've pulled together some information on the folks in this small town that seems to be the focus of all the attention."

Connor flipped through the photos. Typical ranchers…rugged, craggy faces that evidenced years of being outdoors; salt-of-the-earth men and women…

Well, well. What was this?

Connor paused, studying a photo. He was aware of Harry droning on, telling him what he thought about the reports, but he wasn't listening. He was busy studying the picture in front of him. There was a typical group of cowboys gathered together, talking and laughing; but standing to the side, watching, with a small smile on her lovely, slightly exotic features, was a woman. Connor couldn't explain it, but something about her caught him…drew him. He couldn't make out her eye color, but he had the oddest feeling they'd be brown—velvety brown…

"Yo. Camera Man. Are you with me?"

Connor's head jerked up. "Uh, yeah, sure. You were telling me why I should be interested in all of this."

Harry gave him a sideways look and reached out to pluck the photo from Connor's fingers. An unexplained heat surged into Connor's face, and Harry's eyes widened.

"You blushing, boy?"

Connor couldn't sit still. He stood and paced. "Of course not."

Harry's gaze went back to the photo. He flashed Connor a wolfish grin. "Looks like a pretty good reason to be interested right here, eh?"

"Very funny. She's probably just a tourist who happened by when your spies snapped the shot."

Harry waved away the accusation. "Spy, schmy. We're just doing our job, old boy. Besides, she looks like a local to me. No doubt about it. And who knows, she might even be involved somehow." His grin broadened and he waggled his eyebrows. "If you're lucky."

Connor grabbed the picture from Harry and shoved it back into the folder. "You were saying…?"

With a guffaw, Harry slapped the desk. "Boy, it does me good to see your feathers ruffled by a pretty face. Even if it's a total stranger. This could be one of those blessings in disguise. You know the old saying, 'All work and no play makes Jack—'"

"Very good at what he does." *Let's see him argue with that.* "Now, you were *saying…?*"

Still chortling, Harry gave in. "I was saying, circumstances being what they are, I figured it would be a good idea for you to go take a look. A purely unofficial look, mind you. One where no one knows who you are or why you're there. Don't want to get the locals any more worked up than they already are, now do we? And who better to send on such a delicate project than my most experienced field rep?" The man was thoroughly pleased with himself.

Connor sat down again, his heart sinking. He hated doing "unofficial" investigations. There was too much deceit, too much concealing of facts. It went against everything he believed in. "No way, Harry. You know how I feel about this kind of thing."

"I certainly do. I'm well aware of your stand on honoring God and truth and all that stuff. That's why you're going to be completely aboveboard with these folks."

Connor looked at him. It sounded good, so why wasn't he buying it?

"You're going to tell them you're a roving photographer out to shoot some great pix, who has just discovered the wonders of Wyoming."

"Harry…"

"It's the truth, isn't it?" Harry's eyes dared him to deny it.

"Well, sure, but it isn't the whole truth—"

"So *what?* You're not lying to anyone. After all, isn't it the Good Book that says something about being sneaky as snakes and innocent as doves?"

"Shrewd." Connor restrained a laugh. "Shrewd as snakes."

"Whatever! Well, you're just going in there as quietly as possible, thereby avoiding upsetting people unnecessarily. And if anyone happens to ask you if you're there to check out the wolf rumors, you can honestly tell them you are." His eyes gleamed as he played his trump. "I mean, what wildlife photographer wouldn't jump at the chance to get shots of the first wolves to come to Wyoming in sixty years? And that's not even mentioning the local beauties—"

Connor glared at him, and Harry held up his hands in surrender.

"Okay, okay, the local beauty, as in of nature, that you can photograph."

Connor sat there, his arms crossed. The thought was attractive. Extremely. The image of brown eyes flitted through his head again, and he pushed it aside. *Forget the girl!* There were more important matters at hand here. Besides, he wouldn't actually have to lie to anyone.

So why did he feel so uneasy?

He let out an uncertain breath. "I don't know—"

"Great!" Harry looked like the Cheshire cat. "I knew you wouldn't let me down. After all, Wyoming has a lot of unexplored wilderness. Heck, it's the least populated state in the union! It's nothing but unexplored wilderness. And what better time to go than in the spring when all the pretty flowers are blooming." He pulled a face. "Just be sure to credit me for leading you to what are sure to be award-winning photos." A sly grin creased his face. "And maybe the love of your life."

Connor ignored that. "And if the wolves really are there?"

"Then we notify Wyoming Fish and Game or our friends at U.S. Fish and Wildlife, and we send one of our teams to the area to start a host of public education and awareness programs." Harry leaned forward. "If there's even one wolf out there, we'll do our best to put people's fears to rest, and hopefully keep our furry friend from ending up as a rug on someone's floor."

"Or buried beneath the daisies in someone's back-yard."

"So, it's settled then. Here are your tickets." Harry slapped an envelope down on the desk in front of Connor. "You leave tomorrow at 7:00 A.M. Sharp."

Connor looked from the tickets to Harry's expectant face, then gave in with a resigned chuckle.

Harry beamed. "There's a rental car waiting for you at the airport. A Jeep Wrangler from Rent-A-Wreck, I think. Wouldn't take anything less than a four-wheeler into that area! See Irene about your expense check—" A pained expression crossed his face—"and try to keep costs down, Con. Your last trip almost broke us. That money tree we planted in the backyard still hasn't bloomed."

"I don't know why not." Connor took the ticket and started for the door. "There's enough horse manure flying around this office to keep a dozen trees in bloom."

THREE

"TAYLOR MOIRA, YOU'RE AN AMAZING AND COURAGEOUS woman!"

Taylor cocked an eyebrow and looked over her shoulder at her brother, Ryan. He sat at the kitchen table, his booted feet resting on her clean tablecloth, his chair balanced on the back two legs.

"Clearly a lead-in of some sort, Taylor." Lisa, Ryan's wife, grimaced at her from her seat next to Ryan. "I'd avoid it if I were you."

"You're probably right, but I can't resist." Taylor turned to her brother. "So I'm amazing and courageous, am I?"

He waggled his eyebrows at her and grinned. "Either that or you're plumb daft."

"She's not daft!" This quick defense came from Ryan's eleven-year-old son Mark.

Taylor leaned toward him with a smile. "Of course I'm not, sweetie. And I'm glad you're smarter than your daddy and can see that."

Ryan snorted, then yelped when someone delivered a sharp rap to the back of his head. He turned wrathfully, then stopped in midrant when he spotted his mother standing behind him. At her slightly reproachful expression, he turned sheepishly to take a drink of his coffee.

"Really, Ryan," Donelle Camus chided as she moved to the stove to pour hot water into a mug. "I should think you'd try to be a better example for your sons. Instead, you sit in your chair like a monkey, put your filthy boots on the table, and talk to your sister in tones that could hardly be considered respectful. Sasha is exhibiting better manners than you are."

At the sound of her name, the black-and-white Siberian husky who was curled up in the corner of the kitchen, her bushy tail draped over her nose, lifted her head and fixed her intense blue gaze on Taylor's mother.

Taylor laughed. "Never mind, Sash. Mom doesn't have any treats for you."

The Siberian's velvety pointed ears perked, and her gaze switched to Taylor expectantly, her tail giving one hopeful thump.

"Oh, dear, you used the *t* word." Her mother chuckled as Taylor knelt to scratch the dog's broad head.

It was always fun to have her family visit—which happened often since her parents also lived on Galloway Glen, about a half-mile away in a log home of their own, and Ryan and Lisa lived just a few miles down the road. Some people might not like having their family so close, but Taylor loved it.

"Now, Ryan, where were we…?" Their mother

looked pensive. "Oh yes. Your manners…" Her gaze rested pointedly on his feet. "Or should I say, the lack thereof?"

Taylor couldn't restrain her grin. At fifty-seven, her mother was one of those women who always seemed at ease. Her dark curly hair was cut in a flattering short cap, and Taylor thought the occasional fleck of silver only added a touch of sophistication. Mom's green eyes sparkled with humor and wisdom, and her manner was warm and welcoming to anyone she encountered. Taylor knew all too well that little escaped her mother's notice, though she seldom offered advice where it wasn't requested. The emotional anchor of their tight-knit family, Donelle Camus was the very picture of elegance, vitality, and patience. All factors that made her especially effective when dealing with her spirited, fun-loving children.

"You're absolutely right, Mother mine." Ryan removed his offending feet from the table and set his chair in place, then gave Taylor an intent look. "Now let me see…" His brow creased in concentration. "There must be something respectful I can say about you."

Taylor shot him a glare, tempted to throw the dish sponge right between his twinkling eyes.

"Come on, Dad!" Mikey, Mark's twin brother, urged. "How 'bout saying she's pretty?"

"Okay, guys, time for another topic of—" But Lisa didn't have a chance. The twins were off before she could finish.

"Yeah!" Mark clapped his hands. "Her hair's pretty

too. Same color as Chestnut, and all shiny, just like his coat after we treat it for a show."

Ryan considered his sons. "Okay, I can go for that. Taylor, you're as pretty as a greased-up show horse."

Temptation won out. The sponge hurtled through the air and connected with a satisfying, squishy thud squarely in the center of Ryan's broad, muscular chest.

"Taylor!" her mother scolded, but this time she had little effect. The twins exploded into laughter as their father vaulted out of his chair and went after his sister, who fended him off with another sopping sponge.

Seeing that her offspring were out of control, Donelle settled back in her chair and sipped her tea.

"Better not hurt her, Dad, or Sasha will take your leg off!" But the Siberian was far too accustomed to such events. She was lying, unconcerned, her head resting on her paws.

"Well, I thought for sure we were in the midst of World War III," a deep voice remarked from the doorway, "but I see Mother has her tea, so all must be right with the world."

Taylor, who was locked in her brother's bear hug and suspended a good foot off the floor, grinned at her father. "All's right except that Ryan is being his typical, juvenile self."

"Right! You're an angel. That's why my shirt is soaking wet and smells like dirty dishes."

"Exactly."

Taylor's father stepped into the kitchen, his amusement evident.

Lisa smiled sweetly at Ryan. "You can't say you didn't ask for it."

"Ryan, be a good lad and put your sister down, please"—their father took the seat next to his wife—"so she can tend to her duties as hostess."

"And do it gently, dear," their mother cautioned, seeing the gleam in her son's eyes at his father's request.

With a disappointed sigh, Ryan lowered his sister to the floor. She tossed him a triumphant smirk and went to hug her father. His blue eyes were bright with merriment as he hugged her back.

She loved the way her father looked. Tall, broad shouldered, and solid. He had more the appearance of a lumberjack than a minister, but his gentle eyes were a clear window to a heart that was totally dedicated to serving the Lord. Taylor had seen the way that her father's devotion to God, his quick sense of humor, and his caring heart could win over even the most cantankerous parishioner. He was uniquely designed to shepherd God's people.

"Thanks, Daddy. You know how hard it is to control the brute. Not even Lisa's wonderful influence has made him fit for civilized company."

Ryan ignored Taylor, choosing instead to walk back to his seat and lift his coffee cup, holding the handle between his forefinger and thumb, keeping his pinkie out.

"Oh, yuck, Dad!" Mark and Mikey protested together. "You look like a sissy!"

"Not at all, my dear lads," he replied in affected tones. "I'm simply being snivilized."

"Ry, old boy, read my lips." Taylor blew a less-than-ladylike raspberry.

"Uh-oh, Dad, sounds like a grudge to me!" Ryan's expression was full of mock horror.

Taylor fixed him with a glare. "Why don't you just sit there and—"

But Ryan held up a hand, cutting her off. "Father, if you please. Your wayward child is in desperate need of words of truth and wisdom."

Taylor looked at her father. "Dad! Don't you dare…"

Her father merely smiled serenely, his eyes brimming with laughter, then tilted his head and tapped his chin with a long forefinger, as though deep in thought. "Ah, I have it. 'Therefore, as God's chosen people, holy and loved—'"

"'*Dearly* loved,'" his wife pointed out, and he looked at her, a slight frown creasing his brow.

"'Dearly'? Are you sure?"

"Oh, for heaven's sake!"

Sasha started at Taylor's blurted comment, jumped up, cast her mistress one disgusted look, and padded from the room—most likely to find some peace and quiet.

"Taylor, please." Her mother's smile was the epitome of patience. "Your father is talking. You should know better than to interrupt." She turned back to her husband. "'Dearly loved.'"

In good-humored assent he went on, "'Holy and *dearly* loved, clothe yourselves with compassion, kindness, humility, gentleness, and patience—'"

"*Nobody* could have all that with this family." Taylor crossed her arms.

"'*Bear* with each other—'" her father's voice raised in mock sternness—"'and forgive whatever grievances you have against one another. Forgive as the Lord forgave you—'"

"Now, *there's* a wonderful idea," Taylor's mother joined in. Taylor merely huffed in response.

"'And over all these virtues—'"

"I know, I know..." Taylor crossed her arms. "'Put on love.'"

Her dad gave her an indulgent smile. "Good counsel, don't you think?"

Ryan clapped his hands. "Perfect choice, Father dear. Colossians always has been one of my favorites. Especially for putting one certain brat in her place."

Taylor studied her family. "Has anyone ever told you people that weird runs in this family? Because it does. It definitely does."

At her father's laugh, Taylor leaned over to give him a hug. "You're a beast, Dad. I can see where Ryan gets it from." She kissed his cheek. "Now, how 'bout some tea?"

"Coffee will do me fine." Her father leaned back and slid his arm along the back of his wife's chair. "And you can tell me what started the ruckus this morning."

"Dad said Aunt Taylor looked like a horse," Mikey replied around a mouthful of Cheerios.

At his father's raised eyebrows, Ryan grinned. "I said she was as pretty as a show horse, to be exact. But that's not really what started the whole thing. It was Taylor taking exception to my calling her daft, which I still think she is."

"And why, exactly, is that?" Taylor asked in saccharine tones as she poured her father's coffee.

Ryan regarded her with humor mixed with compassion. "Because you're determined to push ahead with the repairs and preparations for the upcoming retreat season."

Taylor gave a nonchalant lift of her shoulders, setting the cup of hot liquid in front of her father. "It's only May, Ry. There's plenty of time to get things done before July. I don't want to delay the opening this year."

"Why?"

His quiet question stopped her cold. She could give him a million reasons, but she knew he'd see through them all. No matter what she said, Ryan would know she wanted to push ahead because she needed to. She couldn't stand being immersed in grief and letting life pass her by any longer. She met his understanding gaze.

He leaned forward to touch her arm. "Sis, I know how much these retreats mean to you. And normally I'd be behind you a 110 percent; you know that."

Taylor knew it was true. Ryan was one of her staunchest supporters. He always had been. For as long as she could remember, he'd been there to cheer her on, to offer encouragement, or just to listen.

"But to push ahead with your plans when you know you'll have to handle a lot of the preparations yourself..." He shrugged. "I'm just not sure it's wise."

Taylor started to reply, but her father spoke up first. "Ryan may be right, Taylor. Don't you think you should give yourself more than a few months to get things done? There's a lot to accomplish, hon, and not enough people to do it."

Taylor looked at her father considering his words, then shook her head. "I don't know, Dad." She was a bit surprised at how tired she sounded. "I just know I don't want to put the retreats off again."

Silence fell over the room as she went to perch on the counter and sip her cocoa. She was touched that her family was so concerned about her yet determined to stick to her plans. If there was one thing Taylor Sorensen was not, it was a quitter. Especially when it came to the retreats she and Josh had developed, designed especially to give families in ministry a place to be refreshed and nurtured.

With her family's help, she and Josh had built small, cozy cabins just east of the ranch house and converted the old bunkhouse into a caretaker's cabin for Luke Narbona.

Luke had been a part of Galloway Glen for as long as Taylor could remember. He'd come to the ranch as a young man to work for her grandfather and had never left. When her father married her mother, Luke had helped open the way for her father to be accepted in his new congregation. When Ryan and Taylor came along, Luke appointed himself their guard and playmate.

Taylor had been Luke's shadow since she started walking. And, as though recognizing the girl's lonely spirit, Luke took her under his wing. He regaled her with tales of his Navajo ancestors, taught her the Songs of Talking to God, and listened as she shared her thoughts and dreams.

When Luke heard about Josh and Taylor's plans for retreats on Galloway Glen, he had been full of creative ideas for transforming the ranch into a retreat center, for making things work more smoothly and efficiently. He'd even helped out with the public relations and advertising, commandeering several local young people to help send out mailings and put up flyers.

So far, the retreats had been a success. Numbers had grown steadily, and now Taylor had families scheduled for a year in advance. Because of Josh's death, however, she'd had to cancel last year's sessions. She'd been too emotionally raw, unable to go ahead with their dream without Josh.

Now…now she was ready to start again. It was time to get on with life.

Which was why she was so hesitant to delay the much needed work or the start of the coming retreat season just because her work crew was deserting her.

Ryan came over and slipped his arm around her

shoulders. "I'm not trying to be the voice of doom here, Sis, but facts are facts. When we're all here, we can divide the work into reasonable amounts. But with this wilderness expedition Dad and the boys and I are going on, and Lisa heading out to visit her folks for a while, you're pretty much on your own."

Ryan worked as a guide for Wilderness Outfitters, an operation that took people on expeditions into the wilds of Wyoming. Ryan's love for and knowledge of the out-of-doors and his easygoing manner had made him a favorite of the firm's clients. Because of that, the company let him take his family for a trip once a year. This year he was taking the twins and his father on a rafting expedition.

"You and Dad will be back in three weeks, Ry. And I've handled at least a week or more of the preparation on my own in previous years."

"No, not on your own." Ryan's quiet correction stopped her, and her throat constricted. Ryan went on. "Josh was here. He was able to take on a lot of the physical work and leave the administration to you and Mom. But that's changed now."

Taylor fell silent. It was hard to believe it had been a year and a half since Josh's death. It frustrated her that every time she thought she was finally getting used to him being gone, the reality would once again sucker punch her and leave her feeling empty and cold. Well, this time it wasn't going to get to her. She had spent the last eighteen months doing her best to get along on her own, and she wasn't going to let this setback make her feel hopeless again.

"I'm sorry, Sis. I just want you to take a realistic look at the situation. As much as you'd like to think you can, you can't do it all yourself."

"It's okay, Ry." She willed her voice to be steady. "You're right. Josh took up a lot of the slack. But I've still got Luke. He can help some, even if he isn't as young as he used to be." She surveyed her family's concerned faces. If only they wouldn't worry so... "Besides, I already realized things were going to be a bit much this year. So I took the proverbial bull by the horns—"

"There's a bull here?" Mark looked up with interest.

"Not a real bull, dummy. A *figurative* one."

Taylor just grinned at Mikey's oh-so-superior tone and went on. "—and put an ad in the paper for a temporary handyman and ranch hand."

At the stunned silence in the room, her grin broadened.

It didn't happen often, but the Camus clan was speechless—and the fact that she was the one who'd rendered them so brought Taylor a surge of gleeful triumph.

For once in her life, she'd actually had the last word!

FOUR

"DON'T LOOK SO SHOCKED, EVERYONE," TAYLOR FINALLY SAID into the silence. "I can show common sense from time to time."

"It's just so novel." Ryan's retort didn't miss a beat. "At least give us time to get used to the idea."

"Har de har." She made a face at him.

Her mother sipped her tea before offering her encouragement. "That's a good idea, Taylor."

Uncertainty washed over Taylor. "I thought so, too, at first. But I haven't had any calls, and the ad's been out for a week. I thought I'd at least get some high schoolers responding, but no one's called." She lifted her shoulder. "Unfortunately, the odds of anyone from out of town even seeing the ad aren't exactly high."

Ryan leaned back in his chair. "You don't think someone would come to the booming metropolis of Wilson looking for a temporary job as a handyman and ranch helper, eh? Not even if he'd have the prettiest boss in the area?"

"I hardly think that would be a draw." Taylor batted at her brother's arm. "Besides, when you consider that the last time a stranger came to town for any length of time the news made the front page of the local rag, it doesn't exactly bode well for my poor little ad."

Ryan's chuckle was gleeful. "Hey, there are strange men walking through our town all the time! I mean, they don't get much stranger than some of the tourists who come here!"

Taylor laughed and took a sip of hot chocolate. "Oh, now there's an idea. Say, mister, I know you came to Wyoming to ride horses, soak in the hot springs, and follow your wife around to every shop in the county, but wouldn't you rather come on over and dig some post holes? Or muck out a few stalls?"

"I'd rather muck out stalls any day than go shopping." Disgust was ripe in Mark's young voice.

"That's my boy!" Ryan gave him a slap on the back.

Lisa held up her hands, looking at the others. "I do my best with them, but you can see what I'm up against."

Taylor went to pat her arm in mock solicitude. "It's okay, Lisa. Ryan was hopeless long before you came onto the scene. But I doubt I'll have any tourists lining up to answer the ad. At any rate, I'll know this afternoon if I've had any luck. I'm going to check out the post office box when Gavin and I go into town today."

Her mother looked up with interest. "You're going in with Gavin MacEwen again, hmmm?"

"He asked me to go along for company while he

picked up supplies. I've got to return some books to the library, Mom. It's no big deal."

"I'm glad you're getting out more, Sis."

"Gavin is a friend." The words came out between clenched teeth. "Nothing more."

"Hey, I think it's great you're spending time with Mr. Scottish Hunk."

Taylor eyed her brother. Surely that remark wasn't as innocent as it sounded. "What are you up to?"

"Nothing. Honest." Ryan's eyes were open and frank. "I'm just glad to see you getting away from the ranch for a while."

"Well, it's not like that's so terribly unusual."

"Actually, hon, it is." Taylor turned to look at her father at this surprising comment. His eyes held a tender concern as he said, "You've kind of hidden yourself away here for the last year, Taylor."

"I love Galloway Glen." What was the problem with spending time in her own home, for heaven's sake?

"We know you do, dear, and we're glad." Her mother's voice was kind but firm. "But you need to be around people."

"I go to church! There are all kinds of people there."

"Sorry, Taylor, but Mom and Dad are right," Lisa said. "No one ever gets a chance to talk with you. You come in as the first hymn starts and leave as Dad is finishing up the benediction." The understanding expression in her eyes softened the words. A little.

Taylor stared at her cooling chocolate, her lips pressed together. It had been easy to socialize when Josh was with her. His vibrant personality and warm heart drew people to him like bees to honey, and Taylor had benefited from that appeal. But without Josh, she felt herself falling back into old patterns. As a child she'd often struggled with feelings of not fitting in, of being somewhat different, even odd. Since Josh's death, those feelings had come back in force, compounded by the fact that she was now a widow. A young widow. If she'd felt odd as a child, she felt downright freakish now.

"I suppose they're talking about me." She knew she sounded bitter, but she couldn't help it.

Her father's eyes chided her. "Sweetheart, I'm not concerned about what people are saying. I'm concerned about you, about how much time you spend alone."

"Which is why we're pleased Gavin is coming over," her mother added.

"Though why a good-looking fella like him would want to be around a prickly pear like you is beyond me!"

"I like Gavin!" Mark piped up, forestalling his aunt's heated response to his father. "I like his accent and some of the funny words he uses—"

"Yeah, like *canna* and *ken* and stuff!" Mike turned to his mother. "He's Scottish, you know."

"Yes, dear. I know. He's charming."

"Yeah, but that's okay. I mean, he's not a sissy or anything. He can fight real good. I saw him once with Dancy Blocker—"

"Okay, sport, that's enough." Ryan tried to put a halt to the story, but Mark could be stubborn when he wanted to make a point.

"I *did*, Dad. Dancy said something about Aunt Taylor, and Gavin told him to hold his tongue or he'd be eating it—"

"Marcus Riley!" His eyes widened and his mouth clamped shut at his father's rebuke.

Ryan sighed. "Sorry, Mom."

She patted his shoulder. "It's all right, dear. I'm well acquainted with men and their set-tos, especially when they have to do with young women." She glanced at her husband, and Taylor was surprised to see a dull blush creep across her father's face.

"Yes, well, I'm sure Gavin was only doing what he thought was best."

"Right, Grandpa." Mark cast his father a cautious glance. When Ryan nodded, he went on. "Gavin's always doing something nice for people. He even lets me drive his Blazer sometimes. Or steer it, anyway," he amended at the quick frown that crossed his father's face.

"Yeah, Gavin's cool." Mikey reached for another piece of toast. Then he paused, his hand in midreach, and shot Taylor a look. "Hey! I know! You should just marry Gavin! He's big an' strong, and he could do all your work for you!"

"What a good idea, son." Ryan was clearly starting to enjoy the conversation. "Or, better yet, we could have a contest. You know, invite all the able-bodied, eligible men in the area to compete against each other and see who can do the most work the fastest. The prize will be our very own Taylor as a sweet little bride!"

"Ryan…" Lisa's warning came too late.

"Sure!" Mikey clapped. "I'll bet ol' Mr. Wanamuc would come. He's always watching Aunt Taylor when she comes in his store—"

"Yeah!" Mark's eyes shone with excitement. "And Eddie Running Elk said Aunt Taylor was real pretty, even if she did keep to herself like a wounded cougar hiding out in the woods. He'd come too, I bet!"

"Oh, I'm sure he would." Ryan was laughing so hard there were tears in his eyes.

Taylor grimaced. "You guys are a laugh a minute."

"But I still think Gavin would be the best one," Mikey stated, as though that settled it.

"I've always thought so, though I'd like to know what I'm the best one for."

The group at the table turned as one to stare at the man leaning in the doorway.

"Gavin!" Heat rushed to Taylor's face. "I didn't hear your Blazer pull up—"

"A bit hard to with all the racket you Camuses are makin' in here." He grinned and came to tousle Mark's hair and tweak Mikey's nose.

As the twins jumped from their chairs to wrestle with Gavin, Taylor took the opportunity to regain her composure. With any luck he hadn't noticed her discomfort.

Any hope of that dissolved when he turned to her, grin still in place, dark brows arched. "Now, what's all this about?"

Her embarrassment almost turned to blind panic when Ryan pulled out a chair and patted it. "Have a seat, Gavin, me boyo, and I'll tell you all about it! The twins here just made the most fascinating suggestion—"

Taylor bolted from her perch on the counter, uncaring if she dumped the remnants of her hot chocolate on the floor. She all but slam-dunked the mug into the sink, snagged her jacket and hat from the peg by the kitchen door, and grabbed the pile of library books from the counter—all the while nudging Gavin toward the door.

"Sorry." She paused only long enough to lean down and give her mother and father quick good-bye pecks. "Gotta go! Loads to do! See you later."

"You will let us know about any response to the ad, dear?"

Taylor paused at the door. "Sure, Mom. And try not to worry, okay? God will work things out. Isn't that what you two are always telling me?"

"Hmmm," was all her mother said, and Taylor felt her speculative gaze follow her all the way out the door.

FIVE

As Gavin MacEwen's Blazer bounced over the rough roadway leading to the highway, Taylor eased back against the seat and drew a calming breath.

She loved her family. She really did. But some days she would gladly trade them in, part and parcel, for a pack of basenjis. Not so much because she liked the dogs, although she thought they were delightful, but because that particular breed had the marvelous distinction of having no vocal chords.

The very thought of her family being mute was utterly delightful.

"Ah, a smile. So am I safe in assuming you're not plannin' to sit there in wounded silence the whole ride to Wilson?"

She glanced over at her friend. "Sorry, Gavin. They just get to be a bit much sometimes, you know?"

"Aye, I know. My family's the same way, though I must admit they're even more vocal than yours. Scots are notorious for their volume and verbosity when they're tryin' to prove a point."

"Well then, my family must have some Scot in them somewhere."

"Either that or it's the Irish tryin' to make more of itself than it really is." He winked and reached out to capture her hand in a brief clasp. "For all of their Irish heritage, though, I have to admit your nephews show a rare insight and intelligence."

She met his warm gaze and groaned. "You heard it all, didn't you?"

"Aye. But it's nothin' new, now is it? I've been tellin' you for some time now that we do well together, darlin'. You know it's true."

"Yes, I know…"

"So why don't you marry me, Taylor?" Gavin's broad smile and his dark eyes sparkled with humor and affection. She turned her head and studied him.

Gavin MacEwen had moved into the area about five years ago. Born and raised in Scotland, he had come to help his uncle work his ranch, the Bar T, which was only a few miles from Galloway Glen. When he'd shown up at church on his first Sunday, Josh had been among the first to welcome him. Before long, the two men realized they shared many interests, and a solid friendship was born.

From their first meeting, Taylor had considered the good-humored Scotsman absolutely charming. He had a way of winning people over without really trying, and he'd always treated Taylor with kindness and a winsome courtliness.

Soon they'd become a merry threesome, attending church together, going to movies, and having dinner at each other's homes. Josh and Taylor watched with interest—and considerable amusement—as Gavin dated a steady succession of women. They never knew who would be accompanying him to their get-togethers, but they didn't mind. It kept things interesting.

During the months after Josh died, Gavin's friendship and support became an emotional anchor for Taylor. He was always there to help out, to talk or listen, to nudge her from her depression, or to pray with her.

Remembering those dark days and the blessing Gavin had been, Taylor reached out and squeezed his arm. He was a good friend. But marriage? She just wasn't sure. With Josh, it had been a lightning bolt. A certainty that *this* was the man for her above all others.

With Gavin…she loved him, of course. He was a dear friend. But what she felt didn't really go beyond that. Not yet, anyway.

But Gavin MacEwen wasn't a man to wait forever. Sometimes he seemed more like a dashing lord of the Scottish Highlands—an image strengthened by the thick, shoulder-length black hair that he often wore tied back in a ponytail. While such a style might have looked odd or out of place on many men, it only increased Gavin's roguish appeal. An appeal that she wasn't completely immune to—not when he stared at her that way with those dark eyes…

The direction of her thoughts jolted her, and she felt

her cheeks blush. She leaned away slightly, and Gavin's smile at her withdrawal was gentle.

"It's not unfaithful to Josh, you know. Being attracted to me."

Taylor was amazed that such a quietly spoken comment could cut her so deeply. She turned to stare out the window, trying to blink away sudden tears. She was successful, too. Almost. But an errant tear made its defiant way down her cheek, despite her most determined efforts.

"I know it's hard for you, Taylor. But Josh wouldn't want you to stop living too. He loved you—and life—too much to want that. I may sound like I'm teasing, but you know I'm serious when I ask you to marry me."

She chewed her lower lip, then turned to meet Gavin's understanding gaze. "I know. And I wish I could say yes. You've been so good to me, so kind and patient and abiding—"

"For the love of MacDougal, Taylor, you make me sound like the faithful family dog!"

Laughter bubbled out of her. "You know that's not what I mean."

"Aye, but just once I'd like to hear you talk about my massive shoulders, or rippling muscles, or granite jaw—"

"Or your compelling brown eyes or rakish grin or your really cool Blazer—" she cut in, her mouth twitching with mirth.

"Or *something* that lets me know you've noticed me as a man and not just as a friend."

She crossed her arms and leaned back against the door, giving him a serious appraisal. "Well, I'm not all *that* impressed with the Blazer. I mean, Luke has one, too, you know. And it's blue, not green. I mean, isn't green kind of a sissy color?"

"Taylor." The caution was a growl.

"Okay, okay. Now that you mention it, I suppose you are somewhat...manly in appearance."

"Oh, aye! *Somewhat* is it?" Without warning he pulled the vehicle to the side of the road and shut it off.

"Gavin! What are ya doin', mon? Have ye gone pure daft?" Her exaggerated Scottish accent only fired the determination in his eyes, and he leaned toward her. With one sinuous movement he stretched his arm across the back of the seat, slipped it around her shoulders, then pulled her close. He smiled down at her, his dark eyes full of mischief.

"*Somewhat* manly, is it now? Well, my fine lass, we'll see aboot that..."

His gaze held her captive as he lowered his head. She considered stopping him, pulling away...but something inside her wanted it to happen. She remembered her first kiss with Josh, how the ground had shifted beneath her feet, how her head had spun so she'd thought she'd faint...

Maybe letting Gavin kiss her would show her, once and for all, if they were meant to be more than friends.

She closed her eyes, lifting her lips to his...and

waited for the ground to move, for her head to spin…and waited…

And waited.

When Gavin finally lifted his head and looked down at her, she bit her lip.

Nothing. She wasn't sure what she expected to feel, but it sure wasn't a big, fat zero!

Well, that wasn't entirely true. Gavin was as adept at kissing as he was at most everything else, but all she'd felt was a kind of cozy warmth, like when she wore her favorite ragged pajamas and curled up in her old, worn comforter.

Cozy…comfortable…

Oh, dear. Somehow, she didn't think that was a good sign.

Gavin sat staring down at her, his expression thoughtful. "Well…" His voice was even huskier than usual. Taylor stared up at him in silence. "Well…," he said again, then shook his head and set her away from him.

Taylor scooted to her side of the seat, wondering what to say to fill the sudden silence.

A deep chuckle came from the other side of the cab, and she risked a glance at Gavin.

"I thought to teach you a bit of a lesson." Gavin's eyes glowed with a gentle light. "But I'm thinkin' maybe I'm the one who learned something."

"Oh?" It wasn't exactly the scintillating response she

wanted to make, but it was all her confused brain could muster at the moment.

"Aye." He reached forward to start the Blazer again and ease it onto the road. "Some things aren't meant to be rushed."

Taylor turned to him. "Gavin, I'm—"

He laid gentle fingers over her lips. "No, lass. It's all right. You need time, and I'm willing to wait as long as it takes." His gaze was rueful as he dropped his hand. "But if you can, have mercy and don't take any longer than necessary, will you?"

She blinked back the tears that were suddenly begging for release. "I won't. I promise."

"Good enough, then. Because I'll tell you straight, Taylor, you're the kind of woman who infects a man."

Her mirth bubbled through the tightness in her throat. "Thanks a lot!"

He gave her a puppy-dog look. "Indeed, you are. And I doubt there's a cure for it, either. So you'd better agree to marry me soon, else I'll suffer untold miseries and ailments and die a horrible death from a shattered heart."

"And what a romantic proposal *that* is."

"Face it, lass. We're meant to be together, you and I. Besides, you won't find a more handsome or vigorous man, and you know it."

"Or humble!"

His grin was purely impenitent. "In truth, yer beauty makes me forget myself, darlin'." The brogue thickened until Taylor was sure she could cut it into chunks. "I canna ken livin' without ye, and the mere threat of it sets my mind to whirlin'. So you'd best say yes. You wouldna want me to drive meself off the mountainside, now would ye?"

"Och, the way ye do talk, Gavin MacEwen. And how the clan must miss such a golden tongue."

"Indeed, I'm sure they must."

His warm, rich laughter filled the Blazer, and Taylor leaned back, grateful for his understanding. *I don't deserve him, Lord.*

"And though I hate to say it, we've reached our destination."

She looked up in surprise and saw that they were indeed entering Wilson.

The small town, inhabited by roughly five hundred people, was a study in rugged beauty. As a restless teen, Taylor had given Wilson the disdainful title of The Town that Never Was. But four years attending college in overpopulated L.A. had given her a new appreciation for Wilson's small-town warmth and familiarity. Now she cherished the fact that traffic jams were unheard of in Wilson. And she enjoyed the uniqueness of the town's landmarks—the post office, Hungry Jack's General Store, and Nora's Fish Creek Inn—a far cry from L.A.'s happening, frenetic hot spots.

Of course, if Hungry Jack's didn't carry what she needed, all Taylor had to do was head six miles further east to Jackson. With a population of nearly 7,500,

Jackson was the area's center of commerce. It had definite old-time appeal with its town square, shopping center, and an abundance of Western fronted shops custom designed to send any tourist into paroxysms of delight.

"Supplies or library first?"

Taylor patted the books beside her. "Library. Definitely."

"I love a woman who knows what she wants and goes after it." His eyes twinkled at her decisive response. "Almost as much as I love one who's ready when she says she will be," he added as they pulled up in front of the building.

"And you know it goes without saying, dear Gavin—" she gathered the books, opened the door, and stepped from the vehicle—"that the only thing that matters to me is making your sweet Scottish heart happy."

"That's as it should be, lass."

"I'll be done in twenty minutes. Thirty, tops."

"I'll wait as long as it takes." A spark of some unfathomable emotion flashed in his dark eyes. And as she turned to enter the building, she was torn between relief that they were able to ease back to their typical bantering and a wave of regret.... As much as she'd like to just ignore it, she knew, deep inside, that while the ground may not have shifted during that kiss, the foundation of their relationship had.

SIX

"Well, I was wondering when we'd see you in here again."

Taylor waved at the librarian as she approached the desk. "It has been a while, hasn't it, Linda?"

"Hmmm, longer than usual." The woman's blue eyes wandered to the doorway behind Taylor. "Is Gavin with you?"

Suppressing a grin at the woman's hopeful expression, Taylor laid her stack of books on the desk. "No, he decided to make a quick stop at the hardware store while I'm here."

Linda's mouth puckered, and then her eyes came back to rest on Taylor.

"Congratulations, Taylor." Two dimples appeared in Linda's cheeks. "You returned these just under the wire. No late charges this time."

Taylor leaned on the counter. "I'm turning over a new leaf. The last batch almost broke the bank."

Linda laughed and turned to her computer. "A new book on wolves just came in." She peered at the screen, then jotted the information down on a slip of paper and handed it to Taylor. "Since you've read almost every book we have on wolves, I thought you'd be interested in this one."

Taylor glanced at the paper. Trust Linda to pick a winner. "Thanks."

"By the way," Linda said, "have you heard the latest rumors—that we've actually got wolves around here?"

Taylor stopped cold, her heart pounding in her chest. "Oh?" She hoped she sounded far calmer than she felt.

"Oh, don't worry! I'm sure there's nothing to it. Just like there's been nothing to all the other rumors we've heard over the years about killer wolves invading the area and decimating the elk and cattle populations." Linda smoothed her hair. "I swear, if wolves did half of what people accused them of, they'd have to be able to fly, leap tall buildings with a single bound, and disappear at will."

Taylor smiled weakly. "So who reported a sighting?"

"Oh, no one. But Mylon Hogan said he heard howling a few nights ago. And you know how the ranchers are about wolves. Someone thinks he hears one, and they all head for their guns."

Oh no! Lord, please, don't let this happen.

"Did Mylon send a report to the officials?" Taylor dreaded the answer. If the government agencies found out about her wolves, they'd be pounding on her door.

Linda snorted. "Think about what you're saying, Taylor."

Taylor's brows came together. Then realization

dawned—and her sense of dread doubled.

When Linda saw the light of understanding in Taylor's eyes, she nodded. "Right. You know what they say: 'Shoot, shovel, and shut up.' I doubt any of the ranchers would even consider reporting a sighting. They don't want the government coming in to catch and move the wolves."

"You think that's what they'd do? Capture them and move them someplace else?"

"I would certainly hope so. But they'd have to do it fast if they wanted to find the wolves in one piece."

What Linda said was true. The ranchers were much more inclined to "take care of things" themselves, rather than let the government agencies and their restrictions in the door. Understandably so. Taylor had heard the debates all her life: The government had no right to tell people what they could and couldn't do—or kill—on their own land. Especially when what they wanted to kill was a predator, one that many would willingly risk fines—and even possible imprisonment—to kill.

Like wolves.

Taylor sat on the bench outside the library, wishing she'd told Gavin five minutes rather than thirty. Her conversation with Linda had left her with a heavy heart, and all she wanted to do was go home.

Shoving her hands in her jacket pockets, she leaned back, watching the clouds dance by in the sky. The sun was warm on her face, and she drew a deep breath of the clean, crisp air—as a shiver traveled up and down her spine.

She sat up straight. She couldn't explain it, but she had the oddest feeling...as though she were being watched. She glanced around, hoping Gavin was parked nearby, waiting.

Her gaze paused for a moment on a tall form a little distance away. A stranger—and a handsome one from what she could see of his profile—was leaning against the side of the general store, looking around with a casual air. Taylor studied him. Who was he? What was he doing in town? Had he been watching her?

Come on, Taylor, you're being paranoid.

She started to look away—but just then he turned toward her, and their gazes collided. A shock jolted through Taylor at the intensity—and interest—sparking from the man's dark blue eyes.

Heat surged into her face and she turned away. What was wrong with her? How could she have been caught staring at a complete stranger like that—

The thought died when she saw a young man coming up the sidewalk toward the library. Though his head was down, his chin all but buried in his chest, something disturbingly familiar about the way his thick, shaggy hair fell over his face like a black curtain blocking his features made her heart constrict. Taylor felt her breathing grow ragged, her heart start to pound. The boy's walk…the straight way he held himself, the over-all impression of grace and contained strength…it could only be one person.

As though sensing her scrutiny, the young man looked up at her. A wave of nausea flooded Taylor, followed quickly by a furnace blast of pure loathing.

Brad Momadey.

She wanted to turn and run. Or to scream and rage at him. She did neither. She simply stood there, stiff with emotion, holding his stunned gaze.

Somewhere in a corner of her mind it registered that his dark eyes were haunted, his face gaunt and strained. His coppery skin was pale, as though all the color had been siphoned away. He wore the anguished expression of someone consumed by a burning, unrelenting pain. She knew because it was the same expression she had seen many times over the last year in her mirror.

Faint stirrings of sympathy brushed at her heart, and she shoved them away. She would not feel sorry for him. She would not! She was glad he was suffering! It was only right after what he'd done.

"Forgive whatever grievances you have against one another." Her father's voice echoed in the black stillness of her mind.

No! The rejection came fierce, determined.

"Forgive as the Lord forgave you."

Her heart twisted with pain, and she turned away from Brad with a jerk.

How do I forgive him, Lord? It's his fault Josh is dead. His fault my heart is dead!

The cold, bitter thoughts ran through her, and she closed her eyes, sickened by the realizations washing over her.

Gavin deserves an answer, Father, but how do I give him one? I have nothing to give him! No love. No trust. Just an empty, dead heart....

She wrapped her arms around herself, fighting the emotions that threatened to envelop her.

That boy killed my heart, Father.

She felt a gentle touch on her arm and jerked away, turning, ready to fight.

"Whoa!" Gavin's eyes were wide. "It's only me, Taylor."

Her breath came out in a rush, and she put out a shaking hand. He took it in his own and drew her against him, cradling her, sharing his warmth with her suddenly chilled body.

"I'm sorry." The words were hushed and ragged. "I—it just was a shock to see him—Brad, I mean."

Gavin nodded. "I see him." The sadness in his voice disturbed her. "The boy looks like he's in a bad way." She stiffened, and his hold tightened. "I'm sorry, lass. I'm sorry it still hurts so much."

"Take me home, Gavin." Her voice was flat. "Please...just take me home."

He didn't question, didn't remind her they hadn't

gotten supplies yet. He simply led her to the Blazer, opened the door, and helped her get in. As he came around to the driver's side, she cast a quick glance out the window.

Brad was still there, his face ashen,…and as the truck pulled away, she was hit with the terrible realization that the boy's face was streaked with tears.

Connor stood staring after the Blazer, willing his pulse rate back to normal.

The woman had been even more exotic, more beautiful in person than she'd been in the picture. He wasn't even disappointed that her eyes weren't brown but green…at least, he thought they were. He hadn't been close enough to see, really, but he'd had the distinct impression of gold-flecked emeralds. And the impact of meeting her gaze head-on had left him feeling as though he'd been nailed on the side of the head with a sledge hammer. Twice.

It wasn't just her looks that had pierced him. He'd seen his share of beautiful women. Usually that didn't faze him much. No, it was deeper than that. There had been something in her expression, something in her eyes, that had reached down inside of him and taken hold.

And then, when she'd turned away, he'd seen her stiffen as though someone had struck her. She'd stared at the kid walking down the street, and he'd stared back, defiance warring on his face with what Connor would swear was shame.

Connor had been stunned by the strong urge he'd felt, the desire to go to the woman, to protect her from whatever was happening. He gave a mirthless laugh. Since when did he want to play the knight in shining armor?

Since I looked into those eyes...

With an exasperated sigh, he walked toward the library. *Keep your focus, Alexander. You're here to find wolves, remember. And that doesn't have anything to do with your mystery woman.*

No matter how much he might wish it did.

Gavin drove in silence. The only contact he attempted was to reach out and clasp Taylor's chilled fingers in his large, warm hand. She leaned her head back against the seat and struggled to hold back the tears. Her empty book bag sat on the floor by her feet.

"Did you find what you wanted at the library?" Gavin ventured after several miles. She started, the memory of her discussion with Linda flooding back.

"No." She was grateful for something to pull her mind away from Brad...and Josh. "I—I left after a few minutes."

He quirked his eyebrow. "Why?"

Instead of answering, she looked at him. "Gavin, do you hate wolves?"

He searched her face, as though a bit concerned about her sanity, and she didn't blame him. The question sounded odd even to her own ears—abrupt and out of left field.

"I'm sorry. I know that sounded weird." She shook her head. "Linda told me some of the ranchers in the area are getting worked up over some rumors about wolves."

"'Worked up' meaning they're getting their guns ready?"

She bit her lip and gave a quick nod. "I couldn't help wondering if you felt that way, too."

"Would it bother you if I did?"

A sharp pang shot through her, and she found herself fighting tears.

"Taylor, to be honest, I don't know how I feel. I've heard tales about wolves since I was a boy. Tales that make them out to be monsters. My grandda used to tell me bedtime stories"—he grinned wryly—"though I seldom slept afterward. Grandda knew how to spin a truly terrible tale."

"About wolves? But why?"

His expression was troubled. "My grandparents, and their parents and grandparents…they saw wolves differently than Americans do now." He glanced at her, a faint smile on his lips. "Most Americans, anyway. In Europe, wolves were considered monsters, killers. I think a lot of the hatred stemmed from the dark days when Europe was devastated by the Black Plague.

Grandda painted a vivid, horrifying picture of wolves roaming to and fro, seeking something to tear apart. He made it so real, I could almost see it."

"Did the wolves actually attack anyone?"

"I don't know. But he told me how when people were dying in droves across Europe, the wolves pulled corpses from shallow graves and devoured them." He angled a look at her. "Believe me, lass, you hear those stories often enough and the last thing you feel for the creatures is compassion. Fear, definitely. Anger, even hatred. But surely not a sense that these are the fine, noble beasts the environmentalists want us to believe they are."

"But stories like your grandfather told are more fairy tale than truth. Myths and legends. Like stories about werewolves."

"Och! Don't even get me started on those!" The teasing laughter shone from his eyes.

"Wolves aren't at all like the stories make them out to be, Gavin. And they don't attack people."

"Here now, are you telling me Red Riding Hood was a liar?"

Her laugh was decidedly weak. "I'm telling you some people are. Real people…though I'm not sure why."

"What makes you say so?"

She tilted her head and thought for a moment. "Did you ever hear about the time, several years ago, when people here got all upset about that wolf attack in British Columbia?"

"Aye, New Chetwynd, wasn't it? Two hunters shot and killed a wolf that came after them."

"That's just it, Gavin." She turned in the seat so she could face him. "The wolf *didn't* come after them."

Surprise touched his features. "But the paper said—"

"I know what the paper said. It was wrong. I read a book that gave an account of the official report the hunters made. The wolf was just following them. They admitted it never made any movement toward them, never demonstrated any aggression, but they got frightened—"

"It's understandable."

"Getting frightened, maybe. But shooting the wolf wasn't understandable. They had the decency to take the dead wolf to the authorities, but they weren't charged with anything. Then the local news magazine picked up the story and splashed 'Wolf Attack in New Chetwynd!' across the front page." She crossed her arms over her chest. "Everything I've read says there's never been a verified account of a healthy wolf attacking any person in North America."

He looked at her disbelievingly. "Never?"

"The only wolves that have attacked people were rabid, and even those instances are rare. So all those tales about the big bad wolf? They spring from imagination and superstition. That's what these guys are basing their fear on. Not the facts."

He inclined his head. "Maybe you're right. I've never been around the beasts myself. They were gone from the area long before my family came here. So I can't say one way or the other what they're really like. But I do know this"—his eyes darkened—"we're a small band here, and we depend on each other to survive and endure. Ranchers like my uncle make their living on their live-stock, and they aren't greatly inclined to risk their families' welfare just to placate some wolf-lovin' environ-mentalist. Or the government, for that matter. And I'll wager that anyone who chooses a pack of beasts over their friends and neighbors is making a regretful deci-sion. If someone is actually hiding the existence of those creatures, he'd best keep it a well-guarded secret. My guess is he'd become as much a target as the wolves."

The words struck Taylor hard. She knew he was probably right. If her neighbors found out about the wolves, they'd be more likely to kill them than anything else. If government officials found out about them, they might take them away. Relocate them. To someplace safer.

Someplace other than Galloway Glen.

She sat back and stared out the window. A fierce determination swelled up and filled her. No one was going to hurt her wolves. And no one was going to take them away from her. The wolves were hers! They came to her; they were on her land, and she'd fight anyone, friend or foe—even Gavin, she realized in amazement— who dared to set foot anywhere near them! True, she'd only seen the large male that one time at Reunion, but she'd heard him and the others several times in the past year, howling, joining their voices in a mournful, discordant, incredibly beautiful chorus. She'd been thrilled to discover that the beautiful beast who had watched her was not alone. And she was fairly certain they were establishing territory on Galloway Glen. She'd hoped against hope that no one else had seen or heard them, that they were as much her secret as Reunion was.

Now she knew that wasn't the case. And she was terrified of what that meant. For her. And for the majestic creatures who had finally, against all odds, defied the dangers and hatred and returned to the area after being completely annihilated over sixty years ago.

"Why does this trouble you so, Taylor?" Gavin's deep voice broke into her thoughts, and she looked at him, caught off guard. It was on the tip of her tongue to tell him, to ask him for his help, for his counsel,...but something held her back.

She believed he would listen, would promise to help her.

But people can't always keep their promises, can they, Lord?

No, this was her battle. She would handle it on her own. She wouldn't ask for help, not from her family, not from Gavin, not from anyone. There was too much at stake to trust anyone but herself to handle things: her relationships with her neighbors, the wolves' lives...

Your hopes, a voice whispered from deep within. *Your heart.*

Keeping her face devoid of emotion, she lifted her shoulders. "I don't know, it just didn't seem fair, somehow. But I suppose it doesn't really matter one way or the other since there's nothing to back up the rumors. I mean, who's really gullible enough to believe there are wolves in Wyoming?" She forced a laugh and settled back in her seat, hoping Gavin was buying her disinterest.

But his dark, probing eyes reflected doubt—and a vague glimmer of hurt and disappointment. She swallowed with difficulty, wishing he would talk about something else.

Instead, he reached for her hand again, closing his strong fingers around it. "Someday, Taylor, I hope you'll realize you can trust me."

"Gavin—"

He stopped her. "It's all right, lass. I understand. You're just not sure of me yet." He smiled into her troubled eyes, and a gently teasing tone filled his next words. "But don't fret. I'm not giving up. I'll just have to work harder at showing you I'm not just the handsomest man you know, but the finest as well."

SEVEN

Linda Williamson loved books—almost as much as she loved men. So when she heard the front door of the library open and glanced up to see a tall, ruggedly handsome stranger walk in, she was definitely in her element.

She put on her most dazzling smile as the man approached. "Welcome to the Wilson library, sir. May I help direct you to something of interest?"

The man studied her, then inclined his head. "I'm interested in anything you have on wolves."

Undaunted by his lack of response to her friendly overture, Linda turned up the dazzle a notch. "Well, you're in luck! One of our patrons just returned several of our best books on wolves. And we just received a new book on the subject. It's a beautiful combination of writings and photographs."

His eyes lit with interest, and she reached for the books Taylor had returned and set them on the desk in front of him.

"I was just about to shelve these, so you couldn't have timed your arrival any better." Her eyes met his with a flutter. *Electric blue,* she decided. *Like a summer sky when a thunderstorm is brewing.* "I'd be more than happy to show you where the new book is located."

He tilted his head to one side and regarded her curiously. "Is the book hard to find?"

"Well, no...of-of course not." She was taken aback as much by the effect of his deep, sensual voice as by the question. "You look well equipped—I mean, well, I'm sure you know what to do—where to go—for what you want."

His eyebrows arched slightly.

"For the *book* you want!" she amended quickly, feeling increasingly flustered under his intense blue gaze. She stuck out her hand, handing him the slip of paper on which she had written the book title and location for Taylor.

He took the paper, glanced at it, gave her a half smile, and then moved toward the shelves.

Oh, my. She watched him walk away, fanning herself. *Oh, my!*

Connor Alexander leaned back in the hard wooden library chair and laced his fingers behind his head. He stretched his shoulders back, trying to work out the kinks in his weary muscles.

Oh, for a night in my own bed.

The flight from D.C. had been delayed a few hours, and they'd experienced considerable turbulence all the way. By the time he finally arrived in Jackson, he was bone weary. Fortunately, the Jeep Wrangler he'd rented was ready, and the drive to Wilson had been uneventful.

His first stop, the general store, had been profitable. He'd noticed a small group gathered as he entered the building. Four or five men stood watching two old-timers play checkers, and Connor's interest had been immediately peaked by their raised voices and heated exchange. He was willing to bet they weren't discussing checkers.

He eased his way to the shelves closest to the group. Doing his best to look engrossed in selecting just the right bag of chips, he focused on the men's words.

"They come on *my* land," a heavyset man declared, "and they'll get a gut full of poison!"

"Or lead," another chimed in.

"I say we follow Brody Camus's lead," a dark-haired man commented. "We kill off as many of the vermin as we can."

"Now there was a hunter!" Mr. Heavyset agreed with relish. "My dad saw old Brody come in once with more than a hundred wolf pelts."

"Did more to rid this area of wolves than ten men combined, so I hear," Dark Hair chortled.

"I want those wolves to come on my land." This comment came from one of the checkers players, an older gentleman whose baseball cap was pushed back to reveal a craggy, weathered face. Clearly he had spent a good portion of his life outdoors.

His bald statement was met with confusion and exclamations of censure from all.

"Sure." A grin splashed across his face. "I been wantin' a new rug in my den!"

At that, a chorus of approval sounded around the laughing man, and Connor restrained a grimace. He grabbed a bag of chips and headed for the cashier.

The talkative young clerk also proved to be a veritable fount of information.

"I heard those men talking about wolves." Connor nodded toward the group of men at the back of the store. "Thought they were extinct around here."

"They musta come over the mountains from Idaho," the clerk, a gum-chewing, fresh-faced teenager, volunteered, explaining that the locals suspected the animals were somewhere to the north of town, on one of the ranches near Phelps Lake. Connor noted the way the kid's eyes gleamed with excitement. "I'd sure hate to have 'em show up on my ranch. I hear tell a pack of them killers can take down a bull!"

"So they say." Connor had paid for his purchase and walked out of the store.

That was when he'd seen the woman from the pictures. He thought he was imagining her for a moment. He stood there, staring at her, wanting her to turn and look at him—when she'd done just that! He barely managed to look away before she caught him watching her.

Then he'd taken a chance and glanced back—and *wham!*

If he hadn't been leaning against something, he was pretty sure his knees would have buckled.

You've got to get this woman out of your mind, pal. Okay, reality check. So she's beautiful. So what? A face that lovely usually means a head that's equally empty. Or totally full of conceit.

Yes, that helped. He needed to fix as unappealing a picture of her as he could in his mind....

Okay, she was a redneck through and through. Yeah, that was it; she was probably the only daughter of twelve kids. And the youngest, which meant spoiled rotten. Probably couldn't put a coherent sentence together. At least, not one that didn't center on her thick, auburn hair or her high cheekbones or her almost almond-shaped, emerald eyes...eyes that he was sure saw into the depths of his soul.

Conner groaned. This was getting him nowhere. Okay, so the safest tact was to not think of her at all.

He turned back to the newpapers spread out on the table in front of him. *Wolves, Alexander. Think wolves!*

He'd come to the library to find out what he could about the town and the surrounding area. He'd scanned back copies of the town's weekly paper—not a big task considering how small the paper was. Still, that gave him a glimpse of local events and topics of interest. If the Help Wanted ads were any indication, things weren't exactly hopping economically. Seasonal help at the resorts seemed to be the big opportunity. Either that or working as a ranch hand.

Connor set aside the paper and looked over the books the librarian had given him.

He glanced at the desk where the librarian seemed engrossed in her work. After that first intriguing encounter with Mrs. Williamson, as her nameplate identified her, the woman had treated him with a professional, slightly distant attitude. But he knew it would take little more than a friendly word, an interested smile, and she would once again be the welcoming charmer he'd encountered when he first came through the door.

He rubbed his temples as he looked down at the table again. A fan of library cards was spread out in front of him. They were the check-out cards from the wolf books, and each one had the same name on it: Taylor Sorensen.

Why did that name sound familiar? He shuffled through the newspapers, finally pulling out last week's paper. He hadn't seen the name in any of the articles, of that he was fairly certain. So that meant it had to be something from the classifieds.

He spread out the newspaper in front of him, reading over the ad in the Help Wanted section. Ah, there it was.

Temporary, full-time handyman/ranch hand needed. Work will last 1–2 months. Mechanical

and riding skills a must. Housing provided.
Good pay. References required. Contact Taylor
Sorensen, Galloway Glen.

A smile tipped the corners of his mouth. Perfect.
Absolutely perfect.

He stuffed the cards back into the books, swept
them and the newspaper up, and headed for the desk.

Linda looked up uneasily at the sound of firm footsteps
approaching. He was coming to talk again. Stiffening her
shoulders, she watched him stroll up to the desk, looking completely at ease.

The least he could do was have the decency to show
some awareness of the way he was affecting her! From
his bland expression, she might as well have been a cold
piece of toast. Without jelly. Or butter.

"Did you find what you were looking for?" she
asked as he set the books on the desk.

"I think so."

"Is there something else you needed?" The second
the words were out, Linda could have kicked herself.
Why was she being so accommodating? The man was
entirely too sure of himself as it was! She should have
turned her back on him.

"If you could direct me to Taylor Sorensen's ranch,
that would be a help."

"Galloway Glen?" She was tempted to ask why, but the quicker she answered him, the quicker he'd be gone—and the quicker her embarrassment could be forgotten. "I'll draw you a map." She pulled a notepad toward her. "It's north of town. Just follow the signs for Teton Village and Phelps Lake." She sketched a quick map and handed it to him. "Are you...a friend of Taylor's?"

"No, never met him. I'm going to see him about a job."

"Him? Oh, but—" She broke off as the last part of his comment hit her. "A—a job? You're going to...stay in the area?" Aware her voice was becoming high and slightly shrill, she clamped her mouth shut, staring at the desk as though fascinated by its wood veneer.

"For a while, anyway."

She clenched her teeth. He was laughing at her. She was sure of it! Looking up, she met his gaze squarely. "Well. Isn't that nice. I hope it works out. So, here's your map." She knew the words had come out rapid fire, but she just didn't care. She shoved the map at him.

"Thanks for your help." He took the paper and turned to head for the door.

"Wait!"

He halted, turning back to her, his eyebrows raised in inquiry. She smiled sweetly. "Just thought I'd offer you some friendly advice. Watch out for Taylor's dog."

A wary look entered his eyes. "His dog?"

Keeping her expression friendly, compassionate, Linda went on, *"Her* dog. Taylor's a woman. And Sasha—that's the dog—is a bit...unpredictable. Especially where men are concerned."

"And how does Mr. Sorensen feel about that?"

"Josh Sorensen was killed a year ago last fall. Taylor's a widow."

"Then she lives on the ranch alone?" Clearly the man was confused. Good.

"No, not at all. Her parents live on the ranch, and her brother and his family are close by too. Her father, Reverend Camus, is the minister here in town."

"Camus?" His frown deepened. "Any relation to a Brody Camus?"

"Brody Camus was Taylor's grandfather. And his father established Galloway Glen."

From the look on the man's face, this information was less than palatable.

"Anyway," Linda pushed on, "watch out for Taylor's dog. One minute she'll seem just fine; the next she'll be snapping and snarling and going for your throat."

The man blinked. "And she lets this animal run loose?"

Linda was all wide-eyed innocence and concern. "You know how some people are about their animals. But I wouldn't say anything if I were you. To Taylor, that is. About the dog. She's kind of sensitive."

He frowned. She could see his mind processing her

words. "Thanks for the warning."

"My pleasure." As the door closed behind him, she could no longer keep the smug smile off her face. She picked up the books he'd been looking at and set them on the reshelve cart. "*Entirely* my pleasure, I'm sure."

EIGHT

Several hours after she returned from town, Taylor stood staring out the tall, elegant windows of her living room. She never grew tired of the view of her home and the wilderness surrounding it. Many people would go crazy in such a remote location, but she thrived on the challenge. As had Josh.

She pictured his face—and felt a pang of sorrow that it wasn't as clear and immediate as it had been. Instead, another image floated into her mind…one of a firm jawline, golden brown hair, deep blue eyes…

Stop it! She couldn't believe one brief glance from a strange man had rattled her so much. What was it about him that stirred her? Those intense eyes? Or the broad shoulders that looked like they could carry any burden she'd care to place on them? Maybe it was the oddly gentle expression on his rugged features?

No, no, no. The last thing she wanted to do was travel down that particular path. Better not to think about it—or him—at all.

With an impatient sigh, she turned and walked to the kitchen. Actually, the living room, dining room, and kitchen were one large room, a spacious floor plan with furniture arrangements defining each area. That was one of the things Taylor loved about her home: the light, airy feel of the open rooms.

When she pulled open the fridge door and took out the milk jug, Sasha rose from her place on the rug and came over, watching Taylor with interest, her tail wagging.

Taylor smiled at the dog. "Hey, you greedy beast. You ate your breakfast already, remember?" Sasha tilted her head to the side, her eyes fixed on the milk jug, and Taylor laughed, patting the dog's head. "Gavin's right. You *are* a walking garbage disposal."

At the mention of the Scotsman, Taylor frowned. As she poured her glass of milk, she thought about the conversation she and Gavin had had on their return from Wilson. *Why didn't I tell him about the wolves?* No answers came.

She moved back to the living room and sank into her favorite overstuffed chair. Leaning back, she took a deep breath, soaking in the sense of peace she so often felt in this room. She loved the openness of the living room, the way it was so often washed in sunlight, thanks to the tall windows on the south wall and the skylights in the high vaulted ceiling. The sheen of the log walls and the wood floor created a richness and warmth; the simple design of the alderwood chairs and couch with their black, oversized cushions offered homeyness and comfort. Decorative pillows scattered across the furniture added a touch of color and playfulness. From the lighting to the plants to the glorious view, it was a room designed to uplift sagging spirits.

Taylor plopped her feet on the ottoman and leaned back, staring at the ceiling. Would the walls around her heart ever come down again? She'd lowered them for Josh, allowed him to come in and draw her out of the inner fortress she'd built as a child. Nurtured by his love, encouraged by his openness, her long-buried desire to find acceptance and friendship had finally pushed through her defenses and blossomed. Until she'd met Josh, she'd always been a loner except around her family and her animals.

She studied the portrait on the mantel of the river rock fireplace. Her family's faces smiled down at her. Her family. They'd always made her feel accepted, as though she belonged. They gave her security, an anchor. Only with them did she feel safe. With them, and at Reunion—her retreat, her refuge.

It didn't matter a bit that she was always by herself. In fact, she preferred it that way. As a child, Taylor had never felt she really fit in with her schoolmates. She was…different. During her teens, she'd thought the girls in her class were scatterbrained, self-involved, and far too focused on their looks and boys. As for the boys, she'd never met one she couldn't outwrestle, outrun, or outthink.

Put simply, she saw little point in spending time with people with whom she had little or nothing in common.

"I have more interesting conversations with my dog," she told her mother once when she inquired why Taylor didn't spend time with any of the girls in her class. Her mother had raised an eyebrow and cast a glance at the husky lying in the middle of the room.

"Have you ever really talked with any of these girls?" Her gaze came back to rest on her scowling daughter.

"Why bother?" Taylor snorted. "All I have to do is watch and listen. They stare at themselves in the bathroom mirrors every chance they get, they moan about how ugly they are, and they sigh all over themselves if Bobby Ravenhill even looks their way."

Her mother had listened patiently, but her expression clearly told Taylor that she wasn't fooled. She knew how hard it was for her daughter to overcome her self-consciousness and reach out. She also was aware of how cutting teenage girls could be, particularly about anyone who didn't think and act the way they did.

Still, whatever Taylor had lacked in social skills, she more than made up for in inquisitiveness and out-and-out daring. Not with people—they were too intimidating. But Taylor was always *trying* things. The proverbial bookworm, she read everything she could get her hands on. But just reading wasn't enough. She had to *do* something with what she'd read.

Once, in the sixth grade, she watched a TV special

on skydiving. Fascinated, she promptly checked out every book the school library had on the subject. Then she'd fashioned a handkerchief parachute for one of her dolls and launched it from her bedroom window. Her delight when the contraption worked convinced her she could do even better. Soon she was perched on the edge of the hayloft, a homemade parachute—a sheet and some clothesline—tied to her back. She barely missed landing on her father as he came in to feed the horses. Fortunately, she didn't miss the hay pile. The stunned look on her dad's face as she sat there, half-buried in hay, sheet and clothesline draped over her head, was a memory that still made her smile.

Then there was the time she slipped though the fence surrounding the field where their nearest neighbor kept their bull. She'd wanted to see how long it would take the nearsighted beast to spot her and react.

Ryan, who had timed the experiment with the new stopwatch he'd gotten for his birthday, said she should go out for track. When he showed her her time for getting from the middle of the field to the fence, she couldn't argue.

"Course, we don't know if you'd run as fast without a bull on your heels," he commented as they mounted their horses and headed for home. She couldn't argue with that, either.

A loud knock on the door pulled her from her thoughts, and she hopped up as the front door opened.

Luke Narbona came in, his dark brown eyes filled

with warmth. "You returned, but you didn't call me to help you unload the supplies, *Yazhi.*"

The Navajo endearment warmed her. *Yazhi.* "Little One." She tossed her arm around her friend's shoulders. Few people would have guessed Luke was old enough to be retired. He had the straight carriage and build of a far younger man. His copper skin glowed with health, and his aquiline features were smooth and free of wrinkles. Only a few streaks of gray in his long black hair, worn in a braid, betrayed him. He was a man who thrived on activity—especially activity that improved Galloway Glen or the retreat center. Taylor's home had become as much a passion for Luke as it was for her.

"That's because I didn't get any supplies, Luke." His eyes were filled with questions, but she forestalled them by leading him from the house to the barn. "But I'm sure we can find something to keep you busy."

"What happened in town, Taylor? Why'd you leave before you got supplies?"

She considered telling him about Brad, but the thought of reliving the experience was too overwhelming. Instead, she told him about the ranchers and their reaction to the rumor of wolves.

"The wolves are gone from this area," he said. "These men are foolish, like worried old women, to think they could return."

"That's what I said," Taylor agreed with a smile. "There haven't been wolves in this part of Wyoming for more than sixty years. I don't know why anyone would believe they'd suddenly come back."

Luke glanced around him. They were in the horse barn. He shot Taylor a pointed look. "Hmpf! Why do I think I know where this is leading?"

She grinned. "That's what I've always liked best about you, my friend." She handed him a shovel. "Your remarkable keen sense of the obvious."

Later that night the moon was high and bright in the sky as Taylor sat and rocked on her front porch. She snuggled into the soft quilted comforter her grandmother had made her, then reached a hand out to rest on Sasha's broad head.

The husky turned, and a twinkle of moonlight caught her ice blue eyes as she looked at her mistress. Affection swept Taylor as she stroked the dog's soft fur.

Sasha was Taylor's second Siberian husky. Her parents had given her a pup, Vanya—a name meaning "gift from God"—when she was ten, and she and the husky had loved each other completely and unconditionally. When Taylor came home from college, new husband in tow, Vanya fixed him with a dubious stare, then moved to sit between the two of them, her unblinking gaze fastened on Josh as though warning him that Taylor was hers and not to be trifled with. Fortunately Josh loved dogs, and it had only taken him a few weeks—and an entire box of dog biscuits—to win the Siberian over.

When Vanya died at the ripe old age of fifteen,

Taylor had been devastated. Josh put up with her moping for a week, then told her to get her coat and get in the car, they were going for a drive. They ended up at the home of a local husky breeder who just happened to have a litter of pups. It was there Taylor found Sasha.

Actually, it was more accurate to say Sasha found her.

Taylor had gone to sit on the back stairs, where she was petting a five-month-old male, when she felt something warm and moist nudge the back of her neck. She turned to find Sasha behind her. The dog looked at her for a moment with the most amazing pair of white-blue eyes, then laid her chin on Taylor's shoulder and licked her neck with the tip of her pink tongue. Taylor was lost. Just under a year old, Sasha had been returned to the breeder by a woman who had developed severe allergies to the dog's thick double coat.

When the breeder saw Sasha's action, he grinned. "Well, the dog's made her choice. I guess the final decision is up to you."

Taylor took her home that very day. And though one dog could never replace another, Sasha quickly became an integral part of the Sorensens' lives. In no time at all it became clear that Sasha was not only thoroughly devoted to Taylor, but also perfectly suited to her chosen mistress in personality and temperament. She enjoyed nothing more than trotting alongside Topaz, roaming the ranch with Taylor. Like most huskies, she was as independent and stubborn as she was loyal and loving.

As Taylor rubbed Sasha's velvet soft ears, she closed her eyes, soaking in the silence—until the sound of movement in the nearby woods startled her. Taylor stilled, staring into the darkness. Sasha stood slowly, her ears twitching, a low growl rumbling in her chest.

Heart pounding, Taylor stood, too, possibilities running through her mind. A bear? Maybe, though it wouldn't have been so quiet. Raccoon? Could be, though it had sounded larger. Actually it could be any number of nocturnal animals....

It could also be human.

The unwelcome thought nudged its way into her mind, and she stiffened. If that were so, it was an intruder. Neighbors or friends would have identified themselves right away.

Her eyes swept the woods, trying to discern any activity in the moonlight.

Sasha growled again and tensed beside her, ready to bound into the trees. Taylor placed a hand on the dog's head. "Stand!" she commanded in a low voice, and the dog obeyed, standing motionless—her eyes fixed on the woods.

"Who's out there?" Taylor put as much confidence in the question as she could. Never let 'em see you sweat. She'd learned that early on.

Silence was her only response—until Sasha turned her head sharply. Taylor jumped.

So much for appearing cool and confident!

"What is it, girl?" Taylor touched Sasha's head, but

the dog didn't look up at her. Something had caught her full attention, and she tilted her head, angling her ears as though listening more carefully to whatever night sound was drawing her.

Taylor strained her ears…and heard the faint rise and fall of a wolf howl.

Relief swept through her, and she looked down at the Siberian. Sasha was lifting her chin, as though tempted to join in the distant song.

"I understand, Sash. I've been tempted, too." She cast another look toward the dark woods, but all was silent. If something, or someone, had been there, it seemed to be gone now.

She lowered herself to sit next to Sasha, draping her arm around the dog and resting her head against the animal's soft, fur-covered neck. With a sigh, Taylor listened to—and was oddly soothed by—the eerie, resonant song that rose and drifted on the wind.

NINE

THE SOUND CAME TO HIM IN THE NIGHT, AND AT FIRST HE thought it was just another nightmare. But it continued even after he awoke, and a shudder gripped him.

He threw off the covers and moved to the window, looking out on the moonlit landscape. He concentrated, listening intently. Had he really heard the howling?

Yes, there it was again, distant and haunting. He leaned his forehead against the cool glass of the window, his long black hair falling like a curtain to hide his face as he fought the sadness welling up within him.

So the rumors were true. He'd granted himself the luxury of not believing, of dismissing what he felt were the tales of old women masquerading as hunters. He knew how quick men were to label any howl wolf howls, even if they knew that it was really just dogs in the area venting their canine angst. It always sounded so much better to say, "Hey! I heard a wolf howling last night," than "Tommy Black Elk's old hound dogs were at it again."

But this…there was no mistaking this haunting,

sonorous song rising in the night. The ever-changing pitches, the discordant symphony that lifted and danced on the wind, as though wooing its listeners to join in. His dark eyes narrowed. This was not Tommy Black Elk's hounds. This was a wild song, full of excitement and an almost seductive entreaty. It was hard not to be drawn.

As Taylor apparently had been drawn.

His heart lurched. She'd lied to him—told him she didn't think there were any wolves in the area. But clearly those howls were coming from her ranch.

The fact that she'd sided with them against him was galling. Didn't she understand what these animals were? It wasn't even so much that they were killers. Many animals could be accused of that fault. No. The greatest danger lay in what they could cost Taylor. If she sided with them, she would be siding against her neighbors. She would become a target. He couldn't let that happen.

He turned from the window and went back to his bed. Morning would begin soon enough. He needed to get some rest, to find some sense of restoration and oblivion before he took up the battle.

His eyes glittered with a fierce resolve as he pictured his adversary: the amber eyes, the falsely sweet expression, the sharp, jagged teeth. And then superimposed on the image of the beast came the reflection of a beautiful smiling face framed by long dark hair and emerald green eyes brimming with laughter and sincerity.

He sighed and turned over, punching his pillow

into submission. For now, he needed sleep. Tomorrow he would plan and prepare.

He would have to be cautious. He couldn't let Taylor know what he was doing. He didn't want to alienate her, to destroy what they were building. He'd have to be as clever and skilled as his opponent if he were to succeed.

Yes, tomorrow he would begin to plan. And by next week he would be ready to do what needed to be done.

On that determined note, he closed his eyes.

TEN

CONNOR TURNED HIS WRANGLER OFF THE HIGHWAY AND drove under a tall arch made of logs. At the top of the arch was a large sign with the name Galloway Glen carved into it. The librarian's map had been clear and exact, a pleasant surprise. He'd half expected her to lead him to the edge of a cliff somewhere.

He eased the vehicle down the long, winding gravel drive, admiring the scenery. Fields of wildflowers bordered the drive. Just beyond the field to the west was a thick forest of evergreens, and beyond that the Tetons loomed in all their craggy majesty. Galloway Glen was a wilderness paradise.

Perfect location for a pack of wolves. A pang of regret shot through him. Too bad such a place was owned by wolf haters.

You don't know that for certain.

The caution breezed into my mind, and he found himself arguing. "I know, Lord, but if her grandfather was what those men say he was..."

People change.

Connor couldn't argue with that. Still, it seemed wiser to follow Harry's instructions, as much as they galled him. He would have preferred to knock on Taylor Sorensen's door and tell her who he was and what he wanted. But until he was sure she wouldn't run him off her land—and then follow in her grandfather's footsteps—he'd just have to play this Harry's way. Fortunately, he had the perfect plan to accomplish his task.

Provided Taylor Sorensen still needed a handyman.

Within a mile or so he saw the ranch buildings. As he drew nearer, he passed a herd of horses grazing in a fenced-in field. The driveway opened into a parking area, and he pulled into a spot in front of a large barn. As he stepped from the Jeep, he looked around enjoying the view.

The buildings were well-cared-for log structures. To the east of the barn were several small cabins, complete with porches and rocking chairs. In front of him, opposite the barn, was a beautiful, ranch-style, two-story log home made of lodgepole pine. The wraparound porch with its rocking chairs and large pots of flowers gave the house a welcoming appearance.

Heavy double doors and a large, circle-head window graced the front entrance, which jutted out slightly from the rest of the house. From what Connor could see, the entryway had to have a vaulted ceiling. On either side of the entrance were windows as tall as the front doors, and these were flanked by double windows topped with fanlights. The overall effect was one of rustic elegance.

In fact, everything about Galloway Glen seemed to proclaim beauty, clarity, and balance. It was a far cry from D.C., that was for sure.

Drawing a deep breath of the crisp, clean air into his lungs, he went up the steps to the front doors. It was time to go to work.

Taylor was sitting at the kitchen table with her mother, just finishing a second cup of coffee when the doorbell rang.

She looked from her mom to the door. "Who can that be?"

"I suppose you could always answer it and find out."

"I suppose so." Taylor got up. It wasn't Luke—he would have pounded on the door, then come in. And Gavin always came to the kitchen door.

The only people who rang the front doorbell were people who didn't know her.

She walked across the living room and peered through the peephole in the massive pine door—then felt a jolt shoot through her.

It was him. The stranger from town. And seeing him this close up was doing odd things to her breathing. And her knees.

"Wow!" She jumped when a hand came to rest on her shoulder.

"'Wow'?" Her mother stood on tiptoe to look out the peephole, then turned to look at her daughter. "Wow indeed."

Taylor went for a second look.

What was a man like this doing in the middle of nowhere—particularly in the middle of *her* nowhere? Before a suitable answer came to her, he rang the bell again.

"Do you intend to stand there and gawk all day, dear, or are you going to invite the poor man inside?"

"I wonder what he wants?" Taylor matched her mother's quiet tone.

"I'm sure I don't know, dear." Her mother turned back to the kitchen. "But you certainly won't find out if you don't let him in." The last three words were spoken in a raised voice, and Taylor swiveled to shoot her mother a warning look.

Her eyes drifted back to the peephole—and she found herself eye-to-eye with the man. The full impact of his intense, blue gaze hit Taylor as solidly as a splash of cold water, and she jumped back, unaware that Sasha had padded over soundlessly to stand behind her. Her heel came down on one of the husky's paws, and Sasha yipped in pain, scrambling out of the way. Taylor gave a yelp of her own as she lost her balance and landed in a heap on the floor.

"Ohhhhhh." She groaned, rolling onto her back and

staring up at the ceiling. "I knew I should have stayed in bed."

"You certainly would have gotten into less trouble." Her mother's tone was a blend of compassion and humor.

With a resigned sigh she pushed to her feet. *Please, God, let him be gone.*

She peered out the peephole again.

He was standing there, completely at ease, his arms crossed, his eyes fixed on the peephole, as though he knew she was there. His thick golden brown hair just brushed the collar of his leather jacket. A slight smile tilted his lips, making him even more attractive—a fact that Taylor found particularly irritating.

Well, nothing to do now but admit defeat. She reached down to turn the handle and, with what she hoped was complete calm, pulled open the door.

"Yes?"

His mouth opened as though he'd intended to answer, but nothing came out. He just stood there, staring at her, mouth agape. So she wasn't the only one affected by their encounter. The satisfaction—and pleasure—that gave her was far greater than it should have been.

When he blinked at her, she had the impression he was trying to make her disappear, like a mirage.

Or a nightmare?

She arched her brows, and he clamped his mouth shut, cleared his throat, then clenched his jaw.

She smiled as sweetly as she could. "May I…help you?"

"Mrs. Sorensen?" Ah, so the man could speak! And quite well. His voice was deep and resonant, and she had the oddest feeling that it was reaching out to wrap around her.

She found herself studying his features. Up close, she saw he was more rugged than classically handsome. A straight Roman nose gave way to a mobile mouth and a square jaw. The set of his cleft chin suggested a definite stubborn streak.

All in all, he gave the impression of confidence, power, and strength. Taylor could easily picture him barking out orders and expecting—no, demanding—immediate obedience. Not that she'd be inclined to do otherwise….

For Pete's sake, Taylor, get a grip!

Now she was the one to clear her throat. "Yes, I'm Mrs. Sorensen."

"Ma'am, I'm Connor Alexander. I'm here about your ad."

She blinked. "My…ad?"

His brows arched a fraction higher. "For a handyman." He spoke with careful diction as though she were either hearing or understanding impaired.

"Oh! Yes. Of course," Taylor tried to sound businesslike. *This* man was a handyman? "Won't you come in, please?"

He stepped inside. "I realize I should have called

you first, but if the job is still available, I wanted to get things moving as quickly as possible—" His eyes were focused on Sasha, who was sitting near Taylor, watching him.

Taylor looked from him to the husky. *What on earth…?* "Is something wrong?"

He looked at her, seemed about to say something, then snapped his mouth shut. "No, nothing."

"Well, why don't you come in." She moved aside, motioning toward the living room. "As it happens, the job is still open."

He moved into the room, keeping a wary eye on Sasha, then stopped with a slight start when her mother came into the room. Taylor saw his eyes widen slightly with admiration. She wasn't surprised. Her mother seldom went unnoticed.

"Mr. Alexander, I'm Donelle Camus, Taylor's mother." She extended a slim, graceful hand. "I couldn't help over-hearing that you're here for the job. I assume you brought references?"

"Of course." Taylor gave the man two points for not being the least bit flustered at her mother's blunt question.

"Well, that's fine then. Please, have a seat." Her mother turned a gracious smile her way, and Taylor noted with alarm the mischievous twinkle that suddenly sparkled in her mother's eyes. "I'm certain my daughter has several questions she'd like to ask you."

At the teasing tone of her mother's voice, Taylor gave her a warning glare.

"About your qualifications." It didn't work. Her mother went on, "experience...*marital status*—"

Taylor grasped her mother firmly by the elbow and propelled her toward the front door, which still stood open.

"Actually—" Taylor tossed over her shoulder— "Mother was just leaving."

"Was I really? Well, I hadn't noticed." There was definite laughter in her mother's voice. When they reached the door, she stopped, and Taylor barely avoided running over her.

Taylor stepped back, her arms crossed, and received one of her mother's haughtiest looks. "For heaven's sake, dear, if you want me to leave, all you need to do is ask."

Taylor felt her cheeks flush as her mother looked at the man, who was now watching them with clear amusement.

"It was a pleasure to meet you, Mr. Alexander. I hope we'll see more of you." With that, her mother turned and made a regal exit.

Shaking her head, Taylor came back into the living room, Sasha padding along beside her. She glanced at her visitor, noting the watchful way his eyes trailed the husky as they approached. Taylor hesitated. "Are you uncomfortable with dogs, Mr. Alexander?"

"Not as a rule."

Taylor dropped into one of the large, overstuffed chairs. The man sat at one end of the couch, his gaze still glued to Sasha as she circled the floor next to Taylor's feet, then plopped down with a contented sigh.

Taylor stifled a twinge of irritation. *This is getting ridiculous!*

"Mr. Alexander, I assure you there's no need to be uneasy around Sasha."

He lifted his eyes, and her irritation increased when she saw the doubt reflected in that blue gaze.

"Now, look—"

Sasha started at the sharp tone of Taylor's voice, coming to her feet and moving between Taylor and Mr. Alexander, a low growl sounding deep in her chest.

In a flash Mr. Alexander was on his feet, tensed and ready for action. Taylor stared at him, dumbfounded.

"Sit!" Sasha obeyed her command; the man did not.

"Okay, I know you don't like to talk about this—" he kept his eyes fixed on Sasha—"but if you can't control your animal, I hardly think you should let it roam loose when there are strangers visiting. You seem to know dogs, so you should be aware how intimidating some of the larger breeds can be."

"If I can't control—" Then she was on her feet as well. "Look, you! My dog is as well behaved as they come—"

"You call attacking people well behaved?"

Taylor felt her mouth drop open. Had she let a nut case into her house? "She hardly attacked you!"

"No, but—"

"For that matter, she's never attacked anyone! She simply wouldn't—not unless I was in danger!"

Clearly that surprised him, and he turned a quick, assessing gaze on the husky. His eyes narrowed suddenly, as though he'd just figured out some perplexing riddle.

"Mrs. Sorensen—" But Taylor had heard enough.

"I don't know where you get off implying Sasha isn't safe—"

"Mrs. Sorensen, I—"

"—when you've never even *met* her before—"

"Please, there's been a mistake—"

"But if she *were* to attack someone, Mr. Alexander, I could certainly understand why she would attack *you!*"

Taylor felt a nudge against her leg and looked down to find Sasha sitting there, staring at her with a worried expression. She laid her hand on the dog's head, trying to calm down—and almost jumped out of her skin when a large, tanned hand covered hers where it rested between Sasha's soft ears. She turned and found herself almost nose-to-nose with her irritating visitor.

"Mrs. Sorensen, I'd like to apologize."

The quietly spoken words struck her as utterly sincere, but before she could formulate a response, the man knelt in front of Sasha and scratched her velvety chin. "And I apologize to you, too, girl. I judged you unfairly."

Sasha leaned forward to bestow a quick lick on Connor Alexander's nose. Her tail thumped approvingly, and she gazed into his eyes with adoration. Taylor sat down, thoroughly disgusted.

What in the world had just happened?

The man's eyes met hers, and he eased into a smile.

"I realize I've hardly made a great first impression, Mrs. Sorensen, but I promise you I had a reason for my…odd behavior."

Taylor pressed her lips together. *This ought to be good.*

But instead of explaining, he rose and moved back to the couch, picked up an envelope he had laid on the cushion, and handed it to her. "My references," he said in response to her questioning look.

"Ah." She lifted the flap and drew out several neatly typed sheets of paper. Scanning them, she found that, according to several previous employers and professional contacts, Connor Alexander was a veritable paragon of virtues.

"So I take it you didn't insult any of their dogs?"

Quick humor sparkled in his eyes. "No, I was more well behaved with them."

"Hmmm." She started to relax a bit. "I see you've had experience on a ranch."

"Raised on one."

"And you worked as a handyman when you were in college."

"Obviously a few years ago." His voice was laced with repressed laughter. "But I remember what I learned."

"Well, it seems you're qualified, but…"

"But?"

She looked at him in silence, then decided to be blunt. "Why do you want the job, Mr. Alexander?"

"Why does a man want any job?"

"Yes, but this is something more suited to a high school or college student. It hardly seems the kind of job that would attract someone of your—"

"Advanced years?" He was smiling again, and she felt her face warm in reaction to that smile. Blast the man! Why did he have to be so ridiculously attractive?

"Experience."

She would not let him distract her—no matter how charmingly he smiled at her. "I confess I'm a bit confused. And I would appreciate some clarification."

That said, she fixed him with a steady look and waited.

Connor held Taylor's gaze, keeping his features as impassive as possible. He settled back in the cushions of the couch and regarded her.

When she'd first opened the door and stood there, he'd almost dropped his teeth. It was the first time in his entire life he could remember being speechless. He thought for a moment that he'd gone crazy, that the image of the woman he'd seen in town had so permeated his mind that he was seeing her everywhere.

Then he'd realized it was really her. Standing there. Right in front of him. And she looked at him then much the way she was looking at him now, as though she wanted an explanation.

What do I say, Lord? He was loathe to lie. So he gave

her as much of the truth as he could.

"You're right on one point. This job does seem well suited to a student. But it also happens to be perfectly suited to my needs at the moment."

Her delicate eyebrows arched, but she remained silent.

You're a tough one, aren't you? He noted the glint of steel in her eyes. They weren't emerald now; they were more of a deep, rich, moss green.

"I'm a freelance photographer. Or I'm trying to be. I've had some success doing shoots in wilderness areas, but I'm still new to the profession. So I decided to take a few months and travel around, checking out different regions, looking for places that are unique and ruggedly beautiful, but for the most part undiscovered. Wyoming seemed an ideal place to start."

It was all true. The fact that it wasn't the *entire* truth hardly bothered him at all. What small pangs of discomfort plagued him, he pushed aside. There was too much at stake to be squeamish.

"But if you're a photographer, why do you want a job as a handyman?"

Connor looked at the woman sitting in front of him. She was sharp. He could almost see the wheels turning as her mind worked to bring the facts in line with reason.

"Because I don't make money until I sell my photos"—that much was true—"and I prefer eating to starving. This job was particularly attractive because you provide housing as well. Another expense I don't have to deal with."

Still all true. The lower he kept his expenses, the better.

"If I hire you, I expect to keep you busy. When do you plan to take your photos?"

"Whenever I can. My equipment is fairly easy to transport. And I assume I'll get a break or two during the day."

"Of course."

"And time for meals."

"Well, yes—"

"So there will be opportunities. Believe me, Mrs. Sorensen, if you hire me, I'll give you a decent day's work. And I'll do my best to stay out of your way when I'm not working. You won't even know I'm around."

"Hmmm." She sounded less than convinced, and she studied him. Despite her closed expression, he sensed something…a certain caution, a vulnerability. It was almost as though she were afraid of him. Or of herself.

She turned her face from him, reaching out to scratch the husky's neck. He took the opportunity to study her profile, taking in the oval-shaped face, high cheekbones, and well-defined brows. Her long, auburn hair was as thick as he'd thought, and it glimmered with red-gold highlights. She wore it parted in the middle, and it flowed in a graceful wave to well below her shoulders.

Dressed in a Henley shirt, jeans, and brown leather boots, she was the picture of simple beauty. He knew how he would photograph her: standing in the woods, trees decked in autumn colors all around her, the wind lifting her hair, those amazing green eyes shining with pleasure and excitement....

She turned to look at him again, and, as had happened in town, their eyes collided. A startling awareness shot through him, and his heart thudded once, then settled back to its natural rhythm. He let out a slow breath.

How could just watching a woman be such a disturbing experience?

"Okay."

He blinked at the short comment. "Okay?" Thank goodness his voice was steady, calm. Not a bit like his erratic pulse.

"Okay. You're hired." Before he could respond, she stood and motioned toward the door. "I assume you have your things with you?"

He stood as well. "Out in the car."

"Good. I'll show you to your cabin." She glanced at her watch, then smiled at him. "While you're settling in, I should have plenty of time to check your references."

"Of course." He wouldn't have expected any less.

"Assuming everything's on the up-and-up, I'll give you a tour of the ranch, and we'll go over meal times and other information. Then we can get started on the work tomorrow, first thing in the morning." A delightful pair of dimples appeared in her cheeks. "There's a fence on the back forty that's been waiting for you for quite some time now."

"And if my references don't check out?" He followed her to the front door and out onto the porch.

She glanced at him over her shoulder, an impish gleam in her eyes. "Then I'll just send Sasha out to get rid of you. Which could mean anything from chasing you off to eating you. After all—" she sounded gleeful as she headed for his Wrangler—"you know how intimidating large dogs can be."

ELEVEN

THE NEXT MORNING, CONNOR WAS STARTLED FROM HIS dreams by a loud clanging.

Sitting bolt upright in bed, he looked around wildly, wondering where the train was. He blinked at the unfamiliar surroundings, his mind struggling to make sense of the rude assault.

With an in-drawn breath, memory returned; he fell back against the mattress. He was at Galloway Glen, settled into a cozy cabin—one bedroom and a bathroom. He closed his eyes, reviewing what Taylor had told him yesterday. He was to mend fences and help renovate and update the small retreat cabins while Taylor's brother and father were gone on some rafting trip. In addition to this work, they would be scouting out new, longer riding trails for retreat day trips. And Taylor's mother would be around on a regular basis—she served as chief cook and bottle washer during the retreat season and had often stayed with Taylor when her husband was away.

The playful interaction between mother and daughter yesterday had filled him with the desire to talk with his own parents. Connor peered into the darkness, and images flooded his mind...his mother laughing, his father running alongside him as he learned how to ride a bike, both of their faces gleaming with pride when he graduated college, their family devotions and prayer times. They loved each other. And the Lord.

He stretched, filling the queen-sized bed with his tall frame, one hand barely missed knocking over the lamp on the bedside table. He stared at the digital clock next to the lamp, and his eyes widened. He threw back the comforter and padded to the dresser, flicking on the small lamp on the top of the dresser. Grabbing up his watch he peered at the dial, then closed his eyes.

The clock was right. It was four-thirty in the morning. He went to the window at the front of the cabin, pushed aside the curtains, and peered out into the darkness. Pitch black. The clanging continued, and Connor's eyes finally located the source. Mrs. Camus, decked out in an apron, stood on the lighted porch of the ranch house, clanging a metal spoon on a large, heavy triangle that hung above her.

With a disgusted snort he let the curtains fall back in place, grabbed a towel from the back of the over-stuffed easy chair, navigated past a small table with its accompanying chairs, and stalked into the bathroom to shower.

▗▚▚▚▚▚▖

"Your new worker isn't exactly a morning person."

Taylor turned at this pronouncement and went to stand beside her mother, peering out the kitchen window with her. Sure enough, Connor Alexander was heading toward the house, his hair still wet and slightly awry, his stride indicating he was less than pleased to be up and about.

Smothering a grin, Taylor went to finish setting the table.

"I take it you didn't tell him when we start working around here, eh?" her mother inquired mildly.

"I told him we get up early," Taylor replied.

"Hmmm, apparently he didn't believe you. Perhaps this will help." She handed Taylor a steaming cup of strong, black coffee.

Taylor planted a kiss on her cheek. "Thanks, Mom. You're a jewel."

"Of course." Her mother picked up a tray of bacon and set it on the table.

The door opened and Connor walked in. "Mornin'," he mumbled as he glanced around the kitchen. Taylor, who had moved to stand next to the door, stuck the steaming mug under his nose.

"Looking for this?" She barely restrained a giggle.

He took one whiff, and an expression of delight broke out over his face. He lifted his hands, cupped the mug as though it were filled with gold, and took several quick sips. His eyes closed in what Taylor could only describe as ecstasy, and he set down the mug on the table. She cocked an eyebrow at him but didn't comment, then grabbed the carafe and topped off his cup.

He drank more slowly this time, then turned a look of appreciation on her. "Thanks." His voice was less rough than when he'd first come in. "I'm starting to feel human again."

She laughed. "Well, that's good. Now have a seat. I've got a whole list of things we need to do after breakfast."

He pulled out a chair and surveyed the breakfast spread before him, licking his lips. Plates of hot griddlecakes, toast, and fresh biscuits were flanked by platters of eggs, bacon, and sausage. Next to these were bowls of grits, sausage gravy, and hash browns. Pitchers of orange juice and grapefruit juice stood watch over a bowl of large, ripe strawberries.

At his stunned expression, Taylor didn't even try to hide her grin.

"I wasn't sure what you liked, Mr. Alexander." Her mother patted him on the shoulder. "So I fixed you a little of everything. Can't have a man facing his first day on the job without a good breakfast, now can we?"

He looked up at her, and Taylor was struck by the appreciative look in his eyes. "No, ma'am, we can't. Thank you."

"Of course," Taylor added, "you don't have to eat it all."

He fixed her with a look of offended amazement. "A man doesn't get this kind of treatment often, Mrs. Sorensen, and I intend to enjoy as much of it as I can." He leaned forward to help himself to something from every plate, then commenced eating with gusto.

Donelle beamed at him, patted his shoulder again, and went to the sink to start washing dishes, humming as she stuck her hands into the soapy water.

"Well, suit yourself. But don't expect me to go easy on you just because you end up with a stomachache."

He paused, a forkful of eggs halfway to his mouth, and regarded her with twinkling eyes. "I appreciate your concern, Mrs. Sorensen, but I have been blessed with a cast-iron, bottomless pit for a stomach. So I imagine the only thing less likely than me getting a stomachache"— he popped the eggs in his mouth, chewed appreciatively, then finished—"is you going easy on anyone. For any reason."

An appreciative chuckle came from the sink, and Taylor glared at her mother's back. As perceptive as always, Donelle stopped washing dishes and looked at her. Seeing Taylor's displeased look, her mouth curved.

"It's okay, dear. You go ahead and shoot sparks at me if it makes you feel better." She turned back to the dishes. "I can understand what a terrible shock it is to get as well as you give." She clucked her tongue. "And so early in the morning."

"Mother!"

Donelle turned innocent eyes back to her indignant

daughter. "Well, you have to admit, hon, you started it." She beamed at Connor. "And I must say, he finished it well." She nodded approvingly. "You made a good choice, dear. You need a man around here with spunk."

"I need—" Taylor couldn't believe what she was hearing. She stood and stared at her mother. "I most certainly do not need a man with spunk!"

"Don't be silly, sweetheart. Of course you do. You'd make mincemeat out of—"

"What I *meant* is that I don't need a man! Period! Spunk or otherwise!" That clarified, Taylor stomped to the doorway, pausing only long enough to spin around and pin Connor with a furious glare. "As for *you!* Be at the stables in fifteen minutes!" Then she was gone.

Connor sat staring after Taylor, then he met Donelle Camus's laughing gaze. "Wow." Her mouth twitched. "Indeed." She went back to her dishes, and he finished eating as quickly as he could. No point annoying his new boss any further. When he rose to leave, Taylor's mom stopped him with a quiet question.

"Are you a praying man, Mr. Alexander?"

He halted, turning to face her. "Yes, ma'am, I am."

The smile she gave him was pure merriment. "Now would be a good time, don't you think?"

A grin split his face and he laughed. "Actually," he said, reaching out to pat her shoulder, "I've *been* praying since the minute I got this job!"

▧▧▧▧▧▧

For the next week, Taylor kept Connor hopping. He would no sooner finish one job then she would give him another. One thing he could say about his new boss: she was true to her word. She was not going easy on him.

In fact, Connor sensed that she was testing him, pushing him to see if he would resist or rebel. So he made it a point to be as accommodating as possible. He accepted each task agreeably, listening carefully as she explained what she wanted and asking questions only when necessary.

The second day, after completing a job, Connor had walked into the stables, looking around at the stalls lining both sides of the building. Horses were munching away happily at their hay.

"One thing about Taylor," a deep voice said from behind him, "she knows horses. Too bad her knowledge of people isn't as refined."

Connor turned. A tall, dark-haired man stood there leaning on a shovel. Connor stepped forward and put out a hand. "I'm Connor Alexander, the new ranch hand."

The man stood unmoving, staring at Connor's extended hand, making no move to accept it. Just then, Taylor came out of one of the stalls. "Oh, Luke, there you are." A warm smile lit her face. "This is Connor Alexander. He's—"

"The new ranch hand. Yes, so he's told me."

Taylor closed her mouth, staring from Luke to Connor. After a moment she tried again. "Connor, this is

Luke Narbona. He's the genius who keeps things fixed here and there before they fall apart."

Connor extended his hand again, and the older man reached out slowly and shook it.

Taylor was watching them, a pensive look in those green eyes. "Luke, I was hoping he could work with you today on the back forty fence."

"I'm not going out there today."

Taylor blinked at Luke's quiet but firm response, and Connor watched two spots of pink tinge her cheeks. He wanted to box the man's ears.

"No disrespect intended, Taylor," Luke went on, "but I'd already planned to finish the plumbing job in cabin two."

She studied him, then shook her head. "Okay. That's fine."

Luke gave a curt nod and moved away.

"But when you're done"—her tone hardened—"come see me about jobs for you and Connor to do together."

His gaze swiveled back to her, then he gave a curt nod and stomped off.

Taylor turned back to Connor. "So," she said, clearly doing her best to recover gracefully. "How are you at mucking out stalls?"

When Sunday came around, Connor showed up bright and early at the breakfast table. Taylor looked at him in surprise.

"It's Sunday. You can sleep in."

"I forgot to ask what time you leave for church. I didn't want to miss it."

"You…want to go to church?" She looked slightly stunned.

He held back his amusement with difficulty. "If that's okay with you."

"Oh. Sure. Of course. I mean, I just didn't realize—"

"That I wasn't a heathen?"

"Ah…well, yes." The admission came with a rueful chuckle. "I suppose that's exactly what I thought."

He helped himself to some coffee. "Well, I'm not. At least not any more than any other believer who's struggling to do what's right."

She started to say something, then paused. Finally, she rose to rinse out her coffee mug. "Okay, then. Drink up your coffee, Mr. Alexander. Dad's not there to preach, but we're still having praise and worship singing. And you won't want to miss the prelude." She grinned at him. "Mrs. Huntsicker plays a mean organ. Foot pedals and everything. Fairly makes the rafters rattle!"

Their time of worshiping together had been peaceful and enjoyable. Connor was pleased to find that Taylor had a sweet alto voice, and she sang the hymns with sincere emotion, as though the lyrics were more than just words. He liked the way their voices blended as they sang. She must have noticed it too for she glanced up at him several times during the first hymn.

After that day, Taylor treated him differently—as though she'd begun to trust him. At least a little. Several times he glanced up from his work and found her watching him, a curious expression on her face. When his eyes met hers, she turned away, busying herself with whatever happened to be at hand. He returned to his task with a chuckle.

The days quickly fell into a routine. They would rise with the sun, head out for the day's work—sometimes with Luke, but more often just the two of them—then return in the early evening to clean up for dinner. Mealtime had become one of Connor's favorite events, and not just because of Mrs. Camus's cooking. He enjoyed watching the affectionate, often teasing, exchanges between Taylor and her mother. From the moment he met her, Donelle Camus had made him feel at home, pulling him into comfortable conversation, listening with interest as he talked, and sharing her own insightful views. As he spent time with the older woman, he discovered that she possessed wit, intelligence, and a remarkable ability to put one in one's place when necessary. All traits she had passed on to her daughter. In abundance.

Along with the company of the two women, the feasts Taylor's mom prepared were a great way to start and end each day. The elegant cook would beam at him as he devoured the food, then pat him on the shoulder as she cleared away his dishes.

Invariably, as he rose to leave, she would give him some words of wisdom: "Patience is the key to victory"; "Soft words turn away wrath"; "The dog that growls the loudest usually has been hurt the most."

The last one had been her comment as he left the kitchen that morning and headed for the stable to meet Taylor. She'd informed him that they were going riding today to check out a new route she wanted to use on trail rides next spring. Once again, Luke had bowed out.

"Got to rewire cabin three," he said and walked away, leaving Taylor staring after him with a troubled expression.

Donelle's earlier words had stuck in Connor's mind as Taylor watched him while he saddled his horse, a sorrel gelding with the unremarkable name of Chestnut. Though he sensed Taylor was waiting for him to make a mistake, he was almost sure she was pleased to see how comfortable he was around the horses. It hadn't taken more than a few minutes, and a carrot stick from Taylor's mom, to make friends with Chestnut.

Connor glanced at Taylor as she rode alongside him in silence. *The dog that growls the most…* He restrained a grin. He would never have equated Taylor with a dog, but she did seem to growl a lot. He wondered if her mother's aphorism were true.

"You know, your mother is quite a lady." Taylor shot him a rueful smile.

"She is that. Sharp, too. She has an almost uncanny

ability to tell if someone is trustworthy or not." Her lips tipped in a slight smile. "Apparently you passed muster. In record time, I might add."

Connor nodded, felt a wave of pleasure, and turned his head to take in the scenery. They were at the top of a hill, and he could see the jagged peaks of the Tetons to the west.

"Yellowstone is north of here, right?" He tried to get his bearings.

"About forty-five miles. Idaho is across the mountains, twelve miles or so as the crow flies."

Connor stared at the Tetons dubiously. "That'd have to be some crow." He took a deep breath of the crisp, cold air. "So you've lived here all your life?"

Taylor nodded. "It was a great place to grow up." He heard the sincerity in her voice.

"Pretty remote."

"Very remote, but I like it that way. It doesn't bother me at all that our nearest neighbor is several miles away." She lifted her shoulders in a self-deprecating gesture. "I'm not exactly what you'd call a social butterfly."

"I've gotten that impression." She laughed lightly at his comment. He watched with interest the way her whole face lit up when she smiled. She was a beautiful woman. Not in the typical fashion-model way, but in an exotic, almost exquisite way. And it was more than her features that stirred him; it was the total, intriguing package that was Taylor Sorensen. In fact, Connor couldn't remember the last time a woman had affected him the way his new boss did. One minute he wanted to throttle her, the next he found himself wondering if her hair was really as silken as it seemed—

Whoa! Hold on there, Alexander! Wolves, remember?

"You know," she went on, thankfully oblivious to his inner struggle, "I actually like it that I can go for days without seeing anyone other than my family." Her grin was easy. "And the only reason I see them is that they live about a half-mile from the ranch house in a cabin they had built several years ago."

"They didn't want to stay in the ranch house?"

"They thought Josh and I needed to have a place of our own. Ryan and his family have their own place closer to town. And since Josh and I were running the retreats, they offered us the ranch house. I was thrilled." Her eyes had a faraway look in them. "I love that house. I grew up in it, and it's full of wonderful memories. I can see images of my family in nearly every room."

"And your husband?" Mrs. Camus had told him about Josh's death and Taylor's struggle to deal with the loss. He watched the emotions drift across her face, the shadows fill her green eyes.

"Yes. Josh, too."

She fell silent, and Connor regretted bringing up the subject. "Are your folks retired?" He hoped to distract her from whatever dark thoughts he'd triggered.

"My mom is retired from teaching. I think my dad will go on being a pastor until the day he drops." A bemused smile lifted her lips. "His church is small, barely more than fifty members, but they're a lively group." Her smile deepened. "They keep him busy anyway."

"Your parents have been in this area for a long time then?"

"Forever." She chuckled. "Galloway Glen was actually settled by my great-grandfather on my mother's side"—she suddenly developed a lilting, Irish accent—"the good and honorable Riley Galloway in the late 1800s."

Connor laughed, caught up in her unexpected playfulness. "Let me guess. Big and hard working with red hair and emerald green eyes."

"Sure, an' you couldn't be more on target if you'd known the fine fellow!" she crowed with delight, her infectious laughter flowing around him. "Seriously, he did have red hair—"

"Which is where yours came from, I suspect. And the green eyes?"

"Guilty. A definite carryover from the Irish side of the family. I have yet to see a green-eyed Ojibwa."

"Ojibwa?"

"Yup. My great-grandmother, the love of Riley's life. He saw her watching him tend sheep one morning, and it was love at first sight. He found her father, offered for her, and they were married soon after. Between the two of them, they took a few acres and built it to more than two thousand. Small by Wyoming standards, but a decent ranch nonetheless."

"Small?"

A small smile graced her lips. "Any good rancher knows you need close to fifty acres a head when you're raising cattle or sheep. The ranches around here average more than four thousand acres."

Connor showed his surprise, and Taylor's humor was clear. "That's why Galloway Glen was considered a nice little spread by the other ranchers. But my grandparents weren't really ranchers at heart. They knew the land was their greatest asset, so from time to time they sold sections off." She glanced around them. "Now Galloway Glen covers a little over six hundred acres, about a square mile, most of which is wilderness."

"No more sheep?"

"Only the one the twins raise to show at the county fair. But that's okay. Riley's work and my grandparents' business acumen have left us pretty well set." She shifted in the saddle. "Which is why I can afford to run the retreat center. And it's a part of why I do it—to give something back."

"How about wolves?"

Taylor started and gave him an alarmed look. "What?"

"Are there any wolves left in this wilderness?"

"No." Her answer was swift…a little too swift. "They were wiped out sixty years ago. Trappers, hunters, men out for the bounty." She urged Topaz forward, ending the conversation.

"That's too bad," Connor said when he caught up

with her. "Galloway Glen seems like the perfect place for wolves."

Again that sharp look came his way, her eyes searching, as though trying to reach into his thoughts. He kept his expression blank, and she turned away with an impatient movement.

"I wouldn't know." Her tone was cold. "I've never seen one." She jabbed her heels into her horse's side, and the buckskin bolted forward, as though startled at the forcefulness of the action.

Connor stared after her. *Now why don't I believe that? And why do I get the distinct impression, Taylor Sorensen, that you're running away from the truth?*

"Did you know frowning causes ten times more wrinkles than smiling does, dear?"

At Taylor's intractable look, Donelle Camus folded her hands. "See there? You just cost your face another ten years or so." She leaned forward, taking her daughter's hand in her own. "Do tell me what's troubling you."

"Nothing, Mom. I'm fine. Just tired, I guess." The smile she gave her mother was anemic at best.

"Taylor—"

But her daughter rose, muttering something about checking on the horses, and left the house.

Donelle settled back in her chair, cupping her mug of tea. It was good to see Taylor so…affected. It had been too long since anyone had gotten close enough to get a rise out of her. With the exception of Ryan—who could send his sister into fits of irritation almost by his mere existence—Taylor seldom let anyone bother her. Anyone outside the family, that was.

Donelle knew it wasn't her daughter's remarkable self-control and patience that allowed her to be untouched by others' foibles; rather, it was that she didn't let anyone get close enough to matter. Josh had been the exception, and a delightful one. When he was killed, Donelle's fears that her daughter would sink back into her somewhat reclusive shell had been more or less realized. Oh, Taylor spent time with Gavin, but even with him she seemed to maintain a certain distance. Donelle wasn't particularly concerned about that. Gavin was a good friend for Taylor, but Donelle wasn't convinced he was the right one to be anything more.

Connor Alexander, on the other hand…

Donelle's delight increased. There was something about the man that she liked. A great deal, actually. She had learned from their talks that he had a heart for God and that he shared many of Taylor's interests and values. He clearly enjoyed life on a ranch and had a passion for animals. His intelligence was evident, as was his sense of humor. He'd even made a few suggestions on how to incorporate wildlife walks into the retreats to teach the youngsters about God's creative genius. Taylor's eyes had lit up with excitement at the idea. Also, he seemed remarkably patient with her daughter—a trait that almost qualified him for sainthood! And several times Donelle had caught him watching Taylor with some indefinable emotion in those wonderful blue eyes.

Yes, indeed. Donelle sipped her tea with pleasure. *Connor Alexander has definite possibilities.*

TWELVE

"I THINK THAT'S EVERYTHING." TAYLOR STUDIED HER LIST, HER lips pursed in thought. "Yup, we got it all."

"Good thing." Connor studied the packed vehicle. "There's no room left in the truck for anything else."

She laughed and pulled the door open, sliding behind the steering wheel. They had come to Jackson for "a quick supply run," and ended up being there most of the afternoon. Connor had been intrigued with Jackson, with its wooden sidewalks and Old West appearance.

"I have an idea." Connor leaned against the door. "How 'bout I buy you dinner?"

Taylor looked at him. "Dinner? Why?"

He laughed. "Mainly because I'm starving!"

"Ah, so your altruistic gesture is really self-serving?"

"Entirely."

"I have a better idea."

"Does it involve food?" He eyed her.

"I promise."

"Then lead on, boss lady."

They picked up sandwiches, chips, and soda at the grocery store, then drove to the town square. Connor stared in amazement at the elk antler arches that stood at the four corners of the tiny park there. He and Taylor sat on a bench, offered grace, and started eating.

"You're right." He munched happily. "This is better than a restaurant." He looked around. "My mom would love this place. She loves touristy towns with shops and atmosphere to the nth degree."

"I suppose you stand outside while she shops."

"Definitely. But she doesn't mind. She just likes to chat as we walk from shop to shop." The image made him grin. "She's the best. My dad, too." He met Taylor's warm gaze. "In a way your mom reminds me of them. Always saying good things about people and laughing a lot."

"Do you have any brothers or sisters?"

He shook his head. "Only child. Spoiled rotten and loved every minute of it. My folks were older when I was born, and Mom couldn't have any more children. So they poured all their creativity and love into me, one another, and the Lord. I think I heard every Bible story about a zillion times."

"Me, too." Taylor giggled. "And I still love them!"

Connor smiled in response, struck by the picture she made. The red light of the setting sun reflected in gleaming highlights in her hair, and her eyes were lit with the warmth of shared memories. She was at ease, relaxed, and completely captivating.

I could spend hours talking to her, laughing with her. Maybe days.

Maybe forever, a small inner voice added, startling him.

"You know, I always wanted to have the kind of relationship my parents share," she said. "I didn't think I ever would…but I did. With Josh."

Connor stilled. She'd never discussed her husband with him before.

"We had such a great time together. I was sure we'd go on forever, that we'd have a passel of kids. Maybe even twins, like Ryan and Lisa." She met Connor's gaze, and he saw tears gleaming in her eyes. "Josh loved kids. All ages."

"Your mom told me he was on a trip with the church youth group when he died?"

"One of the campers went out on a ledge, and Josh brought him back. He saved the boy's life."

The pain in her eyes struck at him. He wished he could hold her close, ease her hurt.

"It shouldn't have happened." The harshness in her tone surprised him. "It shouldn't have been Josh on that ledge. There was another boy, a senior. Brad Momadey. He was supposed to be watching the younger boys. It's his fault Josh is dead."

Connor put a gentle hand on her arm. "Taylor, it was an accident—"

She jerked away. "No. It was Brad's fault. He stopped coming to church. He's all but disappeared. Mom talked with his mother, and she said she hasn't seen him for months…" She blinked rapidly. "He's nineteen years old, and he just vanished. But do you know what?" Her voice choked. "I don't care. I hope he never comes back.

Because when I see him—and I did catch a glimpse of him in Wilson not long ago—all I can think of is what he did, what he cost me. And all I can feel is hatred."

Connor reached out and took her now-cold hand in his own. They sat in silence, until she turned wide, sorrow-filled eyes to him.

"So now you know what a terrible person I am."

Connor rubbed the back of her hand with his thumb. "You're not terrible."

She lifted her eyes, searching his face.

God, give me wisdom. Show me how to help her. "You're hurting. I understand that. And if I can understand that, don't you think God does as well?"

She swallowed convulsively, closed her eyes, and sat in silence. After a moment, she withdrew her hand and stood. "Well, we've been gone a lot longer than I thought we would be. We'd better head back."

He grinned. "Before Luke sends out the state troopers, right?"

"Exactly." She mustered a smile, and he stood to follow her to the truck.

"Taylor, can I talk to you?"

Taylor turned from where she was mending a halter. Luke stood in the doorway of the barn, concern etched on his weathered features.

"Of course." She moved toward him. "What's wrong, Luke?"

He shifted from one foot to another, but his focus never strayed from her face. "Yazhi, what do you know about this man you've hired?"

She hesitated. "About as much as I know when I hire anyone." She scanned his expression, wondering what had him so bothered. It was unusual for Luke to question her decisions. "Why?"

He studied her face for a moment, then shrugged. "I don't like him."

Taylor couldn't hide her surprise, and Luke looked away. She moved to touch his arm gently. "Has he said something to offend you? Because if he has—"

He was shaking his head before she could finish. "No, no. Nothing like that. It's...actually, I'm not sure what it is. But there's something about him, Yazhi, some-thing I don't quite trust. Sometimes people are far different inside than they seem on the surface."

Taylor bit her lip. Connor had been at Galloway Glen for a week and a half now, and he'd been the pic-ture of trustworthiness and hard work. And he'd been nothing but kind and understanding that day when she talked about Josh and Brad. Still, she trusted Luke. He'd always acted in her best interests. So why did she sense that he wasn't being completely honest with her now? That there was something going on beneath the surface, something Luke wasn't willing to share with her?

The thought that her longtime friend might be con-cealing something troubled her far more than his appar-ent dislike of her new ranch hand.

"I'll talk with Mom. She has good instincts. I'll see if she shares your concerns."

Luke seemed satisfied and turned to leave.

"Luke," Taylor said, and he paused. "You know you can talk to me about anything."

"Yes, Yazhi." His dark gaze not quite meeting hers. "I know."

But as he turned to leave, Taylor had the distinct impression that he didn't believe that at all.

Taylor did as she promised. She talked with her mother about Connor that afternoon.

Her mother frowned when Taylor was done. "I don't understand it, dear. Connor seems like a nice man. Kind. Honest."

"I know. It just doesn't make any sense."

"Actually, it might."

She looked at her mother. What did that mean?

"Taylor, you know I think the world of Luke, but he has a definite tendency to treat you as though you belong to him. It might be that he's feeling a bit, well, threatened."

"Threatened? By Connor?"

"By anyone who isn't a part of Galloway Glen. Remember how long it took Luke to warm up to Josh?"

Taylor remembered. She nearly despaired of Luke ever liking Josh. "You're right. I'd forgotten about that."

Her mother patted her arm. "Luke is a good friend

to you, Taylor. And we're told that 'many counselors make a man wise.' Keep what he's said in mind, and let's ask God to show you if there is anything about Connor Alexander that should concern you."

Taylor was grateful for her mother's calm perspective.

"And while we're at it," her mother added, her eyes twinkling, "we just might ask him to bring your father back in one piece. Ryan and the twins could be leading him on a merry chase."

A few days later, during yet another of her mother's marathon breakfast feasts, Taylor announced to Connor that they would be heading for the back forty to repair several sections of a paddock.

"The back forty?"

She bit off a chunk of bagel. "Yup. We take the retreat families out there as a day trip," Taylor explained. "It's about a three-hour ride on horseback through some really pretty terrain. Mom goes out there ahead of us with the truck, and when the group arrives, she's got a picnic lunch all set out and ready to go."

Connor surveyed the spread. "I take it she fixes more than egg-salad sandwiches."

"Count on it." Taylor laughed. "We usually eat the leftovers for the next three nights." She reached for a buttermilk biscuit. "Of course, that's not exactly a hardship." She spread homemade jelly on the biscuit and took a hearty bite. "You haven't really lived until you've tasted my mother's fried chicken. Hot or cold, it beats Colonel Kentucky any day!"

After breakfast, they loaded the truck with poles and tools, then drove westward toward the mountains. As always, Connor was captivated by the beauty of the ranch and the ever-changing terrain. They drove across fields dotted with wildflowers, past stands of evergreens, and around rocky outcroppings. In the distance, the jagged peaks of the Tetons jutted toward the crystalline sky.

They rode in a comfortable silence, something Connor couldn't remember ever experiencing with a woman before. Taylor would speak up from time to time, pointing out landmarks or spots of interest, but for the most part, she simply drove without talking, relaxed and competent.

They had just rounded another small stand of trees when she leaned forward and pointed. "There it is."

A small cabin of rough logs stood in front of them. Other than a picture window and the ever-present rocking chairs standing guard on the porch, the cabin looked as though it could have been in that spot for a hundred years.

"This used to be a sheepherder's cabin." Taylor leaned forward. "We updated it a bit, but tried to keep the authentic, rustic feel."

She pulled up next to a small paddock located at the side of the cabin and shut off the ignition. Near the enclosure were three picnic tables.

"Here's our project for today," she said as they climbed out of the truck.

Several of the main support timbers around the paddock needed to be replaced, and the two went right to work, quickly and smoothly, like a finely tuned team, each understanding what the other needed almost before he or she asked. Connor would no sooner glance around for a tool than Taylor would hand it to him. She would just open her mouth to ask for help when he would stop what he was doing and offer an extra set of hands—or muscle.

Several times, however, Connor noticed Taylor pausing to glance around, a bemused look on her face. After the fourth or fifth time, he said, "What's up, Taylor?"

She bit her lip, giving him a somewhat sheepish look. "Nothing."

He set down the hammer he'd been using. "Uh-uh. Not good enough. You've been looking over your shoulder like a highwayman watching for a posse. What's the matter?"

She leaned on the fence. "It's happening again."

He looked around. "It?"

She let out a slow breath. "I can't explain it, can't even give you a good reason for it, but I'm positive we're being watched." She shook her head. "I know it sounds silly, but the feeling's so strong it's making me as nervous as a three-legged frog on the highway."

Connor turned to scan the surrounding woods, then turned back to her. Clearly she was uneasy. And once again he was surprised at the powerful, protective urge that filled him. "Do you want me to take a ride around? Check things out?"

The way he was feeling now, he knew he'd do so no matter what. Few things had ever felt as important to him as ensuring Taylor's peace of mind.

Quick gratitude swept through her at his accepting attitude, relief that he didn't merely dismiss her feelings or try to talk her out of them.

"No, never mind." She turned to stare into the distance. "Truth be known, if someone is out there, I'd rather have you stay close by."

She turned back to him, then paused at the odd look in his eyes. Something shimmered in the blue depths of his gaze, something protective and so purely male that she felt a sudden tingling in the pit of her stomach. For a moment, the very air around them seemed to snap with electricity. And then he looked away from her, and the spell was broken.

She stood, struggling to get her emotions under control as he turned to pick up the hammer. As she drew a steadying breath and moved forward to help him, she found herself wondering if the man beside her wasn't far more dangerous—to her peace of mind, if nothing else—than anyone who might be lurking in the woods.

"Maybe it was one of those wolves the ranchers have been talking about."

Taylor looked at him in alarm. "What?"

"When I first came to town, I overheard a group of ranchers at the general store talking about wolves. They said they'd been seen in the area."

"Not seen—" Taylor pounded a nail more viciously than was necessary—"heard. There have been a couple of reports about wolves howling." She reached for another nail. "But if you ask me, it's all a bunch of exaggerated nonsense." She positioned the nail and brought the hammer down, then added in a low voice, "I just hope these guys come to that conclusion, too, before somebody gets hurt."

Connor fixed her with a curious look. "Hurt? Why would someone get hurt?"

She concentrated on the nail.

"Taylor?"

She let out a frustrated puff of air, then leaned her arms on the top of the fence and regarded him, debating how much she could safely say.

"You don't know these people like I do. They're good men, Connor, but talk about wolves and some of them get cold. Stone cold. They hate wolves. They call them killers and vermin. Some wouldn't think twice about gunning one down or putting poison out for it."

"Even though it's illegal to do so?"

"They don't care. What matters most to them is their livestock, which is understandable. I mean, it's their

156

livelihood...." He sat back, watching her.

"What do you think of wolves?"

She started at the question. Her eyes flew to his face, but she saw nothing there other than mild interest...and, oddly enough, compassion.

She bit her lip, staring unseeingly into the distance. "When I was a little girl, my grandmother used to tell me the stories and legends of her people, the Ojibwa. She told me how the Ojibwa believed each of the animals had a unique power, an attribute that belonged to it alone. Do you know what the wolf's attribute was?"

"Cunning?"

"Fidelity. Loyalty. From the time she was a small girl, my grandmother was taught that the wolf was a wonderful creature. She often showed me her grandfather's warrior band. It bore a wolf totem for perseverance and guardianship. In their creation story, a wolf befriended and cared for Nanabojo, one of the four most important spirits in the Ojibwa religion. She told me time and again that her people revered the wolf as an example of high family values." She gave a mirthless laugh. "Can you see the ranchers buying into *that*?"

"Let's just say the odds aren't real high."

"Let's just say they're nonexistent. But for me"—she paused, searching for the right words—"for me, wolves have always been a source of wonder. They're remarkably caring and loving to their family members, to the others in the pack. And they seem to find a great delight in living. Sometimes they almost seem to be smiling."

"You sound as though you've seen them."

Oh no! Why wasn't she more careful? "I've seen pictures."

He scanned her face, his eyes intent, and she had the impression he longed to delve into her thoughts, to understand what she was trying to share with him. "You're drawn to their loyalty. I can see that. Loyalty, faithfulness, they're important to you. And they're a part of you."

She looked at him. "What do you mean?"

"Anyone who spends time around you can see that you're loyal to the people you love and the ideals you hold dear. Look at the way you are with your mother, the tone of your voice when you talk about your grandmother. And about God."

His words both pleased and embarrassed her. Once again she had the sense of something passing between them, something powerful and magnetic. She felt her cheeks grow warm and turned away, not sure how to respond. A gentle touch on her arm brought her eyes back to him.

He stood beside her, and the look in his eyes seemed to wrap her in an invisible warmth. It was as though her entire being was filled with anticipation.

"Taylor, I want—I need to tell you—"

Whatever he'd been about to say was cut off by the sound of an approaching vehicle. They turned as one to look in the direction of the engine noise.

When Taylor spotted a Blazer heading toward them,

her eyes widened. *What in the world?* "It's Gavin."

"Gavin?"

"Gavin MacEwen. He's a neighbor. And a...friend."

"Must be coming to check up on the work." Connor knelt to put the tools back in the toolbox.

"Or on the workers," she muttered under her breath.

The Blazer pulled up. Gavin cut the engine and stepped out, pushing his hat back off his head as he did so. "Hey there, beautiful."

"I assume he's talking to you, not to me." Connor eyed her blandly, and Taylor felt a surge of red creep into her cheeks.

"Yes, well, probably."

Gavin came over and slipped his arms around Taylor, giving her a quick kiss. She was so surprised, she didn't stop him. Then he turned to Connor, one arm still around Taylor's shoulders, and held out his free hand. "Gavin MacEwen, at your service, sir."

Connor shook his hand. "Connor Alexander, resident gofer. For the time being, anyway."

Taylor wondered fleetingly at the odd expression of displeasure in Conner's eyes. *Maybe he's jealous.* She dismissed the idea along with the inordinate sense of delight it had triggered. What did she care if Connor Alexander was jealous? The man was nothing more than a temporary employee.

A very attractive, extremely intriguing, ridiculously appealing temporary employee.

159

"Shut up," she muttered under her breath.

"Did you say something, darlin'?" Gavin turned to her, and she closed her eyes. Was this day ever going to end?

"No."

"Well then, lass, put me to work. I've come to offer my services." He crossed his arms, a cocky grin on his face.

Connor straightened, the toolbox clenched in his hand. "Much appreciated, but we're all done." He met Gavin's gaze evenly. "Looks like your trip was a waste of time."

Gavin's eyes flashed, but the amiable smile never faltered. "Not a bit of it!" He gave Taylor a squeeze, pressing her against his side. "It's always worth any effort to see my darlin' girl."

Oh, for crying out loud! This had gone far enough. "Well, now that you're here—" she eased her way out of his arm—"you can help us load the extra poles back into the truck."

"With pleasure." Gavin moved to lift one end of the pole Connor had grabbed. "Anything for you, lass." He cast a knowing grin at Connor. "On the count of three?"

Connor gave him a curt nod.

Together they lifted the timber and walked to the truck. As they slid it into the bed of the vehicle, Gavin gave Connor a casual look. "Ever heard of the caber toss?"

"Gavin—" Taylor started to protest, but the two men ignored her.

"Isn't that a contest of strength you Scotsmen indulge in while you're wearing skirts?" Connor inquired, turning a wide and innocent gaze on the man beside him.

Gavin's eyes snapped. "Those are kilts, mon. Not skirts."

"Ah. Of course." Connor's tone said he was clearly unconvinced.

"But then, it takes a man confident in his masculinity to wear one, so I can see how you'd be a bit wary of them." Gavin sauntered back to the pile of poles.

"For heaven's sake, you two!" She might as well have been invisible for all the attention they paid her.

"Well, now," Connor drawled, bending to grasp the end of the pole. "Since you're such a confident man, why don't you just show me the ropes on this caber game."

Gavin fixed his adversary with a stony glance. "Toss, mon. Caber toss." He straightened. "It's a test of strength and mettle, not a game."

Connor made no reply. He merely fixed the other man with an amused glance.

Gavin's eyes narrowed, and he tilted his head toward an open area in front of the cabin. "Head that way," he said between clenched teeth.

Connor complied, and Taylor could hear Gavin muttering under his breath the entire way. The grin that split Connor's face was one of pure relish.

"Hello? Anyone want to hear my opinion of this little event?" Taylor asked in even, deliberately controlled tones. "Anyone even care that I'm alive?" When neither man responded, she turned with a furious huff, stomped over to pull open the door of the truck, climbed into the seat, and closed the door with a satisfying slam.

The sound of the slamming door brought another grin to Connor's face. Ooooh, she wasn't happy at all. But that was okay. More than okay, since it meant Gavin's inopportune arrival was a source of irritation for her. Why exactly that should delight him so, Connor wasn't prepared to analyze. All he knew was that he didn't care for the Scotsman's proprietary air where Taylor was concerned.

"Well, are you ready?" Gavin asked.

"As I'll ever be. You show me how it's done, and I'll follow suit."

Gavin gave a brusque nod, then moved so his back was to the cabin. "Set your end of the pole down then."

Connor did as instructed and stepped back. Gavin walked forward, pushing the pole, which was a good two feet longer than he was tall, up on end in front of him. That done, he crouched, slid his hands beneath the end of the pole, blew out a few deep breaths, then stood, lifting the pole with his hands cupped beneath it.

Leaning one shoulder into the timber to keep it balanced in front of him, Gavin shuffled his feet, as though dancing with the pole. Then, in one smooth motion, he did a knee bend, tensed, and straightened quickly, throwing his arms up and forward and launching the pole in front of him. The pole rose in a graceful arc, did a complete flip, and landed squarely on its end. It shuddered, then fell with a resounding thud.

"Aye!" Gavin brushed his hands with a proud smile. "Now that was a toss to be proud of!"

"So let me get this straight," Connor said. "You lift and toss the pole so it goes end over end and lands square."

"That's it. Think you can handle it?"

"No sweat."

Do not keep talking so proudly or let your mouth speak such arrogance!

Connor dismissed the thought. There was no reason for that Scripture to be coming to him now.

The Lord hates pride and arrogance.

Connor's brow creased as the two men walked to the pile, took hold of another timber, and made their way back to the field.

What they were doing wasn't pride or arrogance. They were just having a little fun.

A wise man's fun is being wise.

"Ready?" Gavin's question pulled Connor from his thoughts, and he hesitated. A quick, gloating gleam twinkled in Gavin's eyes. "Havin' second thoughts, are you?"

This time it was Connor's face that darkened. "Not a bit."

"Fine, then, off with you!" Gavin dropped his end with a flourish.

Connor walked forward, pushing the timber up on end. When he had it balanced, he crouched and slid his hands beneath the end as he'd seen Gavin do.

"Remember the rules of lifting, lad," Gavin cautioned. "Take the load with your legs, not your back. I'd hate to have to carry you back to the truck."

Connor didn't dignify the comment with a reply. Instead, he focused on the task at hand, regulating his breathing, tensing his muscles...one, two, THREE!

He stood, lifting the pole in his cupped hands. The weight bore down on his laced fingers, and he clenched his teeth.

"Use your shoulder, mon! Don't let the caber get away from you!"

It was good advice. Unfortunately, Connor had no way of following it. The heavy pole swayed back and forth, then began to gain momentum and fall forward. Connor tried wildly to compensate, which only succeeded in bringing the timber back against his shoulder with too much force. He staggered, then started a wild backpedal as the pole fell backward, throwing him off balance as it went.

"Throw it, Connor!" With one fierce effort Connor tensed his muscles and launched the timber over his shoulder. The momentum of his action combined with that of the pole knocked him flat.

Connor slammed onto the hard earth, his head snapping back and smacking the ground with a sickening thunk. The air whooshed from his lungs, and he lay there, blinking, every inch of his body encased in pain, wondering when the stars had come out.

Vaguely he was aware of a crash, then voices.

"Connor? Con? Are you okay?"

Ah. He knew that one. It was a woman…her beautiful auburn hair fell like a silken curtain across her face as she leaned down to him, her moss green eyes filled with alarm.

"Give him room, lass! The man needs some air."

That would have to be Gavin. The idiot who'd gotten him into this mess. The one he'd have to kill…as soon as he could move again.

Slowly, painfully, awareness filled his mind and he was able to focus.

"A wise man's fun…"

He groaned, and then laughed weakly. "Okay, God, you win…" He coughed. "You're right. It was a stupid thing to do."

"He's delirious!" Taylor sounded alarmed, bless her. At least she was worried about him.

Connor laughed harder and rolled onto his side.

"Maybe you're right, lass." Gavin's voice was filled with uncertainty, which only added to Connor's mirth.

"Maybe you should radio for a doctor—"

Connor cut Taylor off by raising a hand. "No—" he

spoke between hoots of laughter and gulps of air—"No, just give me a minute. I'll be okay."

He pushed himself onto his hands and knees, and Taylor moved to slip her arm around his waist. As he stood, she pulled his arm around her shoulders, steadying him.

He looked down at her, amazed that someone so small and slim could be so strong.

"Well, your toss landed, true enough, Alexander."

Connor followed the Scotsman's gaze—and cringed. The timber was lying half in, half out of the cabin. It had gone through the front window as cleanly as an arrow shot from a giant's bow. Regret washed over him, then relief that neither Gavin nor Taylor had been hurt.

"Taylor, I'm sorry." Gavin wasn't an idiot. *He* was.

"The cabin's not a big deal, Con." Her voice was husky with concern, and Connor looked at her in surprise.

He started to straighten, to move away from her support. "I'm okay, Taylor." Then a movement caught his eye, and he glanced behind her to catch a dark look of displeasure on Gavin's face. Connor bit his lip to keep from grinning with delight. Oh, this was too good to be true. He wouldn't have to kill the man after all. He could have his revenge in a much more enjoyable way.

"Then again..." He let his voice sound weak, and she tightened her hold on his waist. He sagged against her, leaning his forehead against the top of her head and speaking into her fragrant hair. "Maybe I do need some help after all."

Gavin sputtered and moved toward them, but—much to Connor's delight—Taylor didn't even notice. She moved toward the truck, still supporting Connor and making sympathetic sounds. He cast a waggish look over his shoulder at the Scotsman.

The sight of Gavin standing there, looking ready to explode, almost made the whole escapade worth the pain Connor knew he'd be experiencing for the next week.

"What are you looking at?"

At Taylor's question, he started, feeling a guilty flush creeping into his face.

"Um, well…"

She glanced back over her shoulder, took in Gavin's stormy expression, then brought her eyes back to Connor. Before he could formulate a believable explanation, she stopped cold. Caught unaware, he toppled forward, landing again in a pile on the ground.

She stood over him, hands planted on her hips, her face thunderous. "I was *worried* about you."

"Taylor—"

"I knew you'd only ask for help if you really were hurt!"

"I—"

"Forget it!"

"Darlin'…" Gavin reached out to put his hand on

her arm, but she brushed him off, angry tears glimmering in her eyes. She pinned the Scotsman with a glare, and he fell silent—a move Connor thought was remarkably wise.

She held out her hand to Gavin. "Give me your keys." He didn't even bother to argue. Again, a wise move.

He nodded toward the Blazer. "In the ignition."

She spun on her heel, stomped to the Blazer, and climbed in. As soon as the engine came to life, she threw the vehicle into drive and stomped on the gas. Gravel flew in all directions, and Connor and Gavin dove for cover.

"Well, laddie," Gavin said after a moment, "looks like we've got a window to fix."

"Aye." Connor stood and brushed off his jeans. He watched the Blazer disappear around a hill.

He gave a weary sigh. *And that's just the beginning of the repairs I need to do.*

THIRTEEN

DONELLE CAMUS WAS JUST STARTING TO SIP HER TEA WHEN the kitchen door slammed open. She looked up with a start to see her daughter storm into the room, stomp over to a cupboard, and jerk a glass from the shelf. Muttering the entire time about ridiculous louts and brainless dolts, she flipped on the tap, filled the glass with water, then spun around to stomp out of the room.

Raising her delicate eyebrows with interest, Donelle smiled.

Ah, love. Wasn't it grand?

Later that evening, after a bath full of Epsom salts, Connor started to think he might actually be able to move again someday without grimacing.

He dropped into the oversized chair and leaned his head back. "I blew it, Lord."

"Your words are truth…"

"Very funny," he muttered, recognizing the verse from 2 Samuel. Rolling his sore shoulders, he rested his elbows on his knees, then pushed himself out of the chair.

No point in putting this off any longer.

Taylor had just settled into her favorite chair and taken a sip of her hot chocolate topped with miniature marshmallows when a knock came at the door.

She looked at Sasha and pulled a face. "Guess who that is." The knock sounded again. "He knows he's in trouble, so he won't come in until I open the door."

Sasha tilted her head, her ears perked, as a third knock sounded, this one a bit more forceful. Taylor leaned back in her chair, giving the husky a pondering look.

"What do you say, girl? Do we let him in?"

Sasha yawned, her pink tongue curling, and then lowered her head to her paws.

"I couldn't agree more." Taylor stood, went to the door, and with a sharp twist of her wrist threw the dead bolt. That done, she padded back to her chair, folded her slippered feet beneath her, and snuggled into the soft cushions.

Take that, Alexander!

Standing on the porch, Connor heard the dead bolt latch. He turned the doorknob, just to be sure he'd really heard what he thought he had. The door was locked.

"Fine! She doesn't want to talk, we don't talk." He

turned, jamming his fists into his jeans pockets and started back to his cabin.

"Well, I must admit I'm disappointed. You give up far more easily than I would have expected."

He spun around. Donelle Camus sat in one of the rockers on the porch, watching him with a bemused smile on her face. He knew he should say something polite, but he was too frustrated.

Her eyes filled with compassion. "I know, dear. She can be a bit trying." Her elegant features creased into a frown. "Sometimes she gets…well…dramatic."

Connor snorted indelicately, and she smiled.

"Yes, I can see you understand. Well, never fear. There are ways around that stubborn streak, which I'm quite certain she gets from her father."

Connor cocked an eyebrow, but he was no fool. No way was he going to argue the point.

She stood and took his arm. "Come along, Connor."

He let her lead him back to the front door.

"Stand right there, if you please." She gave him a gentle push so that he was off to the side of the door. Then she reached out and gave a quick knock and turned the doorknob. At Connor's surprised look, she patted his arm. "She knows I'd knock and just come in. To do anything different now would seem odd, wouldn't it?"

Before he could answer, Taylor's muffled, wrath-filled voice shot out. "Go away!"

"Taylor, it's Mom." She glanced at Connor, and her

smile was severe. "Why is the door locked, dear?"

Connor felt a grin break over his face as he heard scuffling inside, as though Taylor had bolted from her chair and hurried to the door. Within seconds, the dead bolt sounded and the door opened.

Taylor stood there, mortification on her face. "Oh, Mom! I'm sorry! I thought it was—"

"Thank you, dear." She reached out one manicured hand to take hold of Connor's sleeve and pull him forward with surprising strength. "Connor needed to talk with you, and I simply couldn't believe you meant to lock the door."

Taylor stared at her mother, then she began to sputter and protest as Donelle propelled Connor into the house.

"Have fun, you two," she said as she pulled the door shut.

As he stood there in the entryway, Connor could hear her bell-like laughter floating on the breeze.

Taylor was so angry, she was shaking. Her own mother! A traitor!

She swiveled, presenting Connor with her back, and returned to her chair.

"Taylor..."

She was not going to speak to him. Not a word.

"Taylor, please." He came to stand in front of her chair.

She stared right through him.

With a sigh he knelt in front of her, taking her hands in his. The touch of his hands sent an alarming jolt through her, and Taylor finally met his eyes. They were brimming with remorse. "Taylor, I was wrong. I'm sorry."

Ohhhhh, he had to be sincere, didn't he?

She exhaled and sagged back in the chair, her hands still held captive. "You were both silly nits."

He hung his head. "I know."

A smile twitched at her lips. "And you destroyed the window in the cabin."

"It's all boarded up, and as soon as we can get the glass, I'll go back and replace it." He raised his head and met her eyes with a slightly hopeful look.

"So that makes it okay?" she demanded, doing her best to maintain a stern voice.

"No. Not at all. But I believe you are a merciful woman—"

She rolled her eyes heavenward.

"—and you recognize true contrition when you see it." He gave her a hangdog look, his eyes wide and sorrowful, his mouth drooped and quivering, and she laughed. She couldn't help it. He really was appealing when he groveled.

"Okay, okay, you can keep your head," she conceded, and he bent forward to touch his forehead to her hands. Her breath caught in her throat, and her heart felt as though it somersaulted.

"Thank you, milady."

He rose, and she leaned back in her chair. When their gazes met, the expression in his eyes sent her breathing haywire again.

"I discovered something interesting today." He sat in the chair next to her. His low voice seemed to vibrate around her.

"Oh?" Not very original, but it was all she could muster at the moment.

He reached out to take her hand. She laced her fingers with his, surprised—and yet not surprised—at how well their hands fit together.

"I don't like it when I hurt you."

The gentle words wrapped around her, and sudden tears sprang to her eyes. *Father, what's happening here?*

As though aware of her confusion, he released her hand and leaned forward, his gaze coming to rest on the old, leather-bound book that was open on the table in front of her. "May I?"

She leaned forward and handed it to him.

He turned the timeworn pages with great care. "Looks like an antique."

"My grandfather's journal. I like to read through it. It's very soothing. He had a real talent for putting images down on paper. You can almost see his life taking place as you read."

He scanned the elaborate script, and she could tell by his rapt expression that he was soon engrossed. He settled back in his chair and continued to read.

Amazing how comfortable silence can be with some

people. She curled her feet beneath her and hugged herself. Sasha stretched and yawned from her spot on the floor. This felt good.

"Listen to this." Connor's voice was filled with emotion. "'I was made furious by this inexplicable change of heart, this sudden affection some now claimed for wolves. How could they care for such killers? Did the fools not care that the vermin destroyed God's glorious creation? So I thought, with full conviction of the truth of my stand. Then came a day in the woods. A day that haunts me still. I laid my traps with a strategic eye. Surely that day I would capture the killers. And, indeed, I did.

"'As I neared the traps, I saw a gray lump, a furry form lying on the grim, cold earth. Good! I thought. And I hurried forward, anxious to see the end of such evil. I drew near, cautious. Ever I have believed the soul is reflected in the eyes. What better window to peer through to prove I was right? Then and there I determined to look into the monster's golden stare, thereby to determine for myself that this was evil. And so I knelt. And so I looked. And what I saw chilled me to the core.

"'The creature lived indeed. And there, in those amber depths, I found such emotion! Confusion, pain, and sorrow. The deepest of sorrow. So deep as to break the heart. And I understood, as though pierced through with a lance, that the sorrow was not for himself, but for me, for what I had become. I saw myself, reflected in those fading eyes. And, God help me, it was I who was evil. A killer. Cold-hearted. This majestic animal, this creation of the Almighty's hand, was not the monster. I was. God help me, I was. But by God's grace, I will never be so again.'"

They sat, silent, absorbing the words, and Taylor's heart all but melted when she saw tears reflected in Connor's eyes.

"Wow. Talk about a revelation."

Taylor nodded, her throat choked with emotion. "From that day on my grandfather did all he could to preserve the wolves." Hopelessness swept over her. "Not that it did any good. But he tried." She stood abruptly and went to stare out the window, looking through the darkness toward Reunion.

Were her wolves safe? Was there a pack? Were they healthy? Would they suffer the same fate as the wolves her grandfather tried to save?

She heard Connor move, felt him come to stand beside her. "That's all any of us can do, Taylor. Try." He slid a comforting arm around her shoulders, and she leaned against him.

They stood in silence—until Taylor felt a shiver travel down her spine. There it was again! That sense of being watched.

"Cold?" Connor asked, but she shook her head and looked at him.

"Have you ever felt as though someone was…out there?"

He raised a dark eyebrow. "Out there?"

"You know." She turned from his slightly confused expression to look toward the dark window again. "Watching." She wrapped her arms around herself. "It's the oddest thing, but ever since Josh's death, I have times when I get the distinct feeling there's someone, just beyond my line of vision, watching me." Good heavens. She sounded positively paranoid! "Who knows, maybe I've got a second shadow."

Thankfully, Connor didn't make a joke. His eyes were serious as he looked down at her. "Does it frighten you?"

"Sometimes." She let the admission out hesitantly. "It's unsettling, I guess. If I knew who it was—"

"Assuming there's really anyone there."

She inclined her head. "Okay, assuming it's something more than my too-active imagination, it would be nice to know it's a friendly shadow."

He turned to peer out the window. "Seems to me if it weren't, you would have known by now."

The thought surprised her—mostly because it rang true. She'd been feeling this way for over a year, and yet nothing—and no one—had ever threatened her. She bit her lip. "I hadn't considered that."

His smile was quick and easy. "Who knows, maybe what you've got out there is a guardian angel who's new at his job and still needs to learn how to be undetectable."

She laughed, oddly comforted by the idea. "Now *that* would figure. A rookie guardian angel. Well, why not? I suppose I'd be a good case for an angel to cut his wings on, wouldn't I?"

"You'd definitely be a challenge." His eyes twinkled with warm amusement. "But a delightful one."

She looked down, her face growing warm with confusion. She was surprised—and a bit disturbed—at how good his comment made her feel.

"Well—" he stepped back—"I'd better get some rest. My boss is a regular slave driver. Believes in starting the day at the most unearthly hour."

She grinned. "Terrible the things a working man has to suffer."

"Too true. But it's really not all that bad."

"Oh?"

He moved toward her again. "Nope." His gaze roamed her face. "It's not bad at all." He reached out a finger to tilt her chin. "Because this particular boss has the most amazing..." He lowered his head, his warm breath fanning her face.

Taylor's breath caught in her throat, and she was sure her heart had stopped beating. He was going to kiss her. She was sure of it—and an alarming thrill shot through her.

"Cook." He pressed his lips to her forehead with feather softness. Then he stepped back, walked to the door, and left.

She stood frozen to the spot. Swallowing with difficulty, she glanced around and caught her reflection in the window…hair tousled by the breeze, eyes dazed, a bemused smile on her face—

Shaking herself free from Connor's spell, she laughed lightly.

I wonder…

She glanced after him. *I wonder if guardian angels are tall and broad shouldered and have smiles that can melt your insides?*

FOURTEEN

CONNOR GRUNTED AS HE HEFTED A LARGE SACK OF GRAIN from the bed of the truck onto his shoulder.

"Need some help?" The voice came from behind him, and Connor turned to find Luke Narbona sitting in one of the rocking chairs on the front porch of Taylor's house.

"Sure." Connor hid his surprise with a grin. "I never turn down an extra pair of hands."

Luke rose slowly, his gaze resting on Connor in a way that made him feel like a bug under a magnifying glass. Of all the people he'd met at Galloway Glen, Luke was the greatest mystery. The older man had kept a close eye on Connor from the day he'd arrived, but Luke seldom spoke. He didn't even return Connor's greetings when they encountered one another.

Connor was at a loss as to what he'd done to incur Luke's dislike. Which made the older man's offer of help that much more surprising. And interesting.

Connor carried the bag into the barn and dropped it near the feed bin. As he turned, Luke came in with another bag and dropped it next to the one on the ground. As the Navajo straightened, their eyes met and held.

The air was thick with a tension Connor didn't fully understand. He waited. If Luke had something to say, Connor wanted to give him the chance to say it.

After what seemed like an eternity, Luke said, "Taylor is the closest thing to family that I have."

Connor knew it was no exaggeration. "I've seen that."

"I won't stand by and watch anyone hurt her."

"If she were my friend, I would feel the same way."

Luke's dark eyes studied him, and then he nodded brusquely. "We understand each other."

"I believe we do." Connor held his breath, wondering what came next.

"Good. Then let's get to work. That truck won't unload itself."

Connor watched Luke as he walked from the barn and back toward the truck. Well, it wasn't exactly a declaration of friendship, but it was as good a place as any to start.

Later that day Connor was hard at work shoveling out the stalls when he had the sensation he was being watched.

He turned, half-expecting Taylor's guardian angel to

be there, and found himself looking at two boys who were exact replicas of one another, from their strawberry blond hair and bright blue eyes to the smattering of freckles dancing across their noses and cheeks. One of the two stepped forward, gazing up at him with large, solemn eyes. Connor guessed him to be about ten.

"Hi." Connor smiled.

The boy returned his smile. "Hi. Are you the crazy loon Dad says has come to work with Aunt Taylor?"

"He doesn't look crazy," the second boy said, and his twin shot him a disdainful look.

"Well, course not. You can't tell someone's crazy just by looking at them." He turned back to Connor, studying his face. "Least, I don't think you can."

"Did your father happen to mention exactly why he thought I was crazy?"

The boy nodded vigorously. "Uh-huh. He said anyone—"

"Any *man*," his twin corrected, stepping up beside his brother.

The more talkative twin glared at him. "Don't innerupt, Mikey. You know it's not p'lite."

Connor had to look away to hide his amusement. The boy's haughty expression and tone were perfect imitations of Donelle Camus, who, Connor was willing to bet, was this dynamo's grandmother.

"Anyway," the boy said, turning back to Connor, "Dad said any man who was willing to spend every day,

day in and day out, being bossed around by Aunt Taylor had to be crazy as a loon."

"An' if he wasn't, he soon would be!" Mikey piped up.

Connor bent over and whispered conspiratorially, "If I tell you a secret, can you keep it?"

Two blond heads inclined toward him; two pairs of blue eyes widened in anticipation. "Sure!" they chorused.

He looked left, then right, then whispered, "It's not that bad."

They looked at him, searching his face as though to determine if he was being honest, then Mikey crowed. "I told you so, Mark. I told you Aunt Taylor would be fun to work for."

"Well!" Connor looked at the gleeful imp. "I don't know that I'd go *that* far!"

"So you want some help?" Mark peered at him.

Connor raised an eyebrow and nodded toward the stalls. "You'd be willing to help with this?"

"Sure, we do it all the time." Mikey pulled a shovel from the wall hanger. Mark followed suit.

"Right. Dad keeps tellin' us it will help prepare us for what we have to face when we're adults."

Connor's lips twitched again, but the boy's words were so serious and sincere, he kept as straight a face as he could. "I'd say you've got a pretty smart dad." He joined the boys who were already tackling adjacent stalls.

By the end of the afternoon, Connor had two devoted followers. The twins trailed after him from job to job, always willing to lend a hand, always wanting to talk about their Aunt Taylor.

Connor enjoyed listening to them, not only because they were entertaining, but because he learned more about Taylor in that one afternoon than he had the entire two weeks he'd been at Galloway Glen. As they followed Connor to the ranch house in response to the supper bell, the twins finally ran out of revelations about their aunt, so they launched into an animated recounting of the wilderness trip they'd just taken with their father and grandfather.

Connor was still listening and laughing as they entered the kitchen.

"Okay, you two, give the man a break," said a tall cowboy seated at the table.

Connor studied him. "Let me guess, the Marlboro man, right?"

The man's laugh was deep and carefree. "Only if I want to receive a sound dressing down from my mother." He cast an affectionate glance at Donelle, who sat across the table from him, then stood and extended his hand to Connor for a firm handshake. "I'm Ryan Camus. And I take it you're our new ranch hand, come to take on all the work we don't want to do."

"Something like that."

Seated next to Donelle, his arm draped across the back of her chair, was an older version of Ryan. He, too, stood and offered his hand to Connor.

"Hey, Grandpa!" Mark chirped, going to perch on the kitchen counter. "This is Mr. Alexander. He's not crazy at all."

"Yeah, Dad," Mikey tossed his father a superior look. "He's as normal as you are."

"Poor man," Taylor's father muttered, then introduced himself. "Holden Camus, Mr. Alexander. Welcome to Galloway Glen."

"Thanks. It's been a pleasure so far."

"Uh-huh, right." Ryan's expression was knowing. "I can't think of anything more pleasurable than being bossed around by Taylor—"

"As though anyone would believe you could think," came the teasing retort from behind him, and Connor glanced up to see Taylor sauntering into the room. He stared at her, taking in the picture she made, and suddenly he was having trouble breathing. She was surrounded by her family, and happiness glowed in her eyes, giving her a radiance that seemed to shimmer around her. Her high, exotic cheekbones were tinged with pink, and her easy laughter rippled through the air. Connor found his gaze drawn to her lips, which were relaxed and smiling. She was stunning. Gorgeous.

What I wouldn't give to have a woman look like that because of me, especially one particular woman…with emerald eyes and auburn hair…

"Are you okay, Mr. Alexander? You look like you swallowed a bug."

A moment of silence followed this concerned proclamation from Mark, then the room exploded with laughter. Connor's amusement shifted to something far more provocative when his eyes met Taylor's.

A spark flew between them—a surge of awareness—and the pink on her cheeks deepened to a dusty rose. She looked away and went to hug her father, while Connor moved to take a chair before his suddenly weak knees gave way. He was grateful for the distraction when Donelle got up and began setting food on the table.

The meals with Taylor and her mother had always been enjoyable, calm affairs. Not so this particular dinner. Things started out calmly enough, with everyone holding hands and Taylor's father offering the blessing, but the moment the amen was over, everyone launched into animated discussion. In moments Connor saw that every member of the Camus family was blessed with a quick wit and a clever tongue. Yet underlying the teasing and jesting was a warm, deep affection. These people truly loved and respected each other.

Connor found himself struggling with a lump in his throat. His childhood had been fairly typical: hard-working parents who spent whatever time they could with their only child. But what he saw around this dinner table was something remarkable, something rare. And he was grateful he was getting to share in it.

I wonder how welcome you'd be if they knew what you were really up to? The thought struck him, dimming his enjoyment of the nonstop chatter around him. The food, which had tasted so good only a second before, now tasted like sawdust. He took a long swallow of water, then set down his fork.

"Well," he said with forced cheerfulness, "time for this working boy to get some shut-eye."

They tried to coax him to stay longer, but he refused as politely as possible and made his way out the door.

I hate this, Father. He walked toward his cabin. *I hate deceiving such good people.*

"Connor?"

He paused, then turned. Taylor had followed him out. She walked up to him now, concern in her green eyes.

"Are you okay? You seemed...well, you just left so suddenly." A slight blush tinged her cheeks, and she shifted uncomfortably. "I don't want to pry. I was just...uh, well..." She shook her head impatiently. "Oh, never mind."

Before she could spin and hurry away, he put out his hand and caught her arm with gentle fingers. She stopped, and those beautiful eyes came to rest on his face again.

"Thanks." His heart was pounding a rapid beat in his chest. "I'm fine. I just need some time alone."

Her expression softened with understanding. "They can be a bit much, I suppose."

"Not at all. I think your family is amazing. I haven't enjoyed a meal that much in ages."

Her smile was quick and alive with affection—and

it warmed him from head to toe. "They are pretty wonderful, aren't they?"

"They really are...." He stood there, watching her. She had no idea what a captivating picture she made...how her eyes glowed...how her hair danced in the breeze. A sudden, intense longing seized him. He wanted to reach out, take hold of her, and pull her close. Instead, he settled for lifting one hand to smooth an errant wisp of hair from her face. "And so are you."

Her gaze flew to lock with his, and he saw a multitude of emotions reflected there: surprise, awareness, pleasure. She bit her lip, and for the life of him he couldn't keep his fingers from reaching out to tenderly trace the line of her jaw, her mouth...

With the whisper of a sigh, she turned her face into his hand and, closing her eyes, rested her cheek against his palm. His breath caught in his throat and, cupping her face, urged her toward him. He leaned down to brush a gentle kiss across her lips. *Just one, Lord, just one small kiss...*

At least, that's what he'd intended. But it seemed so right when his mouth touched hers that he moved forward, slipping his arms around her, drawing her close, cradling her against him.

She fit perfectly in his arms. Like she was made for him. And the realization sent his emotions reeling. When he finally raised his head, he felt dazed, as though he'd been spun in circles and turned upside down. He looked down at her face. From the look in her eyes, she was in much the same condition as he. And he exulted that she didn't move, didn't step away; she merely looked up at him with a faraway smile—

A sharp pang of guilt pierced him. What was he *doing?* He didn't have the right to do this!

Self-loathing filled him, and he stepped back, dropping his arms to his sides. The look of startled confusion on Taylor's face only compounded the accusing voices hammering at him from within.

"I'm sorry, Taylor." He could hardly believe the hoarse voice was his. "I—"

What could he say? *I shouldn't have kissed you because you don't really know me? I don't deserve to have you care about me because I'm not who you think I am?* How about simple and to the point. *I'm a liar. I'm only here because of the wolves. I'm using you.*

He clenched his teeth, shaking his head helplessly, and took another step away from her.

"Good night," he croaked, then turned and walked away into the darkness.

Donelle leaned against the sink, watching out the kitchen window, her face furrowed with concern.

"If you caught one of the kids spying on someone, you'd have his head," her husband's voice came from behind her. She turned and went to sit beside him.

His eyes roamed her face. Then he leaned forward to stroke her cheek. "Trouble in paradise, love?"

"I'm afraid so." Something just wasn't making sense. "Holden, it's painfully clear that those two are drawn to each other."

"And?"

"And though they haven't known each other long, it feels right for them to be together. There's just something about Connor Alexander…" She put her elbows on the table and rested her chin in her hands. "I'm certain he's trustworthy. But I get the oddest feeling that—"

"That he's hiding something?"

Her eyes met his in surprise. "You think so, too?"

He nodded. "At the beginning of dinner he was fine. In fact, I think he was enjoying himself. Then just before he left, it was as though a cloud passed over his face."

"Exactly!" Donelle was relieved it hadn't just been her imagination. "He looked upset, almost angry. And then he left."

Holden leaned back in his chair. "So, what if it's true? What if he is hiding something?"

"I don't know. I haven't any idea how we could find out."

"Well, I'm certainly not Sam Spade, and neither are you."

Donelle's lips twitched. "Sam Spade? Good heavens, dear, you're dating yourself."

"I'd far rather date you." He reached for her hand.

She entwined her fingers with his, loving the warmth and familiarity of his clasp. He leaned forward, brushing a gentle kiss across her lips.

"It will work out, my love. We've seen God's protective hand at work in Taylor's life more than once. He's not going to stop now."

Gratitude filled her as they bowed their heads, taking their concerns and confusion to the One they knew could make all things right.

I am such a fool.

The thought kept going through Taylor's mind as she got ready for bed, her movements stiff, almost mechanical. She felt like a spring that had been wound too tightly—ready to come completely, totally undone.

Tears threatened, but she refused to cry. She'd given all the tears she intended to give for Josh. No one else was going to get them. Her heart had closed itself off the day Josh died, and she had no intention of letting it open again. No one else was getting in, no matter how tantalizing he might be.

Liar, the voice in her head mocked. *Liar. He's already there.*

"No," she whispered, startled at the agony in her voice. "No!" She swallowed the lump of painful emotions. She dropped onto the bed. Pulling her knees to her chest and circling them with her arms, she buried her face.

You believed what his eyes were saying. You wanted to believe he cared.

"No." She saw again the look in Connor's eyes as he stepped away from her after kissing her…repulsion, disgust, rejection.

You trusted him. You let him in.

"No," she repeated, but the hot tears coursing down her cheeks made it all too clear that she'd lost the battle with humiliation and pain. Tomorrow would be different. Tomorrow she would remember her vow, and her heart would remain safely closed.

No one—not Connor Alexander with his tantalizing smile, not Gavin MacEwen with his assurances of friendship, not even Brad Momadey with his burning, haunted eyes…

No one was going to hurt her again.

FIFTEEN

"WYLIE MARSTEN, YOU'RE A THIEF OF THE FIRST ORDER."

Wylie chortled and rang up the purchase. "Maybe so, MacEwen, but since I own this general store and I'm pretty much the only game in town, I guess that means I can make the rules. Now, hand over your wallet."

Gavin did as Wylie commanded. As the older man pulled the appropriate bills from the wallet, Gavin thought again of Taylor.

He'd called her to see if she wanted to come to town with him, but she'd told him she and Connor had already been to town. To say he'd been less than pleased would be an understatement. Connor Alexander was becoming a definite nuisance.

Gavin hoisted his bag of groceries and headed for the door, only to run headlong into two small torpedoes as they burst through the door.

"Oops!" Mark Camus stepped back to give the Scotsman a sheepish look. "Sorry, Gavin!"

"Yeah, sorry," Mikey echoed.

"No problem, lads. It's clear you were on a mission of great importance."

Two heads nodded vigorously. "We're buying supplies for Mr. Alexander!" Mark said.

Gavin's lips thinned. *Alexander again!* "Are you, now?" He did his best to keep his tone amiable.

"Yup!" Mark turned to glance at the aisle with hand tools. "And we gotta hurry, 'cuz if we get back soon enough, he's gonna show us how to build a birdhouse."

"Is he, now?" Gavin's dry tone was lost on the boys. They just beamed up at him.

"Isn't Mr. Alexander the best, Gavin?" Mikey's adoration was evident in his young eyes.

"He sure is." Mark grabbed his twin's sleeve and tugged him toward the tool shelves. "C'mon, Mikey, I don't want to be late."

They drifted away, and Gavin walked out of the store, a sour taste in his mouth.

"Aye, he's just a peach of a man, I'm sure." He muttered the comment through clenched teeth. "A true gem! Why, it should be an honor that the fine Connor Alexander is tryin' to steal my woman!" He yanked open the door of his vehicle, tossed his package inside, then slammed the door.

He leaned against the Blazer. Just what exactly did he know about Connor Alexander? The longer he thought, the deeper his frown grew. Realization dawned and he straightened.

He didn't know much. Not much at all. And that just wasn't acceptable. Gavin had learned long ago that the only way to deal effectively with an adversary was to know all you could about him. He turned and started down the sidewalk. It was time to pay a friendly, unofficial visit to his deputy friend, Amos Erdrich.

And maybe, just maybe, he'd ask Amos to do some friendly, unofficial checking on Mr. Connor—"the best"—Alexander.

SIXTEEN

THE ANSWER TO DONELLE'S PRAYERS CAME MUCH SOONER THAN she'd anticipated. Oh, she'd believed God would answer, but she'd never dreamed he would do it so quickly—or in such an unexpected way.

It happened several mornings later. Donelle had decided to spend the morning in bed getting caught up on her reading. She had just settled under the covers, her tea on the bedside table, a pile of magazines stacked beside her. She was thumbing through the pile, trying to decide which one to read first, when a cover caught her eye.

It was a wildlife magazine, one of her favorites. The articles almost always presented a balanced view of the issues, which she greatly appreciated. On the cover of this particular issue was a stunning picture of a timber wolf. The title of the article, which was printed on the cover in big bold letters, was, "Wolf: Victim or Villain—or a Little of Both?"

She arched her eyebrows. That was certainly a timely topic, considering the ever-increasing debates among their friends and neighbors regarding the rumored return of wolves to the area. She flipped open the magazine to the page indicated in the contents, settled back in her pillows, and began to read.

Soon she was absorbed, caught in the writer's skillful work and the beautiful photographs accompanying the article. When she finished reading, she turned back to the first page of the article. Her breath caught in a small gasp, and her mouth opened into a silent oh.

She laid down the magazine and leaned back against her pillows, closing her eyes, a gentle smile dancing across her lips.

Thank you, Father. Her heart overflowed with both gratitude and understanding. *You are a wonder.*

Connor wanted to hit something. At the very least, he wanted to go someplace isolated and remote and yell.

Since the night he had kissed Taylor, she had treated him as though he had some contagious disease. Or as though he *were* one. Oh, she continued to work with him, even beside him from time to time, but in almost complete silence. Any conversation with her was stilted and awkward. She answered his questions with curt responses and seldom met his eyes. The easy camaraderie they'd shared had vanished as quickly as snow in August.

It was driving him crazy. At first he'd refused to believe her reserve could last, but it had been four days now, and, try as he might, he couldn't break through the wall she'd erected around herself. Couldn't even chip it.

Today, she was holding the ladder as he climbed to remove storm windows from one of the cabins and replace them with screens. He'd already made several efforts at conversation, and she'd squelched them. Well, he wasn't done yet. If the subtle approach wasn't going to do the trick, then he'd just have to be more direct.

"Where do you keep your rifles?" He felt a flash of satisfaction when she looked at him with a startled expression.

"I beg your pardon?"

"Your rifles." He kept his voice light, unconcerned. He handed her a window, then took the screen she lifted to him and turned to the window. "I mean, I figure you keep them in the house." He snapped the screen in place, fastened it, and started down the ladder. "I was just wondering in which room."

"They're locked in a cabinet in the den. Why?"

He lifted the ladder and walked to the last window, where he set the ladder in place with a great deal more precision than was necessary.

"Connor," she said as he took the screen from her. Her voice had grown just a bit testy. That was fine. Anything was better than that inaccessible, remote tone she'd been using.

"Connor..." Her temper was clearly rising. He snapped another screen in place, his back to her, and indulged in a slight smile. Her rigid control was slipping.

"Connor Alexander! Will you kindly answer my question?"

"Hmmm?" He gave her a bland look as he made his way down the ladder. "Did you ask me something?"

She planted herself directly in his path, her expression murderous, her hands on her hips. Her eyes were burning with frustration, and the color in her cheeks had heightened from a slight pink to an exasperated red.

Now this was more like it! His stormy, exhilarating Taylor was back—for the moment at least. It was all Connor could do not to laugh out loud with relief.

"You know very well I asked you why you wanted to know where I keep my rifles!"

"Oh, that. No reason really." *Other than getting a rise out of you.* He stepped around her, heading for the barn. "I'll put the ladder away." He let his grin loose now that she couldn't see him.

But suddenly she was there, in front of him, her narrowed eyes burning with a dangerous light. "How *dare* you turn your back on me!"

He jerked to a halt, taken aback by the fury in her tone. "Taylor—"

But she wasn't having any of it. "How dare you treat me this way! I thought we were becoming friends. I thought—"

At the catch in her voice, he set down the ladder and took a step forward.

Immediately she backed away. *"Don't."* The desperation in the one word froze him in his tracks. "Don't you dare come *near* me. And from now on, *Mister* Alexander, keep this in mind. When I ask an employee a question, I expect an answer."

Her tone was clearly insulting, clearly condescending, and Connor's anger ignited in response. "Is that so, *Mrs.* Sorensen?" He ground the question out in carefully measured tones.

"Unless, of course, you have a problem with that." Her angry eyes challenged him.

He started to answer, but she cut him off. "Because if you *do,* then maybe it's time to find yourself another boss."

He stared at her, and his fury almost choked him. "Actually, Mrs. Sorensen—" he kept his tone deceptively mild—"I don't have a problem with your request." He took a step closer, bringing them almost nose to nose. "However, I do have a problem with you."

He wasn't sure what kind of response he'd expected— a kick to the shins wouldn't have surprised him—but what happened next did. She met his glare, held it for several seconds…then a sob caught in her throat, and suddenly there were tears running down her face. She spun around and fled from him, looking for all the world as though the hounds of hell were on her heels.

Every impulse inside screamed at him to follow her, to stop her and work through what had happened between them…not just today, but over the past few weeks. He wanted, needed, to understand what she was feeling. What *he* was feeling. But now was not the time. He had to give her a chance to recover, to get her emotions under control.

And then he had to tell her the truth.

So he stood there, watching her run, and as the sound of her sobs drifted back to him, his lips compressed into a thin line. *The deceit ends here, Lord. Tomorrow I tell her why I'm here. It's up to you where it goes from there.*

He put his hands in his pockets and walked toward his cabin. *She'll probably hate me. I wouldn't blame her if she told me to pack my bags. If she does, I'll just have to respect her wishes.* He dropped into one of the old-fashioned rocking chairs outside his cabin door and stared up at the sky. *I can do that, Father. I can leave. This is nothing more than an assignment. If I fail, I fail. Regrettable, but not the end of the world.*

He believed the reassurance, was convinced it was true. So he found it especially confusing, and irritating, that the thought of losing Taylor left his throat dry, and his heart constricted with sudden, blinding fear.

SEVENTEEN

THE NEXT MORNING IT WAS STILL DARK WHEN CONNOR emerged from his cabin. He rolled his aching shoulder muscles gingerly, stretching his neck one way and then the other as he walked. The dull pain that rewarded every movement brought a grimace to his face.

He'd spent most of the night tossing and turning, which hadn't improved his state of mind. Even Taylor's crack-of-dawn mom wouldn't be up this early, so there wouldn't be a warm breakfast to greet him.

Please, God, at least let the coffee be brewing.

He entered the still dark kitchen and turned on the light over the sink. Glancing around, he spotted the coffee maker already brewing a pot of the elixir of life, thanks to the timer Taylor had set.

God bless your socks off, Taylor. With a grateful smile, he started to feel uplifted. God was, indeed, merciful. He sniffed the air appreciatively and rummaged in the cupboards for a mug. He finally found a "man-sized" one and set it on the counter, waiting. Coffee makers were never fast enough.

He eyed the filling carafe, then grasped the handle

with one hand and held the big mug right next to it with the other. With one quick movement he whipped the carafe out from under the stream of coffee and replaced it with the mug.

Didn't miss a drop—

"Bravo, Connor. That was masterfully done."

He jerked around and found Taylor's mother watching him from the doorway.

"Morning." He bit his lip. "I, ah…I wasn't expecting anyone else up so early."

"Oh, I had some trouble sleeping last night." She smiled at him. "Too much on my mind, I suppose. And you?"

"The same." She nodded as though she understood. Connor wished she did. He caught her looking at the rapidly filling mug he still held under the coffee maker. "Uh, it was taking too long…" Her face broke into an amused grin.

"Of course it was." She came forward to set several magazines on the table. Her eyes twinkled. "Anyone knows that three minutes is far too long to wait for one's first cup of coffee."

"Actually—" he switched the carafe back under the drip—"it was more like a minute and a half, since the pot was about half full."

She filled the cream pitcher from the carton in the fridge and set it, along with the ceramic sugar bowl, on the table.

"Either way, I agree. It was ridiculous to wait.

Though my first preference is tea, I have suffered from the occasional craving for coffee. On such occasions, I find a mug works quite well."

"Ahhh, so you've done the same thing, eh?"

She looked at him around the edge of the cupboard door as she got down her own mug, and he almost burst out laughing at the mischievous gleam in her emerald eyes. For a brief moment Connor had the feeling he was looking into Taylor's green gaze.

"Let's just say that while I strive to be the epitome of restraint and self-control, patience is not my strongest virtue." She poured a mug of coffee from the now partially filled carafe, then came to sit next to him at the table.

He sipped his coffee. "I understand. Far better than I care to admit," he said with a low chuckle.

"Indeed?" She watched him carefully. "So you share my struggle with impatience, Connor?"

He considered her for a moment, and the look in her eyes told him there was some vague undercurrent to the question. He inclined his head slightly.

"And do you struggle with other virtues as well?" His eyebrows shot up at the unexpected question, but before he could compose an appropriate response, she went on. Her tone was casual and relaxed, as though she were discussing something commonplace like the weather. "I find that integrity can be most troublesome at times, don't you? Somehow it so often seems as though honesty is...well, risky, at best. Hazardous, at worst."

Connor shifted in his seat but kept his expression blank, trying not to look as though he were squirming.

"Isn't it odd?" She cupped her mug with both hands. "For all that God directs us to use honesty, it's remarkable how much easier it seems to be to act with caution, perhaps even a touch of deception." Her gentle smile was filled with compassion, and he felt an unfamiliar heat in his face.

This couldn't be happening! He couldn't be sitting here blushing!

"Oh, not true deception, of course," she continued with amiable ruthlessness. "Nothing cruel or evil. Just a small, harmless deception, one in which the entire truth isn't told. That way, a person could—" she frowned slightly. "What is that term Ryan uses? Oh yes! Scope out! That's it!" She regarded him triumphantly. "Not revealing hurtful or difficult facts might give one time to *scope out* a situation, to evaluate how those involved might react to the entire truth." She tilted her head and regarded him. "Don't you think so?"

"I suppose it's possible," he said slowly.

"Hmmm." She held his gaze, a pensive look in her eyes. "Yes, I'm sure that seems wise, perhaps even kind, to most people." Her eyes met his, her look direct. "It is a shame we can't use such tools, isn't it? I mean, if we're to follow God's leading in our interactions with each other."

Connor was fairly certain this was how bugs felt when captured and skewered by entomologists. He'd never considered the practice unkind before, but if those insects felt a fraction as uncomfortable as he did, he would write his congressman tomorrow to stop the senseless suffering. He swallowed hard, trying to manage a feeble answer, but she didn't give him a chance. She just went on as though totally oblivious to the fact that she was driving darts of doubt and uncertainty deep into his conscience.

"I am thoroughly convinced that you are as devoted to honoring God as we are, Connor."

Her smile was positively beatific, and he floundered before the brilliance of that look. "I…well…Mrs. Camus…" The words died in his throat when she reached to pat his arm.

"Of course you are. I can tell by your eyes. I know you understand, as I do, that it's best, easier even, to deal in the truth from the very beginning. There are no lies to remember, no fabrications to cover, no relationships to mend."

He felt as though a tidal wave of emotion had come crashing down on him, grinding him into the dirt. Chief among the sensations was a deep sense of regret. And shame.

"My," she said with a contented sigh, "this is good coffee."

He blinked, almost dizzy at the abrupt change of topic. His eyes narrowed, and he studied her sweetly smiling countenance—and at that moment understanding dawned. Donelle Camus's wide-eyed innocence was merely a smoke screen. Beneath that guileless facade was the shrewd mind and well-honed instincts of an experienced hunter, one who recognized vulnerability and opportunity at a glance—and used them to perfection.

"Would you like more?"

The simple question hit him like a semi, and his eyes flew to meet hers. He cleared his throat with difficulty. *"More?"*

She held up her mug. "More coffee?"

"Ah." He was out of his league. Entirely. This woman was a master. "No. Thank you. I...uh...I think I've had plenty." He pushed back his chair and went to set his empty mug in the sink. "I should be heading out, anyway. There's a lot of work to do, and I figure I can get a good bit done if I start before breakfast."

"Whatever you think is best." He started for the door, anxious for escape. A few more steps—

"Oh, Connor."

He paused, his hand on the knob. He'd come so close. Two more steps and he'd have been gone. Letting his breath out slowly he turned to face her. "Yes, Mrs. Camus?"

She rose and came to him, holding out the magazines she'd brought in with her. "I read the most interesting articles last night in a few of our wildlife magazines. I thought you might enjoy them as well."

He accepted the magazines and glanced at them—

then stood there stunned, shaken. He recognized both of the magazines. Each carried an article on wolves. Articles he had written.

"I particularly enjoyed the articles on wolves. The author is quite good." Once again he met her eyes. He expected to see anger, accusation. Instead, there was only kindness. "His passion comes across clearly, as does his intelligence. He presents a balanced perspective on the issues. I daresay he would be most convincing in person, particularly if a person were already predisposed to his views." The warmth of her expression enveloped him. "Or predisposed to the man himself."

He nodded, unable to speak around the lump in his throat.

She patted his arm. "Now, off with you. As you've already said, there's a good deal of work waiting for you. And for me."

He turned and went out the door, the magazines clutched in his hands, his heart beating a rapid, pained rhythm.

Donelle turned and found her husband leaning in the doorway, his head cocked, a pensive smile on his generous lips.

"So, think you got through?"

"The issue isn't whether I've gotten through, dear—" she went to the fridge and pulled open the door—"It's whether God gets through. And I'm sure he will. Connor merely needed a little push in the right direction."

She pulled a carton of eggs and a package of bacon off the shelf, balanced a loaf of bread and tub of butter on top, and stepped back, bumping the door shut with her hip.

"Hmmm." Her husband's lips twitched.

"Oh, please, Holden. Don't 'hmmm' me!" She set down the food with a thud on the counter and turned her back on the love of her life.

"Yes, dear." His smile broadened.

"I just couldn't sit there and watch this charade continue."

"No, dear." He moved from the doorway.

"But if I had told Taylor the truth about her 'handyman,' she would never have given him a chance to explain himself. I swear, I don't know *where* that girl gets her temper!"

"Yes, dear." The laughing response came from just behind her ear, and strong arms slipped around her waist and pressed her close. She sighed and leaned back against her husband, loving the warm familiarity of his embrace. He tucked her tight against him, resting his chin on the top of her head.

"She loves him, Holden. I don't think she even knows it yet, but I see it every time she looks at him. And I think he loves her."

"I think you're right," he said. "And I think you did the right thing."

Quick tears pricked Donelle's eyes, and she turned

to slip her arms around her husband's still trim waist. She buried her face against the soft flannel of his shirt.

"I want her to be happy," she mumbled, her words slightly muffled.

He reached out to tip her chin up. Their eyes met, and they smiled.

"As happy as God has made us." He kissed her softly, his eyes glowing. "You've done your part, my love. The rest is in God's hands. We need to wait and watch. He won't let us, or our girl, down." His eyes drifted to the counter, and he waggled his eyebrows at her. "Now, how 'bout some grub, woman? Your man is here, and he's hungry!"

Thoughts raced through Connor's mind as he walked toward his cabin. He pulled the door open and went inside, flicking on the light and tossing the magazines on his bed. Then he sank into the overstuffed chair and leaned his head back wearily.

God, I've messed everything up. Big time. Once again he swallowed the bitter reality that he was in a mess of his own making. *How do I make this right, Lord? How do I tell Taylor the truth without hurting her?* The image of her beautiful eyes, blazing with anger, floated before him. *She's going to hate me. And I deserve it, Father. How can I find a way to be worthy of her trust...and the trust her mother just showed me?*

Silence answered him, and he stood, going to stare

out the window. The sun was just beginning to peek over the mountains, its red glow coloring the sky in brilliant hues and tones. But the beauty was lost on Connor. His eyes focused unseeingly on the landscape, then came back to scan the room. He needed guidance, direction, something that would give him some glimmer of hope.

"God, I know you don't drop answers from heaven on a string, but could you give me a hand here?" The desperation in his muttered request surprised him, and a heavy realization cloaked him.

There was much more at stake here than the wolves. For the first time in years, the animals weren't his first concern. Taylor was. Though he was determined to protect the wolves, their importance paled when compared with hurting Taylor. He'd be angry, upset, disappointed if he lost the pack, but if he lost Taylor...

His reaction to that thought was more violent than it had been last night. It was frightening—and exhilarating. His heart thudded in his chest as the devastating truth hit him squarely. Somewhere between wanting to shake Taylor until her teeth rattled and discovering the wonder of who she was in all of her unpredictable, irrational, infuriating glory...he'd fallen in love.

He stared blankly around the room. He was in love. One side of his mouth twitched, then quirked up, as though drawn by an invisible string. *He* was in love. Suddenly he was sure of himself and his rightful place in the universe. He would go to Taylor and tell her how he felt. He'd fold her in his arms, cradle her against his chest, and gaze down into her beautiful face. And she would look up at him and…and…

Who was he kidding? She'd look up at him and welcome his pronouncement of lifelong devotion with a sucker punch right in the gut; *that's* what she'd do!

"Oh, God." He raked his hands through his hair. "God, help me." He sat down on the bed with a defeated sigh and reached for his Bible. Then his eyes fixed on a small plaque on the wall just above the table.

Curious, his heart beating with an anticipation he didn't entirely understand, he moved closer and read the beautifully scripted words: "Do not let kindness and truth leave you; bind them around your neck, write them on the tablet of your heart. So you will find favor and good repute in the sight of God and man."

The words washed over him, easing the self-recriminations and anger he'd been allowing into his heart. He read the plaque again, then opened his Bible to the reference, Proverbs 3:3–4, and settled back against the pillows to read and to prepare.

Come hell or high water, before the day was out, he would tell Taylor the truth.

EIGHTEEN

SEVERAL HOURS LATER, CONNOR HEADED FOR THE KITCHEN for the second time that morning. This time, however, he was filled with resolve.

He opened the door, walked in, then stopped in his tracks. Taylor sat at the table, deep in what was clearly a heated discussion with Gavin MacEwen. They looked up as he entered the room, and the expression on Gavin's face when he saw Connor could only be described as predatory. Warning bells sounded softly in Connor's head.

"Connor. I'm glad you're here."

At Taylor's carefully controlled words, the warning bells went from soft to blaring. Her eyes raked him, and he saw hurt and disbelief reflected on her face. His heart sank.

He wasn't going to have the chance to tell Taylor anything. The Scotsman had done it for him.

"Gavin has the most interesting bit of information," Taylor said as Connor pulled out a chair and sat down.

Connor drew a breath and met her eyes squarely, waiting.

"It seems there's a gentleman who works for an organization, the Wildlife Awareness Coalition, I believe"—she glanced at Gavin and he nodded—"a wildlife biologist. He's a field representative, apparently. When Gavin spoke with a secretary at the organization, she said this man is on an assignment. Something to do with wolves in Wyoming. But the most interesting fact is that…he has the same name as you do."

Connor's gaze didn't waver.

"Gavin has the idea that you're here under false pretenses. That you weren't looking for a job at all, but for wolves. On Galloway Glen."

The slight tremor in her voice as she spoke those words pierced Connor. *Oh, Taylor…I'm so sorry.* "He's right." His words were calm and steady. He gave no indication that they cost him everything.

Taylor's face drained of color. He started to rise to go to her, but she held up a shaking hand, halting him. Her eyes, which had never left his face, now blazed with contempt.

He eased back into his chair. *Lord…what do I say?*

"I see."

He hadn't realized how cold—how dead—two words could be.

She rose from her chair and walked to the doorway of the kitchen. She paused for a moment, her back to him. When she finally spoke, it was in a low, hoarse whisper.

"I want you gone. As soon as possible. And I don't ever want to see you again." She spun back around, her eyes large and dark in her white face, and hurled words at him. "I *trusted* you! Believed in you! I even let myself care—" She closed her eyes against him.

Even as she closed her heart. He knew it as surely as if he'd heard a door slam shut and a key turn in a lock.

She walked from the room, her back stiff and straight.

Connor sat there, silent, absorbing what had just happened. He wanted to hate Gavin, wanted to jump up and beat the man to within an inch of his life,…but he couldn't deny the fact that all he'd done was reveal the truth.

Without giving the Scotsman a glance, Connor stood and left the house. He walked to his cabin, his steps slow and heavy.

He had lost her. Before he'd even had a chance to tell her he loved her.

He'd never felt so sick in his life.

Taylor sat in the living room, in her favorite chair, curled into a ball. Her face was awash with bitter tears.

Stupid, stupid, stupid! How could you trust him? How could you trust anyone like that?

Footsteps sounded behind her, and Gavin came to kneel in front of her. He looked into her face, searching.

"I was a fool."

"No, Taylor. You were trusting. That's all."

"I should have known better. You can't trust anyone, not if you don't want to be hurt."

There was a flicker of emotion in his dark eyes. "Did he mean so much to you, then, lass?"

She couldn't answer. She closed her eyes against the tears that threatened to overwhelm her. Oh yes. Yes, he'd meant that much to her.

A gentle touch on her face brought her attention back to Gavin, and when their gazes met, she saw sadness—and loss—in his mahogany eyes. Remorse swept over her.

"Gavin, I'm sorry. I didn't mean—"

He stopped her words with a slight shake of his head. "Taylor, it's okay." He took her hand in his, studying her face, taking in the feelings she couldn't hide. "You're sure?"

Tears slipped down her cheeks. "I don't know. I wish I did. All I know is that he matters. A lot."

He exhaled slowly, as though breathing were painful. "So. Your heart has chosen then."

His eyes were dark with emotion, and she wanted to reach out, to comfort him, ease his pain,…but she couldn't. She was the reason he was hurting.

"It's not what I would have wished for, but lass, I trust God to lead you to the right decision." His smile was gentle. "And the right man. If you're meant to be with me, you will be. But first I think you need to find out what this man really means to you. And you to him."

"I can't mean too much—" a sob caught in her throat—"otherwise he wouldn't have lied to me." Gavin gathered her close, cradling her against his broad chest. She leaned against him, giving in to the grief that washed over her in bruising waves.

"It's okay, darlin'," he said, his arms tight and protective around her. "It's okay."

But it wasn't. It couldn't be. Not when she had just sent away the man she loved. Despite his deceit, despite the sense of betrayal that swept over her, she could no longer deny what her heart had been telling her for weeks.

She was in love with Connor Alexander.

It would never be okay again.

"Sasha, you idiot dog! Where are you!"

Taylor seldom got angry with the husky, but she couldn't hold back her irritation. Sasha *would* pick tonight of all nights to disappear. It wasn't enough that Connor was gone. Now the Siberian was as well.

What do you want from me, God?

She stomped out of the house, calling the dog's name, peering into the darkness. The moon was high in the sky, and the stars painted the gloom with twinkling light. Taylor stepped off the porch, moving toward the cabins. Maybe Sasha was with Luke.

She started to pass Connor's empty cabin, then paused. The door was ajar.

Her heart thudded in her chest at the possibility that Connor might still be there, and a sudden, wild joy surged through her. She moved forward, pushing the door open and turning on the light as she entered.

Sasha blinked at her from where she lay on the empty bed. Keen disappointment filled Taylor, and she went to sit beside the husky, circling the dog's thick neck with her arms. As she buried her face in the dog's soft fur, she felt the tears begin again.

Prayer poured from her heart. For strength, for guidance, for understanding…and for Connor. And before she could stop herself, a plea slipped from her heart and flew heavenward.

Bring him back. Please, bring him back.

NINETEEN

THE WIND BLEW IN WARM GUSTS AS THE MAN TRUDGED along, his traps dangling from his long, lean hands.

He had considered using poison instead of traps, but that would risk killing other predators unintentionally. Besides, he wanted to be sure there was as little chance as possible that Sasha would become an unwitting victim. If he used poison, Taylor's beloved dog could be drawn to the scent of the meat. He shuddered at the thought.

No, the traps were safer. Less indiscriminate.

He set the traps, glancing around periodically, reassuring himself he was undetected. He'd done his best to ensure that Taylor had no idea what he was doing. When he knew he would be hunting the next day, he made it a point to talk with her, to find out where she planned to spend the coming day. Then he would give that location a wide berth. Just to be sure he wouldn't be recognized, he wore a bandana tied around the lower part of his face.

He'd been hunting the wolves for weeks, covering

acre after acre of land on the ranch, watching for any small sign. But without the assistance of snow, it was a difficult proposition at best. Sometimes he stayed out all night, forcing himself to stay awake until dawn, listening, straining his ears for the faintest howl. But the sound had come only once since he'd first heard it, carried to him on the wind. He had guessed at its source, traveled there the next day, and found nothing.

No prints. No scat. Nothing that indicated wolves were—or ever had been—there.

He'd set out a line of traps, just to be sure. But he couldn't leave them out long, couldn't chance Taylor coming across them.

So far, when he'd retrieved the traps he set, he'd found them empty, mocking him, laughing at him for his ineptness. But let them mock. He would not give up.

One day his enemy would make a fatal error.

TWENTY

CONNOR WALKED DOWN THE SIDEWALK, HAMMER IN HAND, flyers tucked securely under his arm. He had been posting the notices about the town meeting everywhere he could think of. Area stores had been surprisingly cooperative. As had the officials at the town hall.

When Connor had first phoned Harry to tell him of his failure, the older man's booming voice had reached out to reassure him. "Don't sweat it, buddy. There's more than one way to deal with this issue. If you can't find the wolves themselves, at least you can hold a town meeting to discuss the wolves and what's happening with restoration. Let the locals know we're aware of the reports, maybe make 'em a little less likely to take a shot if they happen to see a wolf. And you can give the ranchers a chance to air their concerns."

It sounded like about as much fun as a root canal. Connor knew he would be considered the enemy, the target for any shots from those who were angry or unhappy about the wolves. Still, Harry was right. It was a place to start.

So he went to the town hall, talked with the officials, and got their okay. Now all he had to do was post the notices. The meeting was set for Thursday night. That gave him four days to get ready.

He paused by a telephone pole, pulled out a flyer, situated the nail, and started pounding. He leaned back to survey his handiwork. The flyer was designed to catch attention. A large drawing of a wolf head was at the top, just below the words "PUBLIC NOTICE." A brief explanation of the purpose and topic followed, along with the date, time, and location. "Any and all are welcome to attend" was the final proclamation.

"So you're not hiding what you're here for any longer?"

Connor turned to find Gavin standing behind him, looking at the flyer. A brief jolt of anger shot through him, then was gone. Gavin had only done what he thought was best for Taylor.

"I've had enough of coming in the back door, Gavin."

"As have we all."

Connor inclined his head. He turned to leave, then paused. "Is...how's Taylor?"

Gavin's brows arched, and he regarded Connor in silence. Connor turned away. He hadn't really expected a response anyway.

"She's goin' on, livin' her life."

Connor winced. He'd hoped he would be harder to get over than that.

"But she's like a woman walkin' in her sleep."

Connor faced the other man, and the expression in the Scot's eyes made him pause. He'd expected the anger, though it was so intense he thought it would reach out and strike him. But what surprised him was the pain, deep and bruising, reflected in Gavin's dark eyes.

"I never meant to hurt her."

"Aye, but hurt her you did." His eyes hardened. "You've cost her dearly, Alexander. You've taken a heart that was wounded to begin with and cut it to the core. And it's like she's lost now and can't get back from whatever cold, dark place her heart has taken her."

The words struck hard, and Connor closed his eyes.

"Aye, the truth is far from pretty, isn't it?" The bitterness in the Scotsman's voice slapped at Connor. "You see where your lies have brought you? What a pity you didn't go there alone. But you've taken Taylor along for the ride. So the least you can do is face her and see this through to its conclusion, whatever that may be."

Connor opened his eyes. Was Gavin saying what he thought he was saying? "See it through?"

Gavin's voice snapped at him. "Believe me, if I had my way, you'd be run out of town and never allowed back. I'll do anything I can to keep Taylor from being hurt, to protect her. From you. Even from herself."

"From herself?"

Gavin's hard gaze never wavered. "If need be. Sometimes those you love are too close to something to realize it will hurt them."

"A bit arrogant, don't you think?"

A mirthless smile lifted the corners of Gavin's mouth. "Perhaps." The smile died. "But there are some things I can't protect her from. What I've seen in the past few days has made one fact painfully clear."

"And that is?"

"Taylor loves you. Or she thinks she does."

A disbelieving sound escaped Connor, and Gavin fixed him with a steely gaze. "You've been a fool once, Alexander. Don't be one again. Trust what I tell you, mon. It's true. And as much as it galls me to tell you so, you will have a chance to redeem yourself. I see it in her eyes." He crossed his arms. "It won't be easy, by any means. But I'd count any trial worth the effort to gain a woman like Taylor Sorensen."

"Why are you telling me this?" Connor tried—and failed—to fight off the wild hope that was beginning to form deep within him.

"One reason, and one alone: because I love Taylor and want her to be happy." The Scotsman moved to stand directly in front of Connor, his eyes narrowed. "I give you fair warning, though. Hurt her again and it's over. You won't get another opportunity. I'll do everything in my power to make her forget you. And I will succeed."

Connor held Gavin's dark gaze, and the hope he'd been trying to ignore flared to life within him. *Jesus, merciful Jesus, let him be right. Please give me the opportunity to make this up to Taylor.*

"I give you my word, I won't hurt her again. Not if I can help it."

Gavin stared at him a moment longer, then moved to step around him, and walked away without another word. But what he'd said rang in Connor's mind for the rest of the day, then echoed in his dreams during the night.

"You will have a chance to redeem yourself...Taylor loves you...it won't be easy...any trial is worth the effort...."

By the time he rolled out of bed the next morning, Connor knew what he had to do.

Taylor stood near the edge of the pool at Reunion, staring into the clear water.

"I miss you, Josh. I wish you were here to tell me what to do." The incongruity of her statement hit, and a laugh escaped her. "Of course, if you were here, none of this would be happening, so I guess, in a way, it's all your fault."

She sat down, drew her knees close to her chest, and leaned her arms on them. "Thanks a lot," she muttered dryly. "You know, it was bad enough when you died, but this bit about falling in love again is really for the birds." She looked across the pool at the grass and the wildflowers. "Funny thing is, I'm pretty sure you'd like Connor. You two are a lot alike." Tilting her head and resting her cheek on her crossed arms, she sniffed. "You're both funny, and sincere, and strong, and honest—"

Tears sprang to her eyes. "Okay, so you were honest," she said in frustration, rubbing the wetness from her cheeks. "The least he could have done was tell me who he was! But he didn't even give me a chance. He just came in under false pretenses, and he made me believe in him, and he made me love him…." Her voice was choked with tears. "Why couldn't he have been honest? Why did he have to let me down? Like you—"

She stopped, afraid of what she'd been about to say. But not saying the words didn't change what she felt— that Josh had let her down. He had promised to come back, but he didn't. She shouldn't have trusted…not Josh, not Connor, not anyone.

"Trust in the Lord with all your heart, and lean not on your own understanding."

"I know, Lord, I know," she muttered. "But I can't."

Can't…or won't, child?

"I can't! I try! But every time I do, I remember that you let Josh die!" Her tears flowed freely now. "I asked you to take care of him! Asked you to bring him home. And you let him die. Why, God? For Brad Momadey? Then it was wasted. For nothing! Brad doesn't even care, Lord. He doesn't even care!"

The image of Brad's face—his eyes dark with torment, his cheeks drawn and pale—floated in front of her.

"Get rid of all bitterness, rage and anger…. Be kind and compassionate…forgiving…just as in Christ God forgave you."

"So it's my fault I can't trust?" Anger boiled within

her. "It's my bitterness that's keeping me from trusting you?" She jumped to her feet. "I don't buy it, God. Brad killed Josh, and I'm not supposed to be angry?"

"Anyone who hates his brother is a murderer."

She turned, wrapped her arms about herself, and lowered her head. "Then I am a murderer, Lord." The quiet words seemed to hang in the still air, and she knelt on the soft grass. "God...help me."

She knelt in silence, waiting, longing for release but unable to let go of the bitterness that had settled into her heart like a giant boulder. She was caught. Trapped. And unable to free herself. *Father, help me. I don't know how to get beyond this...how to let go. Help me.* Her mind felt congested with doubts and fears and a haunting sense of loneliness. *Lord, are you even listening? Am I as alone in this as I feel?*

A soft sound came from behind her, and she turned, startled. "Oh!" she breathed in amazed wonder.

The wolf stood there, just across the pool, at the entrance to the cave. His ancient, golden gaze was fixed on her, looking for all the world as though he'd been listening to her words and her thoughts.

"Oh," she whispered again, delight filling her. "You're still here!"

He was as beautiful as she remembered. His powerful form and erect posture exuded authority.

"Hi," she said in a gentle tone, and the wolf's sharp ears turned toward her. "It's good to see you again."

As he stared at her with that tawny gaze, a sense of

peace surrounded her, settled over her, and she smiled. She wasn't alone. Even here, in the midst of the wilderness, the Creator was present. And he had stamped his creation with such wonder—like this marvelous creature.

The wolf tilted his gray head as though studying her, then stood and paced back and forth several times, keeping his attention focused on her. He seemed to be telling her something, but she didn't have the vaguest idea what he wanted. When she didn't move, he suddenly sprang up into the air—as though his long, spindly legs were tightly wound springs—then came down again to crouch, his front paws extended out in front of him, his hind end up in the air. His long, bushy tail waved back and forth playfully, and Taylor had the distinct impression he was trying to coax her to cross the pool and come for a romp.

She chuckled. "Okay, so you're a wolf, but that doesn't mean I can't consider you a friend." An idea dawned, and her smile broadened. "That's what I'll call you. *Sikis*. The Navajo term for 'friend.' What do you think?"

The wolf stood, watching her and waving his long tail back and forth, then turned and trotted into the cave.

Taylor hugged herself. "I'll take that as a sign of approval." She rose and walked back toward Topaz, feeling lighter than she'd felt in days.

She wasn't free yet, but she would be. She didn't

know how God would do it, but she believed he would somehow help her out of the hole she'd crawled into. All she had to do was wait and listen…and respond.

She swung into the saddle and turned Topaz toward home.

Several hours later, Taylor returned to the ranch, refreshed and relaxed. She walked Topaz into the barn, then slid from his back and removed the saddle with the ease of years of experience. The buckskin whinnied when the air hit his damp back, twitching his muscles happily.

"Feels good when the weight comes off, doesn't it, boy." Taylor grinned. She led the horse into his spacious stall, refilled his water and oats, then reached for the curry comb. She'd made a couple of long strokes when Sasha came bounding up, thrilled to see her mistress had returned from her ride.

"Well, hello there." Taylor scratched the dog between the ears. "You missed a great ride this morning. Where were you?"

"I'm afraid she was with me."

She spun around, staring. A tall, male form was silhouetted in the doorway of the barn, but with the sun at his back she couldn't see his face. Still, she recognized the deep, resonant voice.

Connor.

As he drew closer, she saw that his face was gaunt, and there were shadows beneath his eyes. He looked like he hadn't slept in a week.

Well, it served him right!

Indignant anger rose in her, and all thoughts of waiting and listening—to Connor or to God—were gone in a heated rush.

"Get off my ranch!"

"Not until we talk."

She snorted in a most unladylike fashion. "Talk? You want to talk?" She stomped out of the stall, brandishing the curry comb like a weapon. "I don't think so."

"Taylor, I'm not leaving until you sit down and listen to what I have to say."

Her jaw jutted out. "Do you seriously think I'd believe you?" He winced, but she didn't care. "I know you'll say anything, do anything, to get to the wolves. Even romance me!"

His eyes blazed. "That's not true and you know it!"

"How should I know *what's* true with you?"

"Ask."

The quiet response took her by surprise. *Ask? Just like that? Okay. Fine.* "Why did you come here?"

"I saw your name on all the wolf books at the library. I figured anyone who was that interested had either seen the wolves or hoped to. Then I remembered seeing your name in the paper. When I found the ad, I knew where to start my investigation."

"I suppose you expect me to believe you care about

me as much as you do the wolves?"

"I care about you a great deal more, but I don't expect you to believe that right now."

"Smart man."

"What I *do* expect you to believe is that I want to help the wolves. And I think you do, too." He stepped closer. "Please, Taylor, if you've seen them, tell me. I'll do my best to protect them. WAC will do everything in its power to do the same. None of us wants to put the wolves, if they really are here, at risk. I promise. You can believe me."

Sudden tears blinded her eyes and choked her voice. "Like I could believe Josh? You're all so quick to make promises you can't keep. Josh couldn't control the ledge he stood on. Do you think you can do any better with the ranchers? Well, I don't. And I don't know anything about your wolves, Mister Alexander. And even if I did, I certainly wouldn't entrust their care to you!"

"To whom, then? To you? You don't even know what you're doing. You've got some naïve notion that you can keep them safe, but I'd be willing to bet some of your fine neighbors have already come onto your land."

"My neighbors, unlike some people, can be trusted. They wouldn't trespass."

"Taylor, you know that's not true. There are ranchers as determined to kill these animals as I am to keep them alive."

"You're not touching my wolves!"

His eyebrows arched. "*Your* wolves? If you keep

going this way, you're going to get them killed. Have you ever seen a wolf in a trap? Or after it's been poisoned? Have you seen what some men will do to a wolf to kill it? The tortures they inflict on it? Well, you will. Count on it. Unless you let me help."

His words struck home, but she refused to let him see the anxiety they had stirred within her. The image of her beautiful friend in pain, being mistreated, was almost more than she could bear. Anger joined with fear within her, and she gave willing vent to it.

"I have a better idea—" the words all but dripped sugar—"Why don't you let *me* help *you*"—a quick, hopeful light sparked in his eyes—"get off my ranch?" She snapped her fingers at Sasha, who looked suddenly alert. "Sasha, protect!"

The husky hesitated, looking from Connor to her mistress as though to say, *"You're kidding, right?"*

Taylor repeated the command. "Sasha! Protect!"

Galvanized by the conviction in her mistress's voice, Sasha moved toward Connor, her usually benevolent features disappearing into a warning snarl.

Startled, Connor took several steps backward. "What are—"

Taylor smiled smugly. "Say hello to a well-trained dog." She moved to stand next to Sasha, who continued a low growl. Taylor's tone hardened. "Now get off my ranch."

Connor backed out of the doorway cautiously, moved to his Jeep, and slid inside.

"Sasha, release," Taylor murmured as Connor turned to look at her one more time before driving away. The husky immediately became her affable self and padded over to sit beside her mistress, looking up at her with curious eyes.

"Good girl, Sasha," Taylor said in a tear-choked voice. "You're a good girl." She stared after the Jeep, watching it grow smaller in the distance. "And you're extremely lucky that you're a dog and not a human." She turned to head for the house. "Believe me, it's not all it's cracked up to be."

TWENTY-ONE

THURSDAY NIGHT, CONNOR STOOD AT THE FRONT OF THE high school auditorium, watching the townspeople come in and take their seats. His heart warmed when he saw Taylor and her family slip into seats at the back of the room. Even the sight of Gavin sliding into the chair next to Taylor didn't bother him.

Whatever they thought of him, he considered them all friends. It helped to know he wasn't on his own here.

The turnout was decent. Thirty or forty people filled the chairs set up before him. Now if he could just get through the night without somebody shooting him.

The head of the town council introduced him, and he stepped up to the podium. "Thank you for coming tonight. I hope you all feel free to take part. This is an open forum, and all questions or comments are welcome."

"Even 'Go home, Scumball'?" one man asked, and laughter traveled around the room.

Connor let his smile show them he wasn't put off. "If it gets the ball rolling, sure."

"C'mon, Frank. Give the man a chance."

Connor glanced at the middle-aged man who had spoken up, hoping his gratitude showed.

The man met Connor's gaze. "Name's Amos Winkler, and I for one am interested in what you have to tell us, Mr. Alexander."

An older gentleman seated at the back of the room stood, his hat in his hands. "I have a question."

Connor relaxed his stance. *Here we go...* "Yes, sir?"

"I just want to know why this all matters so much to you people? This isn't your land. Or your livestock. You talk about 'reintroduction' and 'natural regulation,' but you keep coming out here and sticking your nose in where it ain't welcome." Murmurs of agreement sounded around the room. "Why can't you just leave us and the wolves be? Whatever comes of this will be plenty natural."

Another man jumped up. "I agree with Booth. I mean, what you people want to do is crazy, plain and simple! Bringing wolves into populated areas makes as much sense as bringing back smallpox! There just isn't enough natural prey around here to support bringing wolves back. You all talk about the 'wild ungulate populations' like they're unlimited. But those deer and elk have been replaced by livestock. *Our* livestock. Our livelihood! It's hard enough to make a living out here, without having to fight some crafty, four-footed killing machine that's got the government on its side! There just isn't any room here for wolves."

"Here! Here!"s and "Amen!"s rang out, and Connor pursed his lips. "I understand your concerns, but I admit I'm a bit confused."

"You're a lot confused, son!"

Connor grinned along with the others. "What I mean is, why do you think the ungulate populations are too small to support natural predators like wolves? When's the last time you went through Yellowstone in late February? There are records of more than twenty thousand elk and eight hundred bison crowding the winter range in the northern part of the park."

"That's Yellowstone!"

"True enough, but if wolves are in this area, Yellowstone will be a part of their hunting range. And there are healthy herds of ungulates around here as well. What's more, unless the wolves learn to recognize livestock as prey, they generally don't seem to know what to do with them. Studies have shown they actually prefer their natural prey."

"What you're saying makes sense," Amos Winkler said. "But I think what people here really want to know is, what will happen if the wolves do kill our animals?"

Connor nodded. "That's a fair question. The Wolf Compensation Fund has been set up for a number of years now. It's been a dependable source of money for reimbursing ranchers who lose livestock to predation. If a wolf is found to be a repeated problem, the state wildlife managers will do their best to capture and move it."

"And if they can't?" Amos's expression was expectant.

Connor gave him the truth. "Then the wolf would be destroyed. But only as a last resort, and only when it's been proven that it's a repeat offender."

"What about our kids?" a woman up front demanded. "There are a lot of remote school bus stops out here. I don't know about you, but I'm not inclined to risk my little girl's life just so some wolf can survive."

"I'd be worried, too, if wolves were known to attack people. But it's a fact that, in all of North America, there's never been a verified case of a wild wolf attacking a person."

Scattered boos and hisses sounded, and a wave of grumbling started.

"How's a man s'posed to make a verified report if he's been eaten by wolves?"

"Not willing to have my kid be the first!"

"Bunch of bureaucratic gobbledygook!"

Connor took a couple of deep breaths to calm himself. If he wasn't careful, he was going to lose them entirely. Just then, a tall, tanned man stood up in the center of the room. He scanned the people seated around him with concerned eyes.

"Listen to what you're saying. We aren't talking about government reintroduction programs here. These wolves have come here on their own. They've returned to the land they lived on long before you or I or any of our ancestors came here." He looked from one face to another. "You are my neighbors. I have known many of you since we were children. But these animals are my neighbors, too. I haven't seen them; they're too wise to come out. But I've seen their tracks, heard their howls. They're here already. And we have to learn how to survive together."

A young man jumped out of his seat. "I'll tell you how we'll survive! I'll shoot every one of those killers I can. *Then* we'll survive. And no *environmentalist*"—the kid made it sound like a dirty word—"is gonna tell me otherwise."

Another man in his late twenties spoke up. "I more than heard 'em. I seen 'em."

Everyone started speaking at once, shooting questions. The man stood and turned to glare at Taylor and her family. "I seen one, anyway. A big one. And he was on Galloway Glen."

Taylor jumped to her feet, her eyes blazing. Connor restrained a smile. He knew that combative look well.

"What are you saying, Roy?"

"I'm saying the wolves are on your land, Taylor. And you know it."

"So you trespassed? Came onto my land without asking permission?"

A dull red swath of color started to creep up the man's throat and into his face. "Well, I was tracking—"

"So you did." Taylor's voice was positively frigid. "And you think that's right?"

"As right as protecting them killers!" Several others voiced agreement.

"Taylor's got a point, Roy." Amos Winkler's tone was harder than Connor had heard it all night. "You had no right to trespass."

"Come on, Amos," the man called Booth spoke up again. "You know as well as I do wolves don't belong here. Even Taylor's grandfather knew it. He killed a mess of 'em in his day. My daddy told me he was one of the best wolf hunters in the region."

Gavin broke in then, and Connor was surprised at his words. "I have to agree with Booth, Taylor. My uncle has told me stories about your grandfather and all the wolves he brought in. He felt the wolves were a threat. As these men do."

"Do you think that too?" she demanded.

Gavin tilted his head. "From what I've heard here, they've turned your neighbors against you. There seems to be some threat in that."

"I would like to say something, please."

The quiet request came from Taylor's mother. Connor inclined his head. "Go ahead, Mrs. Camus."

Taylor's parents both rose and walked to the front of the room to stand beside Connor. Donelle laid a gentle hand on his arm, and he was struck by the compassion in her eyes.

"May we?" She indicated the podium.

He stepped aside. "Of course."

The two moved to stand behind the podium, and

Connor noticed the way Taylor's father stood next to his wife. Though he didn't touch her, he was clearly a protective presence. *That's one team I'd hate to mess with.*

"You're partially right, Booth." She nodded at the man. "But what many of you seem to be forgetting is that my father changed his mind on the day he met a wolf. A wolf he had killed."

"The only kind of wolf to meet!" a woman asserted, then sank in her chair at the quelling looks she received from several of those around her.

Donelle regarded her with compassion. "I certainly understand your feelings, Hazel. I've heard them expressed since I was a child. But I can't help but wonder if you would be less sure of that if you saw what my father did. If you ever met one of these creatures instead of basing your opinions on stories told from fright rather than knowledge." She moved her eyes from face to face before her. "Yes, my father hated wolves, until he actually encountered one alive. What he saw in the creature's eyes was powerful enough to change his mind. And his heart. He saw he was wrong. As many of us are wrong."

"What do you think, Reverend?"

Taylor's father tilted his head, his eyes thoughtful. "I think this is an issue that doesn't have any easy answers." Agreement sounded throughout the audience. "Like Donelle, I've heard the stories and the concerns for most of my life, but there's something else that troubles me." He smiled. "The last thing I want to do here is preach a sermon—"

"Here, here!" Laughter rippled through the room in response to the outburst.

Holden's smile deepened, but his eyes were somber. "Still, I can't get away from what I see in God's Word. God made man ruler over all the earth, tells us in Psalms that we're rulers over even the beasts of the field."

"So if we want to rid ourselves of these beasts, it's our right!" Roy's smile was smug.

"That's not what the reverend is saying, Roy."

"No...it's not—" Holden looked around the room— "We are given dominion over the earth, but what we aren't given is ownership. Look at it this way: God has loaned us his world. He put everything in it for our use, to help us survive and thrive. But as often as he tells us we're in charge, he also tells us we have to rule wisely, with kindness and truth."

"Are you tellin' me God cares how we treat a mangy wolf?" It was the woman who'd been shushed by the crowd.

"I'm telling you we're given strict instructions on not being abusive to animals. And we're all very fond of reminding each other that God's eye is on the sparrow, that he watches over and cares for even the smallest of his creatures. Why, then, would he not be interested in a wolf? Or a cougar? Or any animal?"

"So if one of these killers comes after my livestock or my family, I should just step aside and let it do what it wants?"

"Of course not. We're told to subdue the earth, to

use it well and wisely. But there's a huge gap between subduing and abusing. If a wolf is killing livestock, it has to be stopped. Certainly if it attacks a human, it must be destroyed. But we will be held accountable to the Creator for the way we treat his world. And nowhere does he condone senseless destruction. Or torture."

Connor was watching the reactions in the crowd with interest. Several faces were tinged with red, though whether from embarrassment or anger he wasn't sure. Others were listening intently, even nodding in agreement.

Holden's advocate stood again. "I think the reverend's hit the nail on the head, folks. I don't know about you, but I want to be sure when I stand before the good Lord that I can stand tall"—his face creased into a grin—"well, as tall as any sinner can stand before God." He shook his head, chuckling. "But I don't want to have to answer to the charge of cruelty or abuse. Not to humans nor to animals."

"Ruling the earth is a two-edged sword," Donelle added. "We are to use and subdue it, but we are also called to care for it, to keep it well for its true Owner. We're not suggesting that you put yourselves or your families, or even your livestock, at risk. But I do think it is simple wisdom to act out of knowledge, not out of fear. How many of you have ever encountered a wolf? Ever seen one up close or studied their behavior?" No one answered. "Then how can we be so certain we know the truth?"

Connor watched her with deepening admiration. She had them all listening. They might not believe her, but at least they were listening.

Booth crossed his arms. "Well, I'm sure not going to trust some bleeding-heart environmentalist for the truth!"

"'Course not!" Amos gave him a disgusted look. "But you know as well as the rest of us, Booth, that there are other sources. Scientists, biologists, all kinds of folks have studied wolves and their interactions with livestock and with humans. I know this ain't a simple issue, not by a long shot. And I sure ain't convinced the environmentalists or wildlife managers have all the answers. But we gotta start working together, or we're all going to come out losers. You can count on it. And so will our kids."

"At least try to get the facts before you start shooting," Donelle urged. "Let Mr. Alexander and his people tell us what they know. At least your decisions will be based on some reality, not on myth."

She looked at her husband, and he held up his hands. "I suppose it's time to pass the offering plates." Laughter followed the two of them as they returned to their seats.

Connor stepped back to the podium, glancing at Taylor as he did so. Pride glowed in her eyes as she watched her parents. Then he looked out over the crowd. "Our time is about up," he said. "Any other comments or questions?"

"I got one," a teenage boy remarked, jumping to his feet. "What's the best kind of ammo to use on these critters?"

Some snorts of laughter met this comment, but Connor was relieved to see that just as many people scolded the boy and told him to sit down. Maybe they were making some progress after all.

"Well, that was…interesting."

Taylor glanced at her father and grimaced. "I suppose so. I'm always surprised, though, at how quick people are to be afraid and how slow they are to listen to the facts. But the one who really surprised me was Gavin."

Her father slipped his arm around her mother's shoulders. "Facts can be skewed, Taylor. We all know that. And Gavin cares about you a great deal. It's not that unusual that he would be concerned when he sees people who've known you all your life turning on you. The biggest issue these people have is trusting." His eyes rested on her face. "Now that's something I think you might be able to relate to."

She lowered her eyes. He was right. The facts hadn't made a lot of difference for her when Connor came to the ranch two days ago.

"Nice bit of preaching, Reverend," a voice spoke from behind them. They turned to see Booth standing there, flanked by four other ranchers. "But it won't make a hill o' beans worth of difference. Wolves are wolves, and there's no room for them around us." His eyes came to rest on Taylor. "I'm disappointed in you, Taylor. I thought you were one of us, that you would understand what's really important."

Anger flared in her, and she opened her mouth to blast the man, but her father's gentle hand on her arm stilled the caustic response she had ready. She turned to him, and he shook his head.

"A soft answer…" she could almost hear him say.

She drew a steadying breath and turned back to the burly rancher. "I'm sorry you feel that way, Booth. And I hope you believe I have no desire to hurt or anger you. But Galloway Glen is my ranch. If I want to let the wolves come on it, I have as much right as you do to keep them off of yours." She met his steely stare without flinching. "I won't tell you and your friends how to run your ranches"—her gaze hardened—"and I won't come onto your land without permission." Her eyes swept the circle of men, noting how several of them dropped their gazes. "I'd appreciate the same courtesy."

"Your wolves set one paw near my land and they're rugs." At the muttered comment, Taylor had to swallow the white-hot rage that rose within her. "You can do whatever you want on your own land." She stepped closer to him, facing him down. "But not on mine." Her eyes pinned him, and he had the grace to look ashamed. "Not on Galloway Glen. I'd like your word on that, Henry."

The man's lips thinned, but he gave a curt nod. "I won't trespass. I give my word."

She looked at the others, her gaze coldly expectant. One by one they conceded. Finally her eyes came back to Booth. "I've always considered you a man of integrity, Booth. I'd hate to find out I was wrong."

His burning gaze held hers, and Taylor knew the lines had been drawn, and she was in the enemy camp.

"Just keep your wolves away from our land, Taylor, and we won't have any problems."

A wave of despair washed over her. She couldn't control the wolves. They'd go where they wanted. But she didn't voice her concerns. She just gave a curt nod, then watched as the ranchers turned and walked away, their backs rigid.

"You handled that well, Taylor." Her mother's voice was filled with quiet pride.

Taylor looked at her, surprised to find herself blinking back tears. "Maybe so, but we all know I can't stop the wolves from going where they want, Mom. They'll go on Booth's ranch as easily as they came on Galloway Glen. And they'll die for it." She looked away, brushing the wetness from her cheeks.

Her father's arm came around her shoulders. "You can only do your best, Taylor."

She stood silent, then lifted her eyes to his. "You're right. And I think I know what the best thing is for the wolves." She glanced around quickly. "Did you see where Connor went?"

"I believe he was walking with a man toward his Wrangler," her father replied. "Maybe he hasn't left yet if you'd like to catch him."

"Thanks, Dad." She started toward the parking lot. "I'll meet you at the car."

She ran across the blacktop, and when she spotted Connor's tall frame, she called his name. He turned in surprise, his eyes narrowing as she approached.

"Where's your guard dog?"

She felt the blush rise in her cheeks. "She's at home. Still trying to figure out what I was so upset about, I think."

"I understood."

She fell silent, unsure about how to respond. "You were pretty good in there."

He grinned. "Not bad for fighting off a bunch of hostiles."

She couldn't hold back an answering smile. "Not bad at all, and that's what I want to talk to you about."

He leaned against the door of his Jeep. "Shoot." At the look on her face, he gave a deep chuckle. "Figuratively speaking, of course."

"Of course." She hesitated, then plunged in. "Connor, I'm sorry. For a lot of things. And I want you to come back to the ranch."

To say he was stunned would be an understatement. He stared at her as though she'd just sprouted a second head.

"If your offer is still open, that is."

"My offer?"

At his obtuse question she wanted to kick him in the shins. He wasn't making this any easier. "To observe the wolves, to photograph them, to keep WAC informed about their whereabouts." He had straightened quickly when she started explaining, and now his eyes were roaming her face, and the expression she saw in them made her heart pound.

"I want you to get the best photos anyone has ever seen," she said in a rush, emotion surging through her. "I want everyone to see the first wolves to come back to Wyoming. I want people to know how beautiful, how incredible they are. Then maybe they'll have a chance. If enough people hear about them, Booth and his cronies might back off. That might be the only thing that stops them. Even they wouldn't like being known as the cold-hearted killers of the majestic Wyoming wolf." She stepped closer, holding out a hand in entreaty. "Please come back, Connor. Help me protect the wolves."

He didn't reply, and her throat constricted. He had every right to turn her down, every right to walk away. She'd insulted him, raged at him, told him she never wanted to see him again,…and all the time he'd just been trying to protect something precious.

The anger she had felt at his deception dimmed and melted away in the light of sudden understanding. *He didn't know if he could trust me, Lord. He couldn't put the wolves at risk. Please. Please let him forgive me.*

His eyes studied her, intent, seeking, seeming to reach into her thoughts. She stood there, not hiding anything, letting him see in her eyes all she was feeling. Then he reached out to close his strong, warm hand over hers.

"I'll come. But not because of the wolves." His gaze captured hers, and her breathing grew shallow. "I'll come for you."

Relief swept over her, and she moved, almost without thought, into the circle of his arms, burying her face against the softness of his shirt and the hardness of his chest.

She didn't care if anyone saw them. Not her parents. Not Gavin. All that mattered was that Connor was going to help her.

He was coming back.

TWENTY-TWO

W<small>HEN</small> C<small>ONNOR CALLED</small> H<small>ARRY</small> C<small>ROWLEY TO TELL HIM</small> Taylor had asked him to return to the ranch, the president of WAC whooped and hollered with glee.

"See there? You're just too charming to resist! Now get out there and find those wolves."

Connor returned to the ranch the next morning, and he and Taylor spent the day discussing their plans. Harry had asked Connor to observe the wolf—since Taylor had told him she'd seen only the one—for at least a month. They agreed to use the ranch as their base, going out during the day to track and observe.

"I'd like to start out by staying in this valley of yours for a couple of days and nights. Since your wolf has come there twice now, it seems like a good place to find him. I've got a yurt tent in the Jeep," Connor told her, "so I can set it up without any trouble."

"I want to come, too." Taylor had decided she could help him with the wolves for a few weeks and still be ready for the retreat season. "I can set up my own tent—"

"You don't need to. The yurt is large enough for sev-

eral people, and we can section off individual rooms."
Connor smiled. "It's a regular home away from home."

Taylor nodded, but she didn't return his smile.
Though she'd obviously taken a big step in asking him
to come back, Connor sensed her caution and reserve.

*She changed her mind because she knows I'm her best
bet for keeping the wolves safe. Not because she trusts me.*
Well, he had the time now to change that.

"I don't know if it will make a difference." Taylor's
expression held uncertainty. "But maybe if I'm there,
he'll be more inclined to show up."

"Sounds good." And it did. Going there together
suited him just fine.

Two days later, they loaded the tent and other equipment into Taylor's truck and headed for Reunion. Within
a few hours, they had unloaded their supplies and had
set up the tent in a clearing among the trees on the south
side of the pond, a good distance from the cave and as
unobtrusive as possible among the tall evergreens.

Constructed of heavy white canvas, the yurt was
octagonal, domed, and stretched over a collapsible lat-
tice framework of sturdy wood. It had a hinged door and
windows of heavy plastic. Canvas flaps could be secured
over the windows to make the tent as weatherproof as
possible. Inside, it actually felt like a small house. A
wood cooking stove sat near a small table and two

chairs, along with a small generator-powered refrigerator for their food. A gas stove was pushed to the side in case it was needed for heat. And true to his word, Connor had set up individual rooms using canvas and poles from the ranch.

As Taylor surveyed the result of their work, she felt a smile of satisfaction lift her lips. It wasn't the Waldorf, but the spacious tent was far nicer than she had expected. They each had a small bedroom compartment complete with a cot and lanterns. The area they would share for cooking, eating, and studying their notes was fairly large, at least twenty feet across.

"All set?" Connor's question came from behind her.

She turned and caught her breath. He looked so at home out here, so happy. His eyes were glowing with an expression she couldn't quite identify.

Maybe he's as happy to be together as I am.

She pushed the disturbing thought away, refusing to let her mind—or heart—go that direction. No point in it. She and Conner were together because of the wolves. And that was the only reason. No matter how much she might wish otherwise....

His expression altered slightly as he watched her, and she felt heat rising in her cheeks. "So, are we going to get this thing secured or not?"

At the brusque tone in her voice, Connor frowned. Thankfully, though, he simply nodded. They secured the tent, then climbed the path back to the truck and returned to the ranch. There, they saddled Topaz and

Chestnut for the ride back to Reunion, then started out. Sasha loped alongside them.

Taylor was glad the husky was coming along. She'd asked Connor if the husky would be a deterrent to the wolves.

"No. They generally aren't bothered by domestic dogs, especially the nonterritorial ones like Sasha. She'll be fine."

They made it to Reunion in record time, just under two hours. As they crested the rise, the sun was beginning to set. They tethered the horses next to the tent, pulled off the saddles and saddlebags, and got ready for the night. After a quiet dinner, Taylor slipped into her bedroom, Sasha at her side, and lay down on the cot with a sigh.

Connor had wanted to talk; she'd seen it in his eyes as she stood and walked from the table. But she wasn't ready for that yet. Didn't know if she'd ever be. She didn't want to talk about emotions, or hurt, or trust. She didn't want to debate forgiveness.

For now, all she wanted to do was concentrate on the wolf.

For several days and nights there was no sign of Taylor's wolf. Connor told her the animal could be as much as fifty miles away—wolves had been known to travel that far while hunting. Or he could just be watching them from a safe distance. And waiting.

"Waiting? For what?"

His mouth curved in amusement. "To see if we'll get out of his territory. Or to size us up. Wolves are highly intelligent and equally skittish. He won't come around us until he's sure we're not a threat. Maybe not even then. It's actually pretty rare to see a wolf in the wild."

"And I've seen Sikis twice."

He gave a thoughtful nod. "Could be you've used up your quota."

A glance told her he was teasing, and she stuck her tongue out at him. It was the most relaxed exchange they'd had since his return to Galloway Glen, and she felt almost buoyant. Maybe things were going to work out after all.

Then, early the next morning, Connor left the tent. Within moments he was back, his eyes shining with excitement. "Taylor. Come out here." His whisper was urgent.

She hurried from the tent and followed him to the edge of the pool where he stood and pointed to a spot on the other side.

Across the pond was a meadow full of waving grasses, and just beyond that a small stand of trees. And there, lying in the lush meadow grass, looking comfortable and relaxed, was the large gray wolf. And with him were four other wolves!

Taylor watched in amazement as one of them, a slim, medium-sized black wolf, crawled along the ground toward Sikis, its head on the ground, whimpering and wagging its entire body.

"The black one is probably a young male." Connor's voice was low as the wolf reached Sikis and licked repeatedly at the larger wolf's chin and mouth.

Sikis put up with this groveling with regal inattention. The other three wolves were larger than the black wolf, but smaller than Sikis. One was gray, like its leader, and it paced back and forth behind Sikis, watching him, as though ready for the slightest signal. The other gray wolf had a much lighter coat, and this one danced back and forth, making friendly advances toward Sikis, trotting toward him, then darting away if he flinched or twitched. The fourth wolf was a buff-tan color with a darker brown head.

The attention of the entire pack was focused on Sikis, who lay there, his head high, his velvety ears erect, accepting the homage of his followers. The other four kept their tails low, their ears flattened against their heads, and whined with an almost pathetic appeal as they nibbled at Sikis's muzzle, looking like eager children. Taylor could have sworn Sikis's mouth, which was partly open, was curved into a majestic, munificent smile.

"Apparently your friend is the alpha," Connor remarked.

"And loving every minute of it, from what I can see. Typical male."

KAREN BALL

Connor's easy grin warmed her. "That's as it should be." With that, he headed for the tent. He emerged within minutes, his photography equipment in tow.

"Are they still there?" He came to stand beside her, and she nodded.

"It's like they've come for a photo shoot."

He waggled his brows at her. "Well, far be it from me to disappoint them!"

The wolves put on quite a show. They stayed in the meadow for nearly an hour, playing or lazing or just sitting and watching Connor and Taylor with cautious interest. Sikis was the least nervous of the group; the black wolf the least confident. Every time Connor clicked the shutter or Taylor shifted positions, the black wolf would crouch, his head spinning to stare at them, his body already leaning away.

A couple of times Taylor was tempted to holler "Boo!" just to see what the animal would do. But she didn't want to scare the wolf or hinder the growing trust they seemed to be building. Nor did she want to spoil Connor's chances to get his photos. She looked at him, taking in the excitement that was evident in his stance and his face. His eyes shone, a slight smile tipped his lips, and his golden brown hair blew gently in the early morning breeze. If Taylor had been honest with herself, she would have admitted she enjoyed watching him as much as she enjoyed watching the wolves.

But she wasn't ready to be quite that honest.

The next morning, Taylor was awakened by someone shaking her shoulder. She blinked sleepily until her surroundings came into focus.

Above her, Connor's eyes glowed with excitement. "Get up! I have an idea."

With that he left her room, and she rubbed her eyes, then slipped from beneath the covers. She was already dressed—it was cool enough at night that she slept in her clothes—so she pulled on a jacket and went to see what was happening.

"We'll need to leave Sasha here."

Taylor started to question him, then gave in. He was the expert. "Sasha, down." The dog hesitated, and Taylor couldn't stop a grin. No matter how well-trained the Siberian was, she still had a stubborn streak. Maybe that was why they got along so well.

"Down." At the repeated command, Sasha turned, walked over to the table, circled a few times, then plopped down with an exaggerated air of offense.

"Ham," Taylor muttered, then told the dog to stay.

"Come on." At Connor's quiet urging, Taylor followed him, brimming with curiosity. Outside the tent, he grabbed her hand and tugged her along behind him. He led her to the far end of the valley, around the pool, then toward the spot where the wolves had frolicked the day before. Taylor stared at the area, then at Connor. *What in the world?*

His grin just widened. "We're going to see if our friends will come say hello."

She stared at him, not sure she'd heard correctly. "Come…say hello?"

Instead of answering, he took her hand and led her to a spot in the grass. "Sit here." He gently pushed her to the ground. Caught off guard, she landed with a slight thud, but before she could yell at him, he had moved to sit behind her so that their backs were together. "Okay, now we wait. If they're out there, if they're watching, they just might pay a visit."

Taylor sat there, the early morning dampness soaking through the seat of her jeans, feeling completely ridiculous. Not to mention nervous.

"Connor!" she hissed, but he shushed her.

"Be patient!" Then he turned his head to look at her, and the plea in his eyes was clear. "Trust me. You won't be sorry."

She turned back around, biting her lip. She didn't know what made her more uneasy: the idea of actually coming in contact with a pack of wolves or trusting Connor.

"They're here." Connor's hushed voice was filled with jubilation, and Taylor turned her head.

At first all she could see were the trees. Then she realized there were glowing pairs of eyes peering inquisitively from behind the thick trunks.

Alarm shot through her, and she must have tensed because Connor's hand reached out to clasp hers where she had it planted firmly on the ground beside her. "Don't be afraid." His voice was low but confident. "Just stare at your feet as they approach. Don't make eye contact or they'll feel challenged."

Her eyes flew to her boots, and she studied them, then dared to peek out of the corner of her eye. One by one, the wolves emerged from the woods, taking cautious, tentative steps toward the two intruders, ready to retreat at the slightest motion.

Taylor swallowed convulsively as the wolves started to circle them. She'd read the books; she knew what the experts said: Healthy wolves don't attack people.

God, please don't let us prove them wrong!

Finally, Sikis came right up to Taylor's feet, sniffing cautiously at her boots, and then he dropped down into a crouch and started to rub his head all over them, back and forth, with vigorous movements. The light gray wolf approached her next, leaning into her shoulder and rubbing against her, like a grizzly trying to get a back scratch on a gnarly old tree.

Taylor started to laugh. It was the most amazing feeling. She heard Connor's laugh behind her and figured he was getting the same treatment. Soon all five wolves were leaning against them, rubbing their heads and shoulders against them, wagging their shaggy bodies with enthusiasm.

Then Sikis jumped away, gave a sharp bark, and bounded back into the woods. The rest of the pack followed him in a flash, and Connor and Taylor were left to themselves, sitting there, still laughing.

Without thinking about what she was doing, Taylor spun to Connor. He was there, his arms open, and she hugged him tightly.

"That was incredible!" She leaned back to look up into his beaming face. "Thank you, Connor."

He studied her face for a moment, and she saw a deep tenderness in his expression. "Thank you for trusting me." He let her go and stood up. "I know you took a risk in asking me to come back. I don't know if you've forgiven me for deceiving you—" She started to speak, but he shook his head and continued. "I just want you to know that I was wrong. I should have been honest with you from the start. That would have been the right thing...the godly thing to do."

"You did what you thought you had to."

"Yes, at the time. But it wasn't easy, Taylor." He glanced away. "You may find this hard to believe, but my goal in life isn't protecting wildlife. It's honoring God." He looked at her, regret reflected in his eyes. "Deceiving you wasn't in line with that goal. I want you to know that, from this moment on, I will be honest with you. I will treat you the way God calls me to, with respect and truth." He reached out to touch her face, and the tenderness in his warm fingers stirred her deeply. "Taylor, you mean a great deal to me. I want you to trust me. And I'm willing to do whatever it takes to earn that trust."

She didn't know how to respond. She wasn't ready yet to give her trust to God, so how could she give it to

Connor? She decided the truth was the best thing she could give him. "I want to trust you, but I don't know if I can." She rose to her feet.

He nodded. "I've seen that something holds you back," he said as he tilted his head, "something that I don't think involves me. It's always there, in your eyes. Something…hard. Painful."

She fought against the tightening of her throat and turned away. "I don't want to talk about this."

"It's Josh, isn't it? And that boy. Brad—isn't that his name?"

She spun back to face him. "I said I don't want to talk about it!"

His eyes held a gentle warning. "If what's holding you back from me is something I've done, then I can accept that and deal with it. But I won't let someone else keep us apart, Taylor. That wouldn't be fair to either of us." He reached out to touch her face, and she batted his hand away.

"Do me a favor, Alexander. Keep your hands to yourself." She swept past him, pausing only long enough to turn around and snap, "And stick to wolves. You stink as a psychologist." With that, she spun around and headed for the tent.

That night they sat around a low campfire in silence. Usually they spent the evenings reviewing what had happened during the day. Tonight they had nothing to say. The silence was heavy and tense.

They had pulled two camp chairs outside and set them on either side of the fire. Taylor slouched in hers, deep in gloomy thought. One hand was cupped around a metal camping mug full of cocoa, and the other rested on Sasha's head, scratching the dog's ears. Taylor found comfort in the contact. At least Sasha accepted her as she was, without expecting her to make some huge strides toward forgiveness.

"I'm sure the light gray wolf is the alpha female," Connor remarked quietly, gazing into the fire. His eyes came to rest on Taylor, as though debating something. "She looks pregnant."

Taylor's eyes widened, and she sat up in her chair. "You're kidding!" She leaned forward and set her mug on the edge of the ring of stones they'd built around the fire.

"Wolves usually breed by February, so unless I miss my guess, she's nearing the end of her gestation. She'll be looking for a denning area soon."

"I would have thought the time for pups was past."

"Not necessarily. Wolves usually breed in late winter, but they've been known to do so as late as April. So they could be right on schedule."

"Just think of it." She hugged herself, barely able to contain her excitement at the thought. "Nokomis surrounded by pups." She leaned back, then noticed that Connor was looking at her with an amused expression.

"Nokomis?"

She shot him a cheeky grin. "That's what I've named the light gray one, the female. It means 'grandmother.' I figure she's going to be the mother of this pack, so it's appropriate."

"I suppose you have names for the others, too?"

She tossed her head. "As a matter of fact, I do. The black one is Ayasha, 'little one,' because he's the smallest and youngest. The tan one is Tala for 'wolf.' The other gray is Mingan."

"Which means?"

She grinned again. "'Gray wolf,' of course."

His chuckle was deep and warm. "Of course. At any rate, if Nokomis is going to have a litter, my guess is it will be soon. Which means we probably ought to make ourselves scarce."

Disappointment, sharp and quick, pierced Taylor. "You mean leave?" When he nodded, she saw regret in his eyes as well. "But we just got the tent up a few days ago! Do we have to take it down already?"

"Not at all. The tent can stay up. We'll be coming out here from time to time, so we'll just leave it here. You said no one else knows about this place, right?"

"Not as far as I know."

"Then it should be fine. We'll take what's left of the food with us, but everything else can stay." He rose and stretched. "I'll pack the nonperishables up now so we don't have to mess with it in the morning."

"So we're leaving tomorrow?"

He fixed her with a compassionate look. "I think it would be best. We've got to give them plenty of room. There can be a lot of tension when a female births. She gets snappy, irritable"—a broad grin stretched across his features—"kind of like someone else I know."

"Ha ha."

Connor turned away, but not before she heard his chuckle. He paused at the door to the tent. "You coming?"

"Not yet." He studied her for a moment, then went inside.

Taylor leaned back in her chair, chewing on her lip. What was wrong with her? She should be happy to be going back to the ranch. She'd be with her family again, have the chance to tell them all the amazing things that had happened. And she'd be able to see Gavin....

She reached up to massage her suddenly pounding temples. Why on earth did the thought of seeing Gavin make her head hurt?

She'd expected Gavin to be very much against her coming out here with Connor. Instead, he'd kept his dark eyes on her face, an odd emotion floating in their depths, listening when she told him what they were going to do.

"I'll see you when you get back," he'd said at last, then rose to leave. Not exactly a warm parting.

Taylor refused to give in to the tears that stung her eyes. She stared at the stars glittering overhead and wondered why life had to be so ridiculously complicated.

⌄⌄⌄⌄⌄⌄⌄

The song began slowly, with a single, mournful howl rising on the wind and drifting to float all around them. It was so subtle, so faint at first, that Taylor wasn't even conscious of it. But Sasha was.

The husky shifted, then raised her head, her velvety ears cocked. Taylor noted the dog's movement and looked at her curiously.

"Sash?" But the usually responsive husky didn't even look at her. Taylor glanced around uneasily; clearly the dog heard something.

Sasha stood and stretched her throat out, reaching toward the sky with her muzzle. With a frown, Taylor went to kneel beside the dog. She laid a gentle hand on Sasha's neck, burying her fingers in the thick fur. Sasha looked up at her, and Taylor was startled at the intense, faraway look in the animal's ice blue eyes.

Sasha lifted her gaze back to the sky, closed her eyes, and tilted her chin up. After a moment, and a quick look around to assure her Connor was nowhere in sight, Taylor followed suit.

She could tell Sasha wasn't alarmed, but something had caught her attention. Taylor was determined to find out what that something was. She closed her eyes and concentrated on the night sounds.

At first all she heard was Sasha's steady breathing and the myriad crickets and frogs sending messages to each other. Drawing a deep breath, Taylor tried to focus.

The low, keening sound came to her then, and a thrill of wonder raced through her. The sound was deep and resonant. Pure and vibrant, it seemed almost a tangible thing as it drifted all around her.

A wolf was howling. But this time, instead of it being some sound that floated to her from a distance, she knew he was there, in the meadow, just across the pond. And the very air vibrated with his mournful song.

The single howl sounded again, rising, changing pitch at least four or five times. Then a second voice joined in, also changing pitch, creating an eerie harmony that seemed to come from all directions.

Tears pricked Taylor's eyes at the beauty of the sound. Before long, more wolf voices joined in, until the night was immersed in a symphony as ancient and as majestic as the mountains and forests around them.

Suddenly the night fell silent, as though the wolves were pausing, listening, hoping for some response. Taylor looked at Sasha. The dog's eyes were half closed, as though in heartfelt contemplation of what she'd just heard.

"You could join in, you know." At Taylor's whisper, Sasha turned to meet her gaze. "For that matter, we both could." With that, Taylor closed her eyes, lifted her chin, and howled, doing her best to copy the rising and falling of the wolf voices.

Seconds after Taylor began howling, Sasha followed suit. The two of them sang to the night and a shiver of delight surged through Taylor when the wolves once again lifted their voices, as though in response. The eerie beauty of the discordant chorus continued for a few minutes, and then the sound slowly died away.

Taylor sat there, her eyes closed, awash in wonder.

"I don't know about Sasha, but I think you're a bit off the beam."

The deep voice came so unexpectedly that Taylor leaped to her feet. Sasha merely loped over to welcome Connor back to the fire.

That traitorous act, though, wasn't nearly as irritating as the gleam of amusement in Connor's eyes or the cocky grin on his face.

Taylor fixed him with a glare. "I thought you went to bed."

"Nope. Just to pack things up. When I heard the symphony begin, I came back out. And what a show it was!" His playful tone made her want to smile in response, but she refused to give in to the impulse. "You're lucky you didn't kill the howl." He sank into his chair and rested his hand on Sasha's head as she sat beside him.

"Kill the howl?" Taylor raised an imperious eyebrow. "And how would I have done that, pray tell, O Wise One?"

"Your howl was the most pitiful thing I've ever heard, and I've heard some awful ones. So I'm sure the wolves were less than impressed. Maybe even insulted."

"Har dee har." Taylor moved to snatch her cup of cocoa from where it rested on the fire ring.

"I wouldn't—" Connor began in alarm, but he was too late. With a yelp that sent Sasha heading for the shadows, Taylor jerked her hand back in pain, sending the metal cup—and its scalding contents—flying.

Tears sprang to her eyes for the second time that night, but this time they were caused by physical pain. Before she could move, Connor had hold of her arm and was leading her to the nearest seat. For once she didn't argue. The sight of the angry red skin filled her with frustration. She knew better. Even an amateur camper knew you didn't grab anything metal that was near the fire. Not barehanded. She shook her head, silent recriminations flying, and her pain was only compounded by the knowledge that Connor would have a heyday with this act of stupidity.

But Connor seemed too busy dousing a towel in cold water to yell at her. When he came back to her side, the concern on his chiseled features warmed her. He didn't meet her gaze, but concentrated on the burn, wrapping her hand in the cold, wet material and holding it gently.

Taylor hadn't realized tears were streaming down her face until Connor looked at her, then reached out with that same gentleness to wipe her damp cheeks. Their eyes met.

Neither spoke. Taylor couldn't have if she tried, her throat was so dry. All the churning emotions she'd been feeling, all the love she felt for Connor and the depth of her hurt, filled her eyes. She was sure he could see it all, could see her heart, but she couldn't stop it. It just poured out of her.

His eyes widened slightly, and she swayed toward him. For an instant she felt as though she were falling, as though her senses were caught in a spinning vortex, and then the spell was broken when Connor vaulted to his feet and stepped away from her as though she'd suddenly grown fangs and hissed at him.

She blinked once. Twice. Then anger swept over her. "For heaven's sake, Connor, I don't bite!"

He moved to stand near the fire, staring down into the flames, his expression troubled. After a moment of silence, he looked at her again. "I'm just trying to honor your request to keep my hands to myself." He raised his brows. "Unless, of course, you've changed your mind. Again."

She jumped to her feet, careful to keep her swaddled hand clutched close to her chest. "If I live to be a hundred years old, I will never understand men." Her tone was low and furious. "And I especially will never understand you!" She walked away, heading for the tent to hunt up the first-aid kit. It would have burn ointment.

And, if she were lucky, pest repellent.

Connor watched as Taylor jerked open the tent door and disappeared inside. She slammed the door shut, but because of the tent material, the sound was far less than satisfying. Had it been a normal door, Connor was sure his ears would be ringing with the sound of her fury. He chuckled for a moment, then sank down into the chair. Sasha came over to sit beside him, looking at him with a bewildered expression.

He understood her confusion. "Don't look at me, girl. I'm just the wolf expert. I sure can't explain women."

Sasha let out a huff of air and lay down, curling into a circle, resting her head on her paws and covering her nose with her tail.

Connor leaned forward and gazed into the dwindling fire, his elbows propped on his knees and his chin in his hands. "I'm just a man. If you ask me, the only one who really understands the fairer sex is God. He made 'em. He must know what makes 'em tick." He looked at Sasha in exasperation. "You're a female. You explain this to me. Here I am, trying to give her space, trying to give her time to build up trust in me again…and she looks at me with those beautiful green eyes all full of emotion. How's a man supposed to respond?"

The Siberian didn't move; she just looked up at him in mute eloquence. But Connor didn't need an answer. He had one already. A man responded the way he had with an overwhelming urge to pull her close, to enfold her, cradle her against him, and keep her safe.

Either that, or shake the stuffing out of her.

TWENTY-THREE

TAYLOR WAS UNUSUALLY QUIET THE NEXT MORNING, AND Connor wondered if her hand was hurting. After a breakfast of coffee and rolls, she stood at the edge of the pool, looking across at the meadow. The wolves were nowhere in sight.

He walked toward her, wondering if he was risking his head in doing so. But when he drew close, he saw the dejected droop of her shoulders and heard a small sniff. Moving forward, he placed a gentle hand on her shoulder. She tensed momentarily, then relaxed.

When she looked at him, tears glimmered in her eyes. "I'm sorry I got angry, Con."

"I'm sorry I acted like a jerk." That won him a watery smile.

"Well, we seem to be trading off where that role is concerned." She looked back toward the meadow. "Do you think they'll miss us?"

He let out a sigh. "Maybe. I hope so. At least a little."

She turned to head for the tent, then paused, turning her focus to the cave. He saw surprise dawn on her features, and he followed her gaze.

The wolves stood outside the cave, pacing back and forth, whining and scratching at the ground in front of the entrance.

Taylor's quick look was full of alarm. "Is something wrong?"

But Connor was too excited to answer. Before he could think better of it, he reached out to encircle her with his arms, hugging her to his chest. "*Nothing's* wrong! Something's right! The female must be denning. In the cave." He looked down at her, his eyes glowing. "Sikis and Nokomis are going to be parents."

Her head spun to stare at the pack again, then she gave a squeal and threw her arms around Connor.

"When will it happen?"

At her delighted question, he laughed down at her, struggling to catch his breath—in part because she'd hugged him so tightly, and in part because she was so beautiful and so close.

"A few days. Right now the pack is staying close. When the birth happens, the female won't let them inside, and the alpha—"

"Sikis."

"Right, Sikis will be extremely protective of the den." He hugged her again, then set her away from him.

"Can't we stay, Connor?" Her eyes pled with him, and he felt his heart melt at the look in those eyes. He'd love to give her what she asked, but he couldn't.

"No, but I'll make you a deal."

"A deal?"

"We'll come back in a few weeks—"

"Weeks!"

"The pups won't venture out of the den before then, Taylor. The last thing we want to do is make the pack nervous or give Nokomis reason to move her brood."

Despite the pretty pout on her face, he knew she understood. "Okay." The concession was grudging, to say the least. "Three weeks. But no longer."

He didn't even try to restrain his laughter as he threw his arm around her shoulders. "You got it." They walked toward the tent. "And it will go quickly, I promise."

"Right. Mom and Dad used to tell me the same thing about my birthday and Christmas. But they always took forever to come." She cast a glance back over her shoulder.

"Well, it will be worth—" The look she shot him halted his words.

"If you tell me it will be worth the wait—," she ground out—"I'll scream."

He clamped his mouth shut. That was exactly what he had planned to say.

She studied his face and her lips twitched. "I get it. You've decided to exercise the wisdom of the ages and remain silent in the face of a woman's impending fury."

Fighting a grin of his own, he merely nodded.

"See there, Sasha?" she remarked to the dog walking alongside them. "I *told* you he was smarter than he looked!"

TWENTY-FOUR

CONTRARY TO HER GLOOMY PREDICTION, TAYLOR WAS AMAZED at how quickly the next three weeks flew by. There was still work to be done on the retreat cabins, as well as brainstorming for retreat activities. And they spent several days riding around the ranch, looking for places for Connor to take his photos. Galloway Glen was exploding with color. From sunflowers to lupine to phlox and wild irises, the meadows were alive with blossoms.

The warm days and the increase in color and fragrance filled Taylor with a renewed appreciation for God's creative genius. "How can anyone look at this and deny there's a God?" she said as they stood in her living room, enjoying the view.

Connor shook his head. "You've got me. I figure it takes a whole lot more faith to believe this all came about by some cosmic accident than it does to believe in an almighty, all-loving Creator."

Taylor looked at him, unable to hold back her grin. "Two more days and we get to see the pups!"

"Taylor." His voice held a gentle but firm warning.

"It's entirely possible we won't see Nokomis or the pups. I keep telling you that."

"We'll see them." She knew it was true. She couldn't explain why, but she was sure of it. "I know we will."

Connor's lips tilted in a tender smile, and the warmth she saw there made her tingle. She turned to look out the window again, fully aware that he thought her a daydreaming optimist. But she didn't care. They were going to see the pups.

"I think I'd like to get some shots of the sunrise tomorrow." Connor's words broke into her thoughts.

She turned to him. "Oh, Con! I know the perfect place! But it will mean getting up awfully early. I'd like to go on horseback, and it's a bit of a ride."

"No problem!" Connor said, clearly caught up in her enthusiasm.

She just gave him a placid smile. *We'll see about that when 3 A.M. rolls around.*

"Connor."

The soft voice broke into his dreams, trying to coax him away from the comforting darkness. He rolled over and resisted.

"Connor, wake up."

This time it was accompanied by a slight tugging on his arm. He mumbled something uncomplimentary and pulled the covers over his head.

There was blessed silence for a second, and then a huge THING pounced on him, landing in the middle of his chest and punching him in the stomach. Connor sat up with a roar, and Sasha—who happened to be standing on top of him—quickly jumped off and ran for the hills.

Blinking in the sudden light from the bedside lamp, his mind still fuzzy from sleep, he stared at Taylor in disbelief.

"And a happy good morning to you, too," she said in response to his glower. "Now, get up. If you want pictures of the sunrise, it's past time to be on our way."

She strode from the cabin, and he fell back against the mattress with a groan. He had to admit the idea was far less appealing this morning than it had sounded last night. He threw back the covers, shivering in the cold. Fortunately the camera and equipment he needed were already stowed safely in a large duffel bag. He pulled on his clothes, then hauled the bag outside. He found Taylor in the barn. She already had both horses saddled. He tied the duffel to the back of his saddle.

"All set?" Taylor slid her foot into the stirrup and swung herself into the saddle with a smooth, effortless movement.

"Lead on." His eyes followed her in the morning darkness as she urged Topaz forward.

They rode in silence, turning east toward the Wind River mountain range.

As he settled into the saddle, Connor found himself studying Taylor, taking in the picture she made. Even in the dim light he could see that she sat upon her horse with a natural ease and grace. Woman and beast moved in a delicate, barely discernible harmony. Topaz was finely tuned to his rider, responding to the merest touch of Taylor's heels, the slightest lean in the saddle, the barest tug on the reins. As he watched them, Connor wondered what it was like to be so connected to someone…to Taylor.

He shook his head. Was this what being in love did to you? Made you think goofy, flowery thoughts? *Heaven help me. Get your mind on your business, Alexander,* he scolded himself. *You need to think about focus and f-stops, not Taylor—no matter how appealing she may be.*

Appealing. That was certainly an appropriate term for Taylor. As was delightful. Captivating. Enchanting. Guileless. Utterly charming—

You're pathetic! Can't you think about something else? Anything else!

He focused his attention on the deft manner in which his horse was navigating the woods they had entered, on the stunning scenery surrounding them, on anything but the woman riding in front of him. But his traitorous eyes drifted toward her once again, as though she were too compelling, too magnetic to resist.

The first subdued light of morning glinted off her hair, turning it a rich copper. Her eyes, when she turned to him, shone with excitement; he had the impression she could hardly wait to reveal whatever treasure she had in store.

She was so natural, so beautiful, so filled with grace and a childlike eagerness that watching her brought a lump of emotion to his throat. Every day they spent together, the pull he felt toward her grew stronger; he had the sensation of being carried along on the rapids of a river, terrified and exhilarated all at the same time.

Okay, God, how much longer until I can tell her how I feel?

"We're here!" Taylor's triumphant voice broke into his rueful thoughts, and he looked around. They had emerged from the woods and now stood on the edge of a beautiful meadow. Tall grasses swayed in the wind; wildflowers of all kinds and colors created a natural quilt of color and texture. Several tall lodgepole pines stood beside a bubbling stream, which meandered merrily through the meadow. On the opposite side of the stream, 150 feet away, the ground rose to become a small, rocky hill. The grass and flowers gave way at the top of the gradual rise to hard, dirt-packed earth topped with large boulders.

"It's incredible—" he stared, breathless—"absolutely incredible."

She beamed at him, pleasure gleaming in her forest-colored eyes. "We can tether the horses to one of the trees and walk over to the hill. You'll get some great shots of the sunrise behind the trees that way."

The rising sun was just beginning to tint the sky

with brilliant reds and oranges. If he hurried, he could get set up in time to take full advantage of the color changes as the sun came up.

"Let's do it." Excitement filled him with energy and anticipation.

They rode to one of the trees on the edge of the creek, dismounted, and secured the horses. Lifting his duffel bag from his horse's back, he turned and followed Taylor as she leaped from rock to rock to cross the bubbling water and made for the hill. It didn't take long to reach the summit and locate a good vantage point.

As Connor pulled the tripod, camera, and filters from the bag, setting them up with quick, efficient motions, Taylor perched on a nearby boulder, watching him with interest. It didn't seem to bother her a bit that he was entirely focused on the task at hand. She seemed content to merely sit and watch.

Amazing. That's another word that fits. He bent to peer through the viewfinder. *Independent, confident,* his mind went on as he reached forward to adjust the focus. *Creative, adventurous—*

It hit him like a sharp slap that he'd done it again, gotten caught up in his fascination with the woman who was watching him. He heaved a heavy, defeated sigh, resting his forehead against the camera.

"Connor, are you okay?"

Taylor's question brought his head up, and he turned to look at her.

No. Definitely not.

"Sure, I'm fine. Just…thinking." *What a laugh.*

She hopped off the boulder. "You'd better start snapping. You're running out of sunrise."

He turned back to the camera, made the needed adjustments, and "started snapping." The first roll was shot in record time, and he popped it out to replace it. He knelt to the bag and reached inside, then froze.

A low, horrific sound filled the air around them. He lifted startled eyes to Taylor, saw the same alarm on her face that he knew must be reflected on his. It was the most bone-chilling sound Connor had ever heard.

"What in the world…?"

The noise echoed again, and Connor felt the hair on the back of his neck rise. It was unearthly. If Gavin had been with them, Connor was sure the Scotsman would say it was a banshee. Part growl, part scream…the stuff of nightmares.

Suddenly another sound caught Connor's attention. The horses. They were screaming in fear. Full-blown alarm set Connor's nerves on edge, and he looked at Taylor, then glanced around cautiously, scanning the area, seeking the source of the ghastly howl.

Nothing. There was nothing there but rocks.

Taylor stepped toward him. "Con, I think we'd better get out of here."

"I think you're right." He grabbed his equipment and started to dismantle it, when Taylor uttered a muffled scream. He spun to look at her. Her face was pale; her eyes wide and staring. He followed her gaze, and felt his mouth go dry.

There, perched on a boulder about thirty-five feet away, was a cougar. Its lips curled back in a threatening snarl, revealing vicious fangs. Tiny, pointed ears lay flat against its round skull, and it crouched with tense, twitching muscles. Its throat rumbled with its banshee scream as it kept its piercing gaze fixed on them.

"God help us."

Connor echoed Taylor's desperate whisper. He closed his eyes for a second, the image of his rifle, still in its saddle scabbard, dancing in his mind. He'd been in such a hurry to catch the sunrise, he hadn't thought to bring it.

He studied the cougar, noting the way it watched them but didn't advance. If they didn't challenge it, didn't move toward it, the big cat shouldn't come after them. Not unless…

Connor's throat constricted. He let his eyes scan the area. The rocks around them could house a cave…a den…kits…. He swallowed, the action painful in his suddenly dry throat. If they'd come too close to the cougar's young, they were in serious trouble.

"We have to get to the horses, Taylor," Connor told her in a low, hoarse voice. "It's our only chance."

She swallowed, then gave a quick, slight nod.

"Step back, hon. Come toward me. Slowly. Carefully." He watched, his heart pounding in his chest, as she moved. His eyes went from her to the screaming cat and back again. If nothing else, he would put himself between Taylor and the beast. He would do everything he could to give Taylor time to reach Topaz.

When she reached him, he moved as slowly as he dared, positioning himself as a barrier. At his movement, the cougar tensed, as though readying to lunge.

"Mem'ries, all alone in the moonlight…"

Connor jerked a look at Taylor. She was singing!

"What—?" But she just shook her head and kept on. He glanced back at the cougar. It looked about as taken aback as he was.

Connor stepped backward, keeping himself in front of Taylor who kept singing as they moved. The cougar watched them, still angry, still snarling—and, apparently, still flummoxed. It didn't lunge, didn't advance. It just watched them with those wrathful, ebony eyes as they eased away.

Suddenly Connor became aware that Taylor was no longer singing lyrics, but was singing to him.

"I've heard stories of people stopping grizzlies with songs. It was all I could think of to give us time."

"Fine, great," he hissed. "But *Cats?* What if he hates musicals?"

"It just seemed right."

After what seemed like an eternity, they finally moved out of the cat's line of vision. Connor grabbed Taylor's arm, cutting off her singing abruptly and spinning her around. With a shove he propelled her forward.

"Run!" He didn't have to order twice. She exploded into action, and they raced down the hill and across the meadow, toward the panicking horses.

God! God, save Taylor! The prayer flew through his mind, over and over. *Please, Father, please!*

Another horrendous yowl sounded from behind them, and Connor glanced over his shoulder. *O Lord, no!* The cat was coming, running with an almost careless grace, his long legs loping across the ground after them.

Connor looked ahead. They were about a hundred feet from the creek, and the woods were more than a hundred yards beyond that. The horses were pulling at their restraints frantically, eyes wide with terror.

You and me both, guys! A hysterical laugh bubbling up inside him. He assessed the distance left to safety and his heart sank. They weren't going to make it.

"Taylor, keep running! No matter what, don't stop!"

She looked at him in alarm, and he shouted in her face. "RUN!" Without watching to see if she obeyed, he veered off, heading away from the tree where the horses were tied.

Please, God. Let it come after me!

"Connor! No!" Taylor's scream echoed in his mind, but he didn't pause. He looked behind only long enough to see what the cougar was doing, and satisfaction mixed with terror shot through him when he saw it was behind him. Apparently he was the more appetizing prey.

He vaulted across the creek, then sprinted toward the woods, his feet pounding the ground. His breath burned in his lungs, the blood pounded in his temples, and all he could think, over and over, was, *God! God! Help us!*

Taylor watched in horror as Connor led the cougar away. She forced herself forward, splashing through the brook, and raced to Topaz's side.

The buckskin was screaming, tossing its huge head in a desperate attempt to break loose and run. Taylor knew she could get into the saddle, but not without a fight. And Connor was running out of time.

She grabbed at the saddle, screaming at the horse and slapping him on the neck to get his attention. He danced in terror, his eyes wild, jerking the saddle from her hands. She lunged at him, grabbed a handful of mane and pulled for all she was worth, screaming again. Topaz hesitated—and that was all the opening she needed. She grabbed her rifle, jerked it from the leather scabbard, then whirled to run after Connor.

Let me be in time! One look told her the awful truth. Connor was no more than ten feet from the woods, but the cat was almost on top of him. He'd never make it.

"No!" She stopped abruptly and jerked the rifle to her shoulder, knowing even as she did so that it would take a miracle to save the man she'd come to love.

She sighted the cougar—and a terrible realization filled her. Connor and the cat were perfectly aligned. If she shot at the cougar and missed, odds were good she'd hit Connor. A sob escaped her lips.

The sound of a gunshot ripped through the air.

Someone else was shooting!

Taylor watched in stunned amazement as a rock near the running cougar splintered, sending shards flying. The cat uttered a pain-filled scream and jerked to a halt, coiling its sleek body and roaring out its rage.

Taylor was scanning the woods, seeking the source of the shot, when another sounded, and the rock splintered again, peppering the cat with tiny projectiles. It recoiled in fury and pain, raising one huge paw to claw at the air. A third shot sounded, and Taylor felt a cheer rise in her throat.

Who cared who was shooting? The cat had had enough! He turned and raced away, heading across the meadow, away from where Connor had raced into the woods, away from where Taylor stood in stunned amazement.

They were safe.

Suddenly her legs seemed to be made of rubber, and she sank to the ground. She knelt there, her rifle propped up in front of her, leaning her forehead against the cool barrel, willing herself to stop shaking.

Within moments strong hands slid under her arms and lifted her to her feet.

Connor. She opened her eyes, and at the sight of him her rifle slipped from her fingers, and she threw her arms around his neck. He drew her close, engulfing her in his embrace, clamping her in an iron grip that told her he wasn't going to release her anytime soon. And that was absolutely fine with her.

"Are you okay?"

At his hoarse question, she nodded as best she could with her face pressed against his chest. Then his hands cupped her face, and she leaned back to look at him. When their eyes met, her heart swelled with the tenderness of his expression.

"Thank God." He searched her face with anxious eyes. "Thank you, God." His prayer was breathed against her lips as he lowered his head and his mouth covered hers. And suddenly it was as though she came alive. Truly, fully alive for the first time since Josh's death.

Moved by a deep and indefinable need, she leaned into him, her hands clutching his shirt, her senses filled with the emotions he stirred within her. When at last they drew apart, Connor's eyes were dark and burning— and slightly dazed.

She brought a hand to his face and laid it gently against his cheek. "You saved my life." Amazement swept her again at the risk he had taken for her.

He took her hand and pressed his lips to the palm. A shudder passed through her.

His gaze met hers, and when he spoke his voice was low and ragged. "All I could think of was leading the cougar away from you." His eyes darkened. "Taylor, I know you don't want to hear this, but I have to say it. I love you. I don't ever want to leave you, to live without you. You are my life." His voice caught, and shock jolted through her when she saw tears in his eyes. "The thought of you being hurt…of anything happening to you—" He broke off, shaking his head wordlessly as his hands cupped her face with an unbearable gentleness. "I've never prayed so hard in my life."

She smiled suddenly, and her head spun. She felt absolutely giddy, though whether from their escape or Connor's words, she wasn't sure. "I was praying like crazy myself."

His gaze was like a caress, and it was as though warmth enveloped her. "Well, he answered. And he guided your aim, too. That was some kind of shooting."

"It was indeed, but it wasn't mine."

"Wasn't yours?" His brows drew together, and she shook her head, snuggling closer into the warm circle of his embrace.

"I sighted the cougar, but you were in the line of fire." She looked up at him, remembering the wave of despair that had washed over her. "I was afraid to shoot. Afraid I would miss the cat and hit you."

He looked toward the spot where the cougar had stopped. "If you didn't do the shooting—" he turned to look at her—"then who did?"

"I don't know. I can't imagine who would be out here…or why he didn't come over after the cougar left. But I don't really care. All that matters is that God gave us a miracle."

His eyes twinkled suddenly. "Maybe it was your guardian angel."

She tilted her head, slanting a look up at him. "Who knows? I mean, somebody was watching out for us. But it would be the first time I've ever heard of an angel carrying a gun."

"Not me." He gave her a squeeze. "I see one right now."

She felt her cheeks blush and leaned her forehead against his chest. "Connor, I care about you too. I think…" She paused, searching for the right words, and he waited patiently. "I think I love you." She looked up. "At least, I want to. I know I don't want to lose you, no matter what happens with the wolves. But I'm…I'm just not ready yet to give my heart to you. To anyone."

He leaned down, pressed a gentle kiss to her forehead, then stepped away from her. She felt cold, bereft, but his smile warmed her. "I understand, Taylor. I can wait." He moved to pick up her rifle, then held his hand out to her. "Let's get the camera equipment before that cat comes back, and go home."

She grasped his hand, and they walked back toward the horses.

The sun was just setting that evening as Taylor sat in one of the rockers on the porch, pushing back and forth gently. She loved this time of day, when the sky was exploding with color and the evening darkness crept over everything. She leaned her head back against the chair, drawing a deep breath of clean spring air.

Images of the day drifted through her mind…the meadow, the cougar, the kiss she and Connor had shared…

A warm flush washed over her at that last memory, and she hugged her arms around herself. Something was happening here. Something good and right. Between her and Connor. She wasn't sure where it was leading, but she was ready to find out.

"What brings you such pleasure, Yazhi, that your face shines with it?"

She turned slightly to look at Luke, who was coming up the steps of the porch. He pulled one of the rockers over next to her and lowered himself into it, his gaze resting on her face.

She shrugged, wishing Luke weren't so set against Connor. "I don't know, Luke. Just life, I guess."

"It has been a long time since you've had such a look in your eyes. Not since you came home with Josh in tow."

She felt the traitorous color flood her cheeks and looked down at her lap. Luke's large, work-toughened fingers reached to cover her hand where it lay on the arm of the rocking chair.

"Taylor, you know I love you as the daughter I never had."

She nodded.

"And you know I want only what is best for you."

She nodded again.

"I see what this man has become to you, how you feel about him, how he feels about you."

Her eyebrows arched. "How he feels about me?"

Luke's mild amusement danced in his usually sober eyes. "A person would have to be blind to miss the affection he feels for you. But that should not surprise you. Connor Alexander has spent a great deal of time with you these past weeks. It was unavoidable that he would come to love you."

Taylor reached out to pat his cheek. "Oh, Luke, you're so good for my ego."

His hand squeezed hers. "I speak what I know, Yazhi." His eyes darkened with concern. "And that is what makes me uneasy. I do not know who this man is. What he wants from you. From Galloway Glen."

She looked at him thoughtfully. "I won't pretend I know, Luke. Not entirely. I'm still learning who Connor is. But there are a few things that I think are true. He's committed to following God, and he's determined to protect the wolves. And he's become—" Her voice choked with sudden emotion. "He's become very special to me. I can't explain it, but it's true. I care for Connor a great deal."

Luke stared into the growing night around them. When he spoke again, the coldness in his voice surprised Taylor. "I do not want you to go back into the wilderness with him."

"Luke—"

His gaze captured hers, and she was startled by the intensity of the distrust she saw there. "You are too far away. I cannot protect you."

"I don't need protection. Connor won't hurt me—"

"He has before."

Irritation rose within her, and she pushed it down. Getting angry wasn't going to help. *Father, what can I say to help him understand?*

Her mother's words came back to her. *"It might be that he's feeling…threatened."*

Gently she weaved her fingers with his. "You are my dear friend, Luke, and nothing will change that. Josh didn't. And Connor won't. You are a part of my life, a part of Galloway Glen, and you always will be. I am not replacing your part in my life with Connor." She met Luke's eyes, willing him to hear her. "But God brought Connor here for a reason, and he has become a part of my life too. I don't know what he means to me, what he will mean in the future. All I know is that I care for him. A great deal."

Luke stared down at their entwined hands, then looked up at her, letting his breath out in a weary sigh. "I hear your heart, Yazhi. I will do my best to see this man as you do."

"That's all I ask. Just give Connor a chance. I think you'll find you have a lot more in common than you realize."

He squeezed her hand once more, then rose and walked down the stairs and into the night.

Taylor closed her eyes. Luke wanted to please her, she knew that. But the dislike she'd seen in his eyes when he talked about Connor was clear and intense. And she felt a sharp pang of sadness that one who had shared her life and dreams for so long suddenly seemed very far away.

TWENTY-FIVE

Taylor's heart was pounding as she slid from the saddle the next morning. It was early yet, barely after dawn. She waited for Connor to dismount and gather his photography equipment. Then together they walked through the trees and went to stand at the edge of the pool.

At first there didn't seem to be a wolf anywhere around. Taylor looked up at Connor, trying to hide her disappointment, but his smile was reassuring as he set up his tripod and fitted a camera on the top. "Give them some time."

She bit her lip and sank down on the lush green carpet beneath them. She plucked at blades of grass, but that didn't help. A small patch of lupine was beside her, so she picked several of the lavender flowers and pulled the small bell-like blooms off, one by one.

"I hope the pups show soon." There was gentle laughter in Connor's voice as he came to sit beside her. "Otherwise you're going to trash this place."

She looked up to make a retort, but the words died in her throat. Her breath caught in her throat, and her heart raced as she stared at the cave. She opened her mouth again, but all that came out was a small "ohhh…" of utter wonder. Connor spun around, following the direction of her gaze, then moved to his camera and started shooting.

A small bundle of fur stood at the edge of the cave entrance, peering out at them. It shuddered when the cool morning breeze ruffled its downlike fur. Staring at them with curious blue eyes, it took a tentative step forward, only to be run over by another pup from behind. This pup was far more adventurous than its littermate, and it bounded out into the open with a total disregard for any hazards that might be awaiting it.

"Oh no!" Taylor whispered as the pup ambled to the edge of the ledge and peered at the water below.

"It's okay," Connor told her, still taking shots. "Watch."

The first pup squealed in displeasure, its face in the dirt where it had sprawled. Within moments, Nokomis was at the mouth of the cave, her dark eyes scanning the ledge, locating her offspring. In two quick strides she stood over her audacious infant, then leaned down to take the pup's head in her mouth. With tender care, the mother carried the pup back inside the cave.

Taylor gave a relieved sigh, then giggled when the first pup, still sprawled in the dirt, voiced its displeasure in a high-pitched yowl.

"Not much different from human kids, eh?"

Connor said, and she laughed.

"They remind me of Mark and Mikey when they were little. Whatever one didn't get into, the other did."

"Oops, here she comes again."

Sure enough. Nokomis was standing over the fallen pup, leaning down to lick at it with her long, pink tongue. The pup suffered the washing, then opened its little mouth in an enormous yawn. Nokomis nudged it with her muzzle, and the pup struggled to its feet and toddled back into the cave. Without a backward glance, Nokomis followed her offspring.

Taylor sat back, clapping her hands with glee. "They're adorable!"

"And I'm sure you'll have names for them in no time." Connor unfastened his camera from the stand.

"Do you think there are more?"

"Probably. Wolves generally have litters of five to seven pups, sometimes even more. The others are probably still asleep inside." He tucked his tripod under his arm, slipped the camera strap around his neck, then extended a hand down to her. "And we should probably head out. We've disturbed them enough."

Reluctantly she let him pull her to her feet.

"Okay—" she made sure her tone was none too gracious—"but you owe me something wonderful for not letting me stay longer."

"How 'bout a kiss?" He waggled his eyebrows.

"Something wonderful for *me*. That would be wonderful for you."

With a gentle tug, he pulled her off balance and into his arms. Lowering his head, he spoke in a low, rumbling tone, his lips a breath away from hers. "Oh, I think I could make it wonderful for both of us—" his blue eyes sparkled with tender amusement as shivers coursed through her, making her traitorous knees go weak— "don't you?"

Oh, my, yes. She believed that. With all her heart.

She leaned forward, closing her eyes, breathless, anticipating…only to find herself suddenly standing on her own as Connor stepped back, let go, and patted her on the head.

"But, of course, you know best. So you just let me know what I owe you, hon, and I'll be glad to comply."

With that, he walked away, leaving her to follow behind, her only companion her disappointment…and that infuriating deep chuckle that drifted back to her on the breeze.

TWENTY-SIX

LADEN WITH TRAPS, HIS GUN STRAPPED OVER HIS SHOULDER, the hunter knelt in the loose dirt, inspecting the drying tracks. The print was nearly as large as his hand. He guessed it was from a female, one that was several years old. His eyes narrowed in speculation.

It was the right time of year...

He stood abruptly. He had to find her before the beast could reproduce. Odds were good that she was already pregnant, maybe even denning. If so, he'd find the den and finish off the lot of them.

He tracked her for hours, and it took all his skill and knowledge of the old ways to stay on her trail. She was clever, doubling back and doing all she could to cover herself. But it wasn't enough. No matter how clever they were, they were still just animals.

When he followed the trail to a rock formation, he squinted, looking around. Wolves didn't den in the high places. They denned underground, or in a low spot covered by brush and branches. He'd even heard of one female denning in an abandoned beaver dam.

Cursed creatures. They had the most amazing knack for survival.

He studied the trail again. Mud from the recent rain had left a trail of paw prints, and they clearly led up the rocky rise. He hoisted the traps and set them on the ground. The less encumbrance the better. Slipping his gun from his shoulder, he checked the chambers and nodded in satisfaction. If the wolf was there, he was ready for her.

Within moments he was at the top of the rise, and what he saw widened his eyes in amazement. A valley lay below him like a small piece of heaven. Trees, flowers, grasses, and a pool all combined to create a vision of beauty and tranquillity. He couldn't believe his eyes. He thought he'd wandered every acre of Galloway Glen, but he'd never come across this place.

It was then that he spotted the tent at the far end of the valley. So, the biologist was here. Which probably meant Taylor had brought him. Sharp pain squeezed his heart as he thought of her here with Alexander. The sense of betrayal he'd felt the night he first heard the wolves returned and was fed and strengthened by this most recent offense. He and Taylor had never come across this place on their rides because she had made sure they hadn't. She'd kept its existence to herself, willing to share it with no one. Except the intruder.

He glanced down at the tracks. And her wolves.

How could she do this to him?

Calm down. She's deceived. She just doesn't realize

what's best for her. It's not her fault.

The reassurances washed over him, easing the heat in his gut. That had to be it. Taylor had been fooled. Now it was up to him to protect her, to help her see the truth. Before it was too late.

His jaw tensed as he thought about Connor Alexander. The man was trying to move in on territory that was already claimed. Well, first he'd take care of the wolves. Then he'd see to Alexander. With him out of the way, Taylor would be able to understand.

A rustling sound from below drew his attention, and he froze. His heart pumped double time as he watched a slender wolf trotting toward a rock ledge beneath him. He thanked the old ones that he was downwind of the beast, or she would have spotted him long before he saw her. He watched her approach the area just below, then examined the ledge more closely. He smiled in satisfaction. A cave. So that was where the creature had denned.

Moving slowly and soundlessly, he brought the gun to his shoulder. When the wolf was in his sights, he closed his eyes for a second against the sheer adrenaline rush that washed over him. He opened his eyes and sighted the wolf again.

You're mine. Then pulled the trigger.

The sharp sound of rifle fire echoed on the wind, and Taylor spun in the saddle, looking at Connor in alarm. "That sounded close!"

"Too close," he agreed. "Like it came from the valley."

Quick fear suffused Taylor's face with color, then siphoned it off again, leaving her pale and tight lipped. Without another word she pulled on the reins, spinning Topaz back toward Reunion and urging him to a gallop.

The gray form lay on the ground below, unmoving. The hunter released a long, slow breath and stepped forward. Already he heard the whines from the cave. He clenched his teeth. The killing brought him little pleasure, but he would do what he had to do to protect the ones he loved.

He made his way down the incline, then stepped cautiously toward the unmoving form of the wolf. No point in taking any chances. He would make sure she was dead before he killed the pups.

Suddenly he was hit from behind. Someone had tackled him, sending them down in a rolling, struggling heap. Fists flew in his face and several solid punches landed on his nose and his cheeks. Stunned, disoriented, he swung his fist as hard as he could. The satisfying thud and groan that followed told him he'd connected, and his attacker sagged.

Taking advantage of the moment, he rolled away and staggered to his feet. He wiped at his face, pulled the handkerchief down around his neck, and spit blood. He looked at the prone form in front of him, and his eyes widened. Lying there, trying to shake off the blow to the side of his temple, was Brad Momadey.

With muttered oath, the hunter took his gun in both hands, raised it, and brought the butt down with a sharp motion to connect with the side of Brad's head. The boy stiffened, then his eyes rolled back in his head, and he sank, unconscious, to the ground.

Turning toward the cave, the hunter spit again. First he'd take care of the cubs. Then he'd make sure this young fool would be all right before he left. He glanced at the boy's inert form with disgust.

What was Brad doing here, anyway?

The sound of pounding hoofbeats halted him, and he turned, frustration washing over him, hot and fierce. "No!" He looked down at the cave. "I didn't have time!"

He listened carefully, gauging the distance of the riders, and knew with a sinking certainty that they were too close. He wanted to race to the cave and finish what he'd started. Instead, he spun, jumped over the fallen boy, and scrambled up the rocky slope.

He would have to wait for another day.

Racing down the incline he snatched up his traps and headed for the nearest woods.

Brad's head felt as though it were going to explode. He blinked, willing the spinning world to come to a stop. When it did, he pushed himself up, groaning at the sharp pain in his head.

Woozy, he looked around—and saw the still form of the wolf. Memory hit him in a wave. "No!" Struggling to his feet, he staggered to the wolf's side. He knelt beside her, reaching out to touch her muzzle gently. A soft puff of air against his hand startled him, and he felt a thrill of hope. She was still alive!

Slowly she opened her eyes, her breathing shallow and ragged. "Please…" For the first time in a long time, Brad thought he would weep. "Please don't die!"

But the look he saw in the wolf's eyes was all too familiar. He'd seen it before, just before death came to claim its victim. As he watched, the fierce amber light focused on him, blazed for one wonderful moment, then flickered and died. The wolf's eyes glazed, and she was gone.

A sob tore at Brad, and he lowered his head.

He'd failed again.

When Topaz crested the rise, Taylor vaulted from the saddle and ran to look down into the valley. Connor was right behind her, and she felt his hand grip her arm.

"There." His voice was flat and grim. She followed his pointing finger and saw the still, gray form. Her mind was so focused on the wolf that it scarcely registered that someone was kneeling next to the animal.

"No!" A flash of wild grief ripped through her. "Oh no!"

Connor mounted his horse and went down the path to the valley floor. Taylor wanted to follow him, but she couldn't make her legs move. It was Nokomis, beautiful, laughing Nokomis.

Taylor felt sick. She leaned against Topaz's side, squeezing her eyes shut, drawing in deep gasps of air, willing her stomach not to reject her lunch. Her head spun, and she shook with impotent rage and fear. Then one thought pierced through her misery and spurred her into action: *the pups!*

With a cry, she grasped the saddle horn and swung herself into the saddle. Within minutes, she was down in the valley, off the horse, and circling the pool.

Connor was kneeling next to Nokomis's body, his hand resting in her lush fur, his face ashen. When Taylor came toward him, he looked at her, and his eyes glittered dangerously.

"She's dead." He stated in a low, rasping voice what she already knew. She nodded, unable to speak around the knot of grief in her throat. She laid a hand on his shoulder, and he reached up to take it in his. His grip was so hard that it hurt her, but she didn't care.

Then with one lithe movement he was standing, and he pulled her into his arms, as though he desperately needed contact with something warm and alive. He crushed her to him, burying his face in her hair, and she felt him shudder with emotion. She slid her arms around his waist and tried to offer him what comfort she could.

At last he drew a ragged breath and set her away from him.

It was then that she became aware of someone else standing there, watching them. She turned, and her grief exploded into fury.

"You!" Until that moment she'd never realized one word could be the embodiment of violence. But that was what she felt, what surged through her in waves. Violent rage. Wrath.

And all she could think of was making Brad Momadey pay for what he'd done.

TWENTY-SEVEN

WITHOUT THINKING, TAYLOR ADVANCED TOWARD BRAD. "DID you do this? *Did* you?"

Brad flinched as though she'd struck him. "No!" His horrified denial was immediate.

"I don't believe you!" Her hands clenched into fists.

"Taylor, stop." Connor grabbed her arms, holding her firmly.

She struggled against him. "He killed her!" She brushed an angry hand at the tears streaming down her cheeks.

Connor turned her to face him, shaking her slightly. "No, he didn't." The words were quiet but firm.

"You don't know—" She forced the words out, a sob in her voice. "You don't know him like I do. He killed Josh!"

Connor's eyes widened at that, and he looked at Brad's strained, pale face.

"It was my fault." The boy's words were laden with guilt and self-recrimination. "I was supposed to watch the boys, and I didn't."

Understanding dawned in Connor's eyes. "You're Brad Momadey."

"Yes."

"What are you doing here? How dare you come on my land—" Connor's grip on her arms tightened. She looked up at him, and shame swept over her at the look in his eyes. Some small part of her knew she was being vicious, shrewish, but she didn't care.

"Forgive us our trespasses, as we forgive those who trespass against us."

The words echoed faintly in her mind, but she pushed them away. Forgive? How could she forgive this boy for all he'd cost her?

"Forgive as you've been forgiven…"

No, Lord. I can't.

"What were you doing here, Brad?" Connor's voice was filled with gentleness.

"I was watching over the wolves."

Taylor stared at him. "Watching over the wolves? How? Why?"

He looked at her, and she was shocked to see how old his eyes looked. Old and weighted down.

"I knew they were here a year ago. I heard their songs, saw their tracks. I've been following them since they arrived, trying to cover their tracks and make sure the ranchers didn't find them. I wanted to protect them. Keep them safe."

Her mind spun, and she thought she might faint.

Brad had been on her land, following her wolves, for the past year! How could that be? How could she not have seen—?

"It was you!" She struggled to comprehend what was happening. "You're the one who's been shadowing me. You scared the cougar away—"

At his stiff nod, she crossed her arms and looked away. So *this* was her guardian angel, her protector, the one who had made her feel so safe at night? This was the one God had sent to watch over her.

"Why?" She directed a look at Brad. "Why did you do this?"

Emotions swept over the boy's face. His haunted eyes burned with an inner despair, and Taylor was hit with an overwhelming desire to reach out and smooth the anguish from his young face. Stunned by her unexpected feelings, she stiffened and stepped back.

Brad took in her movement and looked away. "I—I wanted to be there...to make sure nothing happened to you because—because it's my fault you're alone. It's my fault Josh isn't here to take care of you." A sob caught at the words, and he closed his eyes, tilting his head back. His jaw was clenched, and his entire body seemed coiled with anguish and tension.

After a moment, he opened his eyes again, and Taylor found herself faced with the rawest grief she'd ever seen. *How does he live with that much agony?* Her heart squeezed painfully with the sorrow she felt emanating from him.

"When I saw how much the wolves meant to you, how much you loved them, I swore I'd do everything I could to protect them too. I knew you were spending every day with him." He nodded at Connor. "So you'd be safe. But the wolves were here…alone…." Despair washed over his face as he looked at Nokomis's body. "I've been staying here, sleeping in the tent for a few hours each night. Then I'd go up on the rise and watch from there. Today, I came out of the tent and saw the man standing on the opposite side, saw him sight his rifle on the female. I didn't have time to reach my gun. To reach him." His eyes came back to hers, pleading with her to believe him. "I would have stopped him if I could. But I couldn't save her. I'm sorry…." He gulped hard, tears slipping down his cheeks.

Connor stepped forward to lay a hand on the boy's shoulder. "You did what you could, Brad. Do you know who he was? Did you see his face?"

Brad's head shook abruptly. "I didn't see his face. I came up behind him when he was going to the female, I think to make sure she was dead. We fought. I caught a glimpse of him, but he was wearing something across his face. Then he hit me with his gun, and all I saw were stars." He looked at Nokomis. "I watched her die." The flat words seemed wrenched from somewhere deep within him. "I saw the light in her eyes go out. She looked at me as though she felt bad for *me*, like she was trying to tell me it was okay, and then she was gone." He moved restlessly, rubbing his temples with shaking fingers. "I'm sorry, Taylor."

She jerked when he said her name. She stared at him, more uncertain than ever. Brad just kept talking, as though he couldn't help himself. "I wanted to stop him. I never wanted him to die."

A jolt of shock left Taylor lightheaded. Brad was no longer referring to the wolf but to Josh. She was sure of it. Her eyes flew to Connor, and he shook his head. *Let him talk,* his eyes seemed to say. *Let him get it out.* He came to stand beside her, his arm slipping around her waist as he offered his strength, his support.

Taylor's heart constricted, and she thought the pain would tear her in two. *God, I can't. I can't bear this! You can't ask this of me!*

Brad paced back and forth, his hands clenched at his sides, his movements quick and strained. "I can't get it out of my mind. I keep seeing him fall, keep seeing his face, the look he gave me." He stopped abruptly and looked at Taylor, his face filled with confusion. "He should have hated me! He should have screamed at me! But he just looked at me with such…understanding. Like he wanted to comfort me, tell me it was okay."

Taylor's chest felt as though it would burst. Listening to Brad's voice, she heard the echo of her own pain; looking at his face, she saw the reflection of her own grief and confusion.

His eyes searched her face, as though hoping against hope to find some answer, some reason there for what had happened. "Josh knew he was going to die," he went on, "I could see it in his eyes. And he just looked at me as though he were worried about *me*." Brad sank to the ground, his knees pulled up against his chest, his face buried in his hands. "I can't get that look out of my mind. It haunts me. It's like he won't rest until I understand, but I don't. I can't."

Connor's arm tightened around Taylor's waist, but she pulled away. She stood there, ready to flee, wanting to escape this nightmare...yet something held her fast. As though she couldn't help herself, she looked at Brad, and his anguish tore at her heart. She clamped her lips shut to imprison a sob of her own.

At last, at long last, her enemy was here before her in agony. But there was no joy, no triumph, no sense of victory.

Why not, Lord? Why not?

He is not the enemy.

With that truth, guilt and regret washed over her in great, drowning waves. *God! O God, forgive me!* She'd thought Brad was going on with his life happily, uncaring that Josh was dead or that he had been responsible. She'd pictured him as cold and cruel, painted him a monster without heart or conscience. And all this time, day in and day out for a year and a half, he had been paying penance, living like a wraith, watching over her. He was as imprisoned in his guilt as she was in her hatred and bitterness.

Father, forgive me. Josh was willing to die for Brad, to

give his life so that Brad might find you. And all I've done is hate. And wish him dead. If anyone wasted Josh's life, Lord, it's been me.

Connor's strong hands gripped her shoulders from behind, and she turned to look into his compassionate eyes. Tears spilled down her cheeks, and she shook her head.

"I was so wrong."

He motioned gently toward Brad. "Tell him. He needs to hear. He needs to be set free, and I think you're the only one who can do it."

She held Connor's gaze, drawing strength from the love she saw there, then turned and went to kneel beside Brad. Carefully, gently, as though he were made of something infinitely fragile, she slid her arms around him.

For a moment he stiffened, and she thought he might bolt. Then, with a broken sob, he sagged against her.

"I'm sorry! I'm so sorry! I never wanted him to die. He was the only one who ever listened to me, who didn't give up on me. And I killed him!"

"You didn't kill him, Brad." The truth was finally clear in her heart. "It was an accident."

"But it was my fault!" He pulled away from her, surging to his feet. Desperation lined his features, and he reminded her of the wolves just before they bolted for the woods. "Billy never would have gone out on that ledge if I'd been watching him. I was too proud, too concerned with showing Josh he couldn't tell me what to do.

I wanted to teach him a lesson."

Taylor waited for the anger and pain to sweep through her, but they didn't. Instead, she felt surrounded with God's peace, cloaked in his presence and forgiveness.

"Forgive, beloved, as you've been forgiven."

She stood. "Brad, listen to me." Though she didn't move toward him, she caught and held his eyes with her own. *Let him hear me, Father. Please, just let him hear me.*

"You're right. It was your fault Josh ended up on that ledge." Brad flinched as though she'd struck him, then closed his eyes as though waiting for her to strike a death blow. "I hated you for a long time for that, even wished you had been the one to die—" She looked away in shame. "I didn't care if you knew God. I even hoped you didn't. I wanted you to suffer for eternity for what you'd done."

Brad opened his eyes, and they were a dark void in his colorless face.

She took a step toward him, extending her hands, palms up. When she spoke, her voice was heavy with regret. *Oh, Jesus, I've been so wrong....* "Please, Brad, will you—can you—forgive me?"

He blinked and his mouth sagged open. She smiled in spite of herself.

"You want *me*...to forgive *you?*" His husky voice was ripe with disbelief and confusion. His sable eyes clung to hers, and she saw that he wanted to believe her. Wanted it as desperately as she'd wanted to trust God again.

It hit her then and took her breath away. They'd

both been in prison, trapped by their emotions.

No more, Father. She was filled with a sudden sense of a locked door being thrown wide open. *It's time for us to be free.*

"How can you ask that? I killed your husband! You should hate me!"

"No, Brad. No. Don't you see? We've both been wrong. I forgot that Josh loved you. I forgot that God loves you—"

"God doesn't love me! He can't! Not after what I've done."

"Yes, he can." She was in front of him now, and she reached out to take his clenched hands. For a moment he kept them clamped, but they began to relax in her warm grasp. "And he does. We've all done terrible things, Brad. Yes, you made a mistake. And yes, Josh died because of it. But it was an accident." She lifted one hand to touch his cheek, wiping away a tear. "What I did was far worse. It was intentional. Determined. I let myself blame you. I feasted on my bitterness and nurtured my anger until I hated you."

Pain was alive and glowing in his eyes, and she squeezed his hand in entreaty. "But I was wrong! If I hate you in my heart, then I'm as guilty in God's eyes as if I murdered you." She was crying again…would she ever reach the end of her tears?

"Weeping endures for a night, but joy comes in the morning."

Yes, Lord…yes. It's time for morning. "But that ends here, Brad. Now. The hate ends here." Her voice gained strength. "I forgive you." A glint of wonder entered his eyes at her words. "I forgive you, and I know Josh forgave you, too, before he died. I know his heart. You know his heart. He loved you, Brad." She reached out to place her palm over his heart.

He caught his breath at her touch, as though it were painful.

She understood. It could hurt to the core when your heart started to thaw after a long, long freeze.

"Josh loved you. You said he knew he was going to die. He loved you enough to give up his life so you could have the chance to know Jesus. That's what mattered most to him. And, when it comes down to it, that's what matters most to me, too."

"Why?"

She gave him a watery smile. "Because it's what matters most to God. He died for you, too, Brad. Christ came for you, to die in your place on the cross because he loves you."

He nodded. "I know. I—I've been reading a Bible my mom gave me. I wanted to believe…wanted to ask God to forgive me, to accept me…" He looked down. "I just figured I wasn't worth it."

"You aren't," Connor said from beside them. Brad looked at him sharply, and his smile was kind. "None of us is. We can't be worthy of God's love. He just gives it because he wants to, not because we deserve it. You don't have to be good enough. All you have to do is say yes."

Brad glanced again at Taylor, and she nodded.

"Will you...will you pray with me?"

A warm glow of praise and gratitude flowed through Taylor. She smiled, and Brad's mouth tipped into a hesitant smile in response.

"Yes, of course." She reached out to take Connor's hand, too. "We both will, if that's okay."

Brad looked at Connor. "I'd like that."

The three of them knelt there together, and Taylor's heart resonated with delight as she and Connor ushered Brad to the throne room of his heavenly father.

She knew, somewhere up in heaven, Josh was singing.

TWENTY-EIGHT

IT HADN'T BEEN HARD TO FIND THE PUPS; ALL FIVE WERE COW-ering at the back of the cave, whining piteously for their mother. Taylor couldn't hold back the tears as they gathered the tiny furry bundles and took them back to the tent.

The other wolves were gone. For now at least. The gunshots had most likely sent them into hiding.

Brad stayed with Taylor and Connor, and all three spent the night feeding the pups every hour, using some dry formula and bottles, supplies Connor had brought in case they were needed.

When he first mixed the powder with water and shook the bottle, Brad wrinkled his nose in distaste. "They're supposed to like this stuff, eh?"

Connor slanted him a knowing grin. "Like it or not, they'll eat it when they get hungry enough."

"I'll believe it when I see it."

At first the pups seemed to agree with Brad. They resisted the bottles, turning their heads this way and that. After several frustrated efforts at coaxing the small, whining bundles, Connor took the bottles and strode from the tent. When he returned, his face was grim. He handed the bottles to Taylor. "Try it now."

She did so, amazed when the pup she held latched onto the nipple, sucking for all it was worth. Taylor looked at Connor curiously.

"You put the mother's scent on them, didn't you?" Brad asked quietly.

At Connor's nod, tears sprang to Taylor's eyes—but mixed with her grief was gratitude for Connor and his willingness to do what was necessary.

The night wore on, and all the pups but one drank their fill, then dropped off into an exhausted slumber. The last pup, the smallest and weakest, continued to refuse the formula. His whimpers persisted nonstop for several hours, but as grating as that was, it wasn't nearly as alarming as when the pup fell silent.

Taylor held him, petting him tenderly. A large hand covered hers, and she looked up to meet Connor's eyes. "Is he going to die?"

"I don't know. He might."

"Please? Can't we do something?"

His eyes held hers. "We can pray."

Her heart swelled with love for him, and she leaned forward, resting her head on his shoulder. Connor's arms slid around her, but she pulled back suddenly. "Wait." She turned to look at Brad. He was sitting in a chair across the room, holding a sleeping pup, watching Taylor and Connor.

"You do it," she said, and a dull red crept into the boy's cheeks.

"Me? I—I can't. Why would God listen to me?"

"Because you're his child now, and he loves you." She held out a hand to him, and he rose, setting the lightly snoring pup on the rug. He straightened and came to take Taylor's hand. The three of them huddled together, bowing their heads.

"God, I don't know what to say," Brad began. "All I know is this little guy needs your help," he said, his voice choked with emotion, "just like I did. Well, you helped me, and I figured I was beyond any help from you or anyone else. So please, help the pup. Don't let the little guy die. Um, amen, I guess."

They opened their eyes, and Taylor smiled at Brad through her tears. "Thank you."

Connor opened his sleep-drugged eyes and reached his arms above his head, stretching. He yawned deeply, peered down at the pups snuggled against him—both of which were snoring away—then glanced around.

Brad was slouched in his chair, two sleeping pups cradled in his arms. Taylor was curled up on the floor, the last pup cuddled close. Connor's heart constricted. Had the pup survived?

He stood up, careful not to disturb the two pups on his cot. He would check on Taylor's little guy. If he were dead, Connor intended to dispose of him before Taylor woke.

But at the sound of his footsteps, quiet as he was, both Taylor and Brad started and woke up. Brad looked at Taylor, his face filled with apprehension—and a loud protesting wail came from the circle of her arms.

She looked down in wonder; then a joyous smile broke out over her face. "I think somebody's hungry!" she exclaimed, and Connor felt like turning somersaults.

He went to Brad and pounded him on the back. "Way to go, buddy! And you thought God wouldn't listen to you!"

"Well," Brad said, a smile crossing his tired face, "I'm glad I was wrong."

Taylor came to stand beside Brad too, and she rested a gentle hand on his shoulder. "I want you to come back to the ranch house with us."

Brad looked up at her in silence.

"Brad, you're a part of this. You've been a part for a long time. I want you to come and help us care for the pups. And I'd like to talk with you about the future."

"The future?"

"I can always use a good ranch hand. And you probably know Galloway Glen as well as any of us now." She grew serious. "Brad, I want you to think about staying on at the ranch. I can use you. And I'd like to have you there. After all, you're family now."

He stared at her, and Connor saw the play of emotions across his young face: amazement, disbelief, confusion, and finally, hope.

"I'd like that." A smile broke out over his weary face. "I'd like that a lot."

TWENTY-NINE

WHEN THE THREE OF THEM RETURNED TO THE RANCH, TAYLOR'S parents took one look at the pups and melted. Then they surged into action. By the time Connor was on the phone to a friend of his, a biologist who worked with captive wolves, the pups were ensconced in a large willow basket lined with soft, fluffy blankets.

Ryan, Lisa, and the twins showed up before long, and they, too, fell victim to the pups' charms. The twins sat on the floor, peering over the side of the basket, watching for the slightest movement or sign of distress.

Figuring the pups were in good hands, Taylor told her mother she needed to go out for a while.

"Are you all right, dear?" Her mother's gaze searched her face.

Taylor gave her mother a reassuring glance. "I just need to talk to someone."

"Gavin?" her mother asked, and Taylor nodded. She should have known her mother would figure out where she was going.

"I want to tell him…about Connor and me. Before he hears it from someone else."

"I think you'll find he already knows, dear. Anyone who cares about you knew how you felt about Connor when he left. But I do think it would be good to talk with Gavin." She patted Taylor's arm. "Gavin has been a good friend."

"Yes, he has."

She drove to Gavin's home, a ranch very similar to her own. When she pulled up in front of the house, she saw him on the porch, sitting on the railing, watching her. She walked up and sat beside him.

"I wondered when you'd be coming," he said quietly, staring into the distance.

"I just got back from Reunion. Where the wolves are."

He slanted her a look. "Your mother told me about the valley, where it was. I went to see it one day." His eyes glowed with the memory. "It's truly a place of beauty, Taylor. I can see why you love it so much." There was no censure, no anger in his voice. Only a quiet resignation.

She wrapped her arms around herself, struggling to find the right words. But there didn't seem to be any words to express what was going on in her heart right now.

Gavin was the one who finally spoke. "Connor is a good man. He'll treat you well." He looked at her then, a wry smile tipping his lips. "He's so besotted, he'll probably spoil you rotten." His dark eyes caressed her face. "But then, that's only right."

The tenderness in his expression pierced her, and

she bit her lip. "Gavin...I'm sorry. I—"

He lifted a hand and pressed gentle fingers to her lips, halting the words. "Lass, I know you love him. And I know you care for me. I won't lie. I wish this had ended differently." His hand dropped. "But I want you to be happy, darlin'. If it's Connor who will make you so, then I canna try to hold you."

"I will always treasure you."

A teasing light jumped into his eyes. "Aye, lass, as is only right. You've a friend of pure gold before you, and don't you ever forget it."

"Sure, an' you know I won't." She smiled through her tears.

His eyes held hers for a moment. "Know this, lass, and never doubt it: You've a friend forever in Gavin MacEwen. I've done all I can to help you, to protect you, darlin'. I've always tried to do what's best for you," he said, smiling wryly, "even when I knew you wouldn't agree with me. Because I care."

She blinked the tears back as he leaned forward to press his lips to her forehead.

"Now get you gone, lass. Your man is probably wonderin' where you've been." He arched his eyebrows. "And it wouldna be right to keep him waitin'."

She turned to leave, then spun around and threw her arms around his neck, hugging him fiercely. "My mother told me today that you've been a good friend to me," Taylor whispered as his strong arms closed around her. "But she's wrong. You haven't been a good friend—you've been my best friend. You helped me survive. You gave me hope." She leaned back, looking up into his dear face. "I love you, Gavin, as I have never loved another friend, man or woman. And I always will."

She squeezed him once more, then stepped back.

He let her go, a sad smile on his handsome face.

Father, you blessed me abundantly when you gave me Gavin MacEwen for a friend, she prayed as she walked back to her truck. She opened the door and stepped up to slide behind the wheel. *Now I ask you to bless him. Please, Lord, bring him a woman who will love him the way he deserves to be loved.*

The answer, swift and clear, rang in her mind and brought a delighted smile to her lips: *"No eye has seen, no ear has heard, no mind has conceived what God has prepared for those who love him."*

When the doorbell rang two nights later, Taylor jumped up to answer it. Connor's friends were here at last.

She opened the door and was suddenly caught up in a gargantuan hug. "Well, you must be Taylor! I swear, Connor didn't even begin to do you justice, little lady."

She giggled breathlessly as the bear of a man finally set her back on her feet. "And you are?" she asked, utterly charmed.

The man gave a deep bow, graceful for all his girth.

"Harry the Harridan, at your service."

The man standing behind him planted one foot on Harry's ample behind and pushed him through the door. Taylor laughed as Harry stumbled inside, tossing a look of mock outrage over his shoulder.

"The caveman here is Alec Stewart, resident biologist and wolf daddy." Connor came up behind Taylor and slipped his arms around her. Alec had agreed to raise the pups for the next four months. Then he would bring them back to Reunion and reintroduce them to the pack. "And whatever else you do, don't believe a word the man tells you about me."

Alec snickered. "Actually, the one you shouldn't trust is ol' Connor here." His jibe was softened by the obvious affection and respect in the look he gave his friend.

Taylor joined in the fun, showing the men to their rooms, then teasing and bantering all the way into the kitchen, where she introduced the two men to her family. Before long the rooms echoed with uproarious laughter as Harry and Alec regaled them with accounts of Connor's escapades in Washington. Taylor found herself mesmerized as she watched Connor trade stories with his two friends. He'd always been so quiet and reserved, but now he seemed to come alive. He mentioned the names of politicians as though they were just a bunch of guys who lived down the block! And her eyes widened with surprise when she discovered he'd actually been to the White House.

"Wouldn't have dreamed of sending anyone but ol' Con, here." Harry beamed. "After all, I taught the boy all I knew—"

"Which took all of five minutes." Connor crossed his arms.

"Yeah, well, that five minutes got you through one humongous verbal battle with those folks at the White House," Harry retorted.

What a job, Taylor thought as she listened. *It's clear Connor loves it.*

Sudden apprehension filled her. She and Connor hadn't really discussed the future, hadn't talked about whether or not he'd be staying around, or when she'd see him again…IF she'd see him again.

The stories that had been so entertaining a moment before now weighed her down, and Taylor soon rose and excused herself, pleading fatigue. She half hoped Connor would come away from the group with her, but he merely wished her a good night and turned back to correct Harry as he launched into another tale.

Swallowing her disappointment, she trudged to her room. Sasha lifted her head when Taylor came in, stretched in her spot on Taylor's bed, then dropped her head back down with a soft whuff.

"Thanks a lot," Taylor muttered. "It's good to see you too." She grabbed her towel and prepared to stomp into her bathroom when a light knock sounded at her door. She spun around and hurried to open it. Connor must have followed her after all.

But it was Brad standing there, his expression troubled. "Can I talk to you?"

"Sure." She stepped aside.

He came in and dropped into the large, overstuffed chair beside the window. "I've been racking my brain, trying to remember something, anything, about the hunter who shot Nokomis." Taylor moved to sit on the edge of her bed as he talked. "Tonight, I remembered something."

She could tell from his voice that he was hesitant to tell her about it.

"And?"

He licked his lips and stared at the floor.

"Brad, what is it?"

He fidgeted, looking down. "I think I know who the hunter was."

"You're kidding!"

He shook his head, but he didn't look happy.

Taylor felt a sudden apprehension. "Is it someone I know?"

"I...I think so. What I remembered was black hair. Long black hair. And broad shoulders."

She felt the color draining out of her face. "Oh, Brad..."

"He was tall," he went on miserably, "and really strong." He shifted his feet. "I'm sorry, Taylor, but I think it was—"

"Gavin." When Brad nodded, she closed her eyes. "That can't be true! You must have made a mistake."

"Maybe." The word was laced with doubt. "I mean, I can't believe Gavin would do something like that. What reason would he have to hurt the wolves?"

Taylor looked at Brad. None. No reason at all…then her eyes widened in sudden understanding. His words from this afternoon floated back to her: *"I've done all I can to help you, to protect you…I've always tried to do what's best for you, even when I knew you wouldn't agree with me."*

"Oh no…"

"What?" Brad leaned toward her, his eyes concerned.

She bit her lip. "I…you may be right."

Brad slumped lower in his chair. "I was afraid of that. What should we do?" He looked as upset as she felt.

She put her hand on his arm. "Don't say anything. Not yet. Give me a chance to think about this."

He looked away for a moment, then rose to leave.

"G'night, Taylor. Sleep well."

As the door shut softly behind him, she sank back on the bed, certain any chance of that had been completely obliterated.

In the clear light of morning as she stood brushing her hair, Taylor realized something terrible. Gavin knew about Reunion, knew the wolves were there, knew where it was. She tossed down her brush and headed for the kitchen. She'd heard Connor's voice coming from that direction a few minutes ago. She needed to talk to him. He'd know what to do.

"Still mad at me for making you take this assignment?"

Connor looked up from his bowl of cereal at his ex-boss, arching one eyebrow. "No."

Harry hooted. "Yeah! Right! You got some amazing photos, every last one of which will probably win you all kinds of awards, and you found the woman of your dreams, who just happens to live in the wilderness, have wolves on her property, and looks like a beauty queen." He looked pointedly around the spacious living room. "Then there's the cruddy shack she lives in—"

"Is there a point to this, Harry?"

"As a matter of fact, there is. I expect an invitation to the wedding. And I expect invitations to visit. I bet they've got great fishing here!"

Connor laughed and leaned back in his chair. "You got it, buddy."

"I still can't believe you won't be coming back to WAC. I am gonna have to calm Irene down, though. The woman's gonna feel terrible that you're dumping her, you know."

Connor slanted his friend a look. "Well, that's just the way it works. She should have known it wasn't meant to last. Besides, I never promised forever."

"Right!" Harry snorted. "I'm not all that worried.

You know how resilient women are. I just can't believe you're jumping ship."

Connor gave a slow nod. "I know. I was afraid it would be hard to leave. But you know, there's nothing to hold me there."

"Well, you're a rascal, old boy."

"Ain't it the truth." Connor's laughter bubbled over. "Ain't it just the truth."

Taylor stood, her back against the wall, in stunned disbelief.

She'd only caught the last part of Connor's discussion with his boss, but it had been more than enough. Connor was leaving, dumping her. He didn't love her. *"She should have known it wasn't meant to last...I never promised forever...there's nothing to hold me..."* She leaned her head back against the wall, refusing to cry.

Resilient, was she? Well, she'd show Connor Alexander just how resilient she really was. She turned and stormed down the hallway, out of the house, almost running over Brad on the back porch.

"Whoa! What's the rush?"

"Do me a favor, okay?"

At the fierce tone of her voice, his eyes widened. "Sure, Taylor."

"Tell Connor Alexander I hope he's very happy in whatever he chooses to do, and that I understand entirely.

If there's nothing to hold him here, then he *should* go. The sooner the better! Got that?"

"Well, yeah…but—"

"Good." She pushed past him.

"Taylor, what's going on? Where are you going?"

She opened the door to her truck. "To stop a killer."

Brad stopped in his tracks, then spun and ran into the house.

"She said *what?*"

Connor stared at Brad, and the boy gave a helpless shrug. "I know. It didn't make any sense to me, either."

"Uh-oh," Harry muttered. "Sounds like she overheard us and got the wrong impression."

"I don't know what happened—" Brad looked from one man to the other—"But what worries me most is the bit about stopping a killer."

"*What?*" Connor surged to his feet, grasping the boy by both arms and all but lifting him from the floor. "Tell me everything you know. And do it fast!"

"See what happens when you trust someone, Father?" She'd been raging for the last hour. "Are you happy now?"

"*Trust in the Lord.*"

"I *did* trust, and look what happened!"

"Lean not on your own understanding."

"What's to understand. I'd say it was all pretty clear. Connor Alexander is a bum. And I never want to see him again. Case closed."

She jammed the gears angrily, bouncing on the seat as she sailed over the bumpy ground. Then her eyes narrowed. Reunion was just ahead. And there was a Blazer parked at the base of the rise.

Oh, God, please! Not the other wolves! Not Sikis!

Taylor pulled up and slammed on the brakes, sending a shower of gravel and dust into the air. She pushed open the door and scrambled out, realizing as she did so that it wasn't Gavin's Blazer sitting there.

It was Luke's.

She frowned in confusion as she ran. Was Luke the hunter?

She reached the top of the rise and looked down, scanning the valley below her. Relief surged through her when she saw no sign of the wolves, living or dead. Then a gunshot rang out, and she looked up in alarm. It had come from the other side of the rock formation, outside the valley.

She raced back to her truck and backed out, spinning the wheels furiously. She stomped on the gas, and the vehicle shot forward. As she rounded the rock formation, she strained her eyes, searching. A glint of sunlight caught her attention, and her heart felt as though it had stopped.

Luke was standing there at the top of a steep, rock formation, his gun to his shoulder, drawing a bead. About four hundred yards away, racing for the woods, was Sikis.

"No!" A sob tearing at her throat. "No!"

She laid on the horn, and she stomped on the accelerator in tandem. Luke spun, and when he saw her truck, he dropped his gun to his side. Taylor glanced back at Sikis and saw him disappear into the woods.

"Oh, Lord!" Her breath caught in her throat. "Thank you!"

Taylor pulled up, threw the truck into park, cut the ignition, and slammed out.

"Are you *crazy?*" She stormed up the rocky incline, struggling not to fall as her feet slid in the loose dust and gravel.

Luke flinched at her fury but stood his ground. "Go home, Yazhi."

She stopped and stared at him, stunned. "Go—" Her hands clenched into fists at her sides. "I'll go home, all right. And you'll go with me. And then we're going to talk!"

"There's nothing to talk about. The wolves have to go. They are not safe, not for you, not for anyone."

"Luke, this is crazy—"

"No!" He turned to her, and the intensity of the emotion in his eyes startled her. "I'll tell you what's crazy. Letting these killers come on your land. Letting them turn people against you. They're the enemy, Taylor. You just don't understand."

"They're animals, Luke—"

"No. They're predators. Instinctive killers. I've seen them." He raised a hand as though to reach out to her, then let it drop to his side. When he went on, his voice was resigned. "Taylor, my grandfather was killed by a wolf. I was young—too young to stop it...but I saw it all. It came out of the woods, just like that one." His eyes went to where Sikis had vanished into the trees. "I was a boy, hunting with my grandfather. We'd killed a deer and were dressing the carcass when the monster came out of the woods. It attacked Grandfather. He didn't have a chance. I ran. I ran and hid in the woods. But I couldn't shut out the sounds of the screams...and the sounds the wolf made—" he shook his head—"they were the sounds of something evil."

Taylor took a step toward him. "Luke, you know animals and their behavior. You know how shy wolves are when they're alone, without a pack. They do everything they can to avoid people." She waited, hoping against hope he'd see the reason in what she was saying. Emotion flickered in his face, but he didn't reply. She raised a hand, reached toward him. "Luke...please, that wolf must have been rabid. You must know that."

His expression hardened. "No, I don't. And neither do you. No one does. Not for sure." He turned to her then. "Has it ever occurred to you that no wolf attacks on humans have been recorded simply because none of the victims lived to tell about it?"

"You know that's not true—"

He looked at her, and his expression grew tender—and then terribly sad. "What I know, Yahzi, is that wolves have brought only sorrow and loss to my life. And to yours. What profit is there in saving these animals when it may well cost you everything—" His voice choked and he looked away. "Maybe even your life."

"My life? The wolves would never hurt me—"

"They already have. Your neighbors are turning against you. Some even speak of violence."

"Against the wolves?"

He met her outrage with a calm look. "Or against you. I can't take the chance, Yahzi."

Sadness and regret filled her…sadness for Luke and all he'd held inside for so long…regret that she'd been so wrong about Gavin, about Brad.

About everything.

"Luke, please, let's go home." She reached out to put her hand on his arm, but he stiffened. She turned, following his glare, and saw Sikis again, standing at the edge of the woods.

With a swift motion, Luke brought his gun up, took aim….

Taylor lunged at him. *"No!"*

With a muttered exclamation, he moved to dodge her, but she hit him broadside. His gun went flying, and he grabbed at her but couldn't get a solid footing on the loose gravel. Neither, for that matter, could Taylor. Before she could catch her balance, they both were scrambling, slipping…and then they were airborne.

She heard Luke cry out, thought she heard her name…but something struck her temple a fierce blow. Light exploded in her head, and then there was nothing.

Someone was groaning. Taylor could hear the sound, but she couldn't see anyone. Or anything, for that matter. But the sound was growing louder.

"Ohhh…" Awareness flooded her, and with it came pain. Incredible pain. Her head throbbed like it was going to explode, and her arm was on fire. Then there was her leg—she didn't even want to think about her leg.

"God, I think I blew it." She glanced around and realized she was behind the rocky hill she and Luke had been standing on. They'd fallen.

Luke?

She turned her pounding head and saw him laying motionless a few feet away. He was unconscious. "Okay, make that, I *know* I blew it."

She grasped her injured arm with her good hand and pulled it onto her chest, gritting her teeth. Oh yeah. It was broken all right. As for her leg, she wasn't sure what was wrong with it, but she wasn't going to be standing up anytime soon.

They were stuck until Luke came to. Or someone found them.

Taylor stared at the sky. Normally she'd be praying like crazy, asking God to help her, to save her. But she wasn't doing that. Wasn't going to.

Because she knew everything was going to work out.

There was no fear, no worry. She felt nothing but a strong certainty that God was at work on her behalf. As he had been all of her life. Tears of wonder stung her eyes. God had finally helped her to see.

All this time she'd been telling God she couldn't trust Josh, or Gavin, or Brad, or Connor, or anyone. Not even God himself. All this time she'd figured the problem was with them. With everyone else. But it wasn't.

The problem was with her. Within her. She hadn't been willing to let go, to trust things she couldn't see, couldn't understand. Everything had to be proven, had to make sense. But that wasn't faith. That was leaning on herself.

"Father, I'm sorry." Tears rolled down her face, making a soggy patch in the dry ground beside her throbbing head. "I thought I knew what to do. Thought I was right about Gavin. Thought I could handle Luke. But I was wrong." She looked back up at the sky, regret heavy on her heart. "And I have a feeling I was wrong about Connor, too, wasn't I?"

"I have loved you with an everlasting love."

"I know, Lord. You've never let me down. When Josh died, you were there. When I thought Connor had betrayed me, you were there. I've probably jumped to conclusions again. You gave me my family and Gavin. You brought Connor into my life. And the wolf. And then Brad." She sniffed, overwhelmed at the enormity of God's care for her. "Even now, Lord, you're with me." She looked up at the hill, studied the fall they'd taken, the rocks where they'd landed. She gave a slightly hysterical laugh. "You kept us alive. Wounded, but alive. Forgive me, Lord. Forgive me for not trusting you. Again."

"Ask, and it will be given you."

The assurance floated through her, and a smile lifted her lips. She had asked, and God had forgiven her.

"Seek, and you will find."

Her smile broadened. Connor. Her family. When they realized she was missing, they would come looking for her. And they would find her and Luke. She knew it. She didn't need to be worried. She was in good hands.

"Do you see her?"

Connor didn't answer Brad's frantic question. He was too busy running up the incline to the edge of Reunion. He reached the top and peered into the valley. His breath whooshed out in disappointment.

"She's not there."

"Maybe she's in the tent."

Connor wished he believed it, but he didn't. "I don't think so…"

Suddenly something caught his attention—a sound, floating on the wind. A mournful, sad, haunting sound.

He looked up sharply, straining his ears. "Do you hear that?"

"Howling. A wolf is howling."

They stared at each other for a moment, listening. "It's coming from the opposite side of the valley," Connor said, and he raced down the hill, not even pausing to see if Brad followed. He pounded around the rocky structure, but when he reached the other side, there was no sign of Taylor. Just the woods, and the dry ground, and a steep, rocky hill.

"Over there!" Brad pointed at the hill. "I think it's coming from over there."

Connor ran, his heart pounding in his chest. If anything had happened to her, if he'd lost her...

No! He wouldn't even allow the thought to form.

The howls grew louder as he and Brad drew closer to the hill. There was no doubting it now. The wolf was behind the hill. Connor grabbed Brad's arm, pulling him to a halt. "Hold it. I want you to stay here."

"No."

"Brad, I don't have time to argue—"

"Then don't." With that he ran around the base of the hill.

Connor followed quickly, then stopped and stared.

Sikis lay on the ground, his head tilted to the sky, howls flowing from his throat. As the last note died on the breeze, the wolf directed his amber eyes at Connor. For a heartbeat he lay unmoving, then jumped up and trotted to a safe distance, watching intently.

That was when Connor saw Taylor, lying motionless on the ground. The wolf had been leaning up against her, covering her.

"Father…" He sprang forward and was beside her in an instant. "Oh, Jesus, please…"

He saw another someone sitting a few feet away from Taylor, his back against the large rock.

"Luke?"

The man watched Connor and Brad approach, his expression filled with pain…and something else. Sorrow?

"She's alive," Luke said to Connor as he knelt beside Taylor, and Brad moved to Luke's side.

"What happened?" Gently he ran his hands over her, checking for injuries.

"Luke's leg is busted. Bad." Connor nodded at this news. Taylor hadn't fared much better. Her swollen forearm told its own story, as did the tear in her jeans and the bruise he could see forming on her shin. Her forehead was badly bruised as well.

"It was my fault." Luke's words were soft.

A towering rage swept over Connor, so potent that he felt dizzy. He fixed the older man with a glare.

"Care to explain that?"

Brad put a restraining hand on Connor's shoulder. "This isn't the time or place. We need to get Luke and Taylor back to the ranch. And get the doctor in to patch them up. You can sort through the details later."

Connor held Luke's gaze. "Count on it."

Luke gave a short, curt nod.

"Con?"

He looked down at Taylor, relief flooding him. She was conscious, and the look she gave him was one of pure calm and contentment.

"Hi there." She tried to smile.

"Hi," he croaked.

"I'm ready to go home now," she told him, and he uttered a short laugh.

"Okay. I think that can be arranged."

Her eyes traveled past him to Brad, then came to rest on Luke. "I'm sorry."

Connor frowned and looked at Luke, then stared in amazement. The man was crying.

Luke shook his head. "I was wrong." His voice was hoarse, broken.

"You two can tell us all about it after we get you home." Brad looked from Taylor to Luke with concerned eyes.

Her light laugh was like music in Connor's ears. "It's okay, Brad. I'm not delirious." Her gaze came back to rest on Connor's face. "Well, no more so than any woman who's madly in love, anyway."

Connor stared at her, torn between the desire to laugh and his urge to slip his arms around her and crush her to his chest. "You're a nut."

The slow smile that eased across her face made his pulse pound. "Well, of course. I'd have to be to fall in love with you."

Stay focused, Alexander. Now is no time to get all weak-kneed! "Taylor, it's going to hurt like crazy when we move you." He touched her scratched face with his fingers. "I'll do my best to be careful."

"It's okay." Her eyes were shining with a light he'd never seen in them before. "I trust you."

When Taylor opened her eyes, she had to blink to bring things into focus. One glance told her she was in her room, tucked safely in her bed. She moved and grimaced at the resulting pain. Looking down, she saw she had a cast on her left arm.

She turned her head, and her eyes widened.

Luke.

He was sitting in a chair, staring out the window, his face drawn and haggard.

She said his name, but it came out in a dry, raspy whisper. He turned quickly, saw she was awake, and grabbed a pair of crutches. Hobbling over, he came to balance on the edge of the bed. She reached out and took his hand.

He pressed her palm to his heart. "Yahzi, forgive me."

She started to nod, then stopped abruptly when fireworks went off in her head. "Are you all right?" She glanced at the cast on his leg.

"I will be." His hand tightened on hers. "The wolf—" He stopped, looked away, then tried again. "I thought I was doing the right thing. Thought I was protecting you. I thought you were deceived, that your heart was too tender, that you'd taken in a pack of monsters."

"Luke—"

"No, child. Let me finish." His face was filled with remorse. "We both were knocked unconscious when we fell."

"I suppose landing on rocks will do that."

He smiled at that, and she squeezed his hand as he continued.

"When I came to, I saw you were hurt. I tried to move, to go to you, but I couldn't. The pain was so bad, I passed out twice just sitting up. The last time I came to…"

She waited, watching the emotions in his features.

He cleared his throat. "The last time I came to, I saw the wolf. He was standing over you. I didn't have my gun…couldn't protect you…" He closed his eyes, and she could see how awful that had been for him. When he spoke again, his voice was low and hoarse. "But he wasn't there to harm you. He was protecting you." He opened his eyes, and there was a stark awareness there as he met her gaze. "He *protected* you, Yahzi. He lay down beside you, stretching out as though to keep you warm. And then he began to howl. I thought I would go mad with the sound…."

Taylor's mouth fell open. "That's how Connor and Brad found us."

Luke nodded. "The wolf led them to us. And when they came, he stood and walked away. As though his mission was over." He stroked her face gently. "I was wrong, child. Wrong in so many ways. Can you forgive me?"

Tears held her mute for a moment, so she placed her hand over his where it rested on her cheek.

They sat that way, in silence, until Taylor drifted off to sleep.

THIRTY

"Taylor Moira, you're an amazing and courageous woman."

Taylor looked at her brother and laughed. "So I'm amazing and courageous, am I?"

His grin was impish. "Either that or you're—"

"Plumb daft. I know. Seems to me we've been through this before. So what have I done now?"

Ryan leaned back in his chair, plopping his booted feet on Taylor's kitchen table. "Well, you agreed to marry Connor, which takes an incredible amount of courage right th—"

The rest of his sentence was cut off when he received a sharp smack to the back of his head. Ryan spun around to find Connor standing behind him.

"For crying out loud." Ryan rubbed his head. "You're already acting like a member of the family."

"I've always been a bit of an overachiever," Connor replied smugly as he moved to wrap his arms around Taylor, cast on her arm and all. "That's why I'm marrying the most beautiful, most intelligent, most wonderful—"

"Puh-leeze!" Ryan crossed his eyes in disgust.

"—woman in the world," Connor finished, and Taylor smiled up at him demurely.

"See?" she told Ryan. "I told you he was brilliant."

"You two are pitiful."

"Yup," Connor agreed. "So, you guys ready to go?"

"All set." Ryan dropped his feet on the floor with a thud. "Mom and Dad and Lisa and the boys are outside." He grinned, wagging his eyebrows. "Let's go howl with the wild ones."

The sun was just setting as Connor drove up to a line of trees and put it into park.

"Well." His eyes met hers, filling her with warmth. "The moment of truth."

They got out, then went to stand beside her family and Luke.

"Wow!" Mark stared in wonder at the line of cars coming behind them. "There's a zillion cars there!"

"Maybe even a trillion zillion!" Mikey's face shone. "And they're all coming to see your wolves, Aunt Taylor."

"God's wolves," she corrected him gently. "They belong to God, not me."

Mark cast a quick glance at the cars again. "Yeah, well I hope God told his wolves to show up tonight."

"Me, too," Taylor said, laughing. "Me, too."

"There aren't exactly a *zillion* cars." Connor shook

his head in amazement. "But there are sure a lot more than I expected."

"Looks like about fifteen or twenty all together," Luke said. "I guess they're wanting to learn about these animals as much as the rest of us."

Taylor smiled at him, grateful he was still with them, still a part of their lives. The change in him had been dramatic. Luke had helped them in every facet of working with the wolves. He'd become invaluable to Connor during the education and management process. It was as though he'd traded one passion—his hatred for the wolves—for another—understanding them.

"Well, I hope everyone fits in the clearing." Ryan walked toward a group of ten or so people who were gathered in a circle, chattering excitedly. "This way, folks." They turned to follow him to the newly created path that led into the woods.

"I sure hope Sikis and the gang decide to cooperate tonight." Taylor watched as more cars pulled up.

"They howled last night, so the chances are good that they're still in the area. But even if they aren't, Brad's got a great program set up to show everyone." Connor wrapped his arm around Taylor's shoulders and squeezed.

"Thanks in large part to the slides made from your pictures," Taylor's mom said with a proud smile.

Taylor slipped her arm around his waist, looking up at him with eyes that also shone with pride. "They are wonderful photos, Con."

He smiled. "I had some wonderful subjects. By the way, Harry sends his regrets, but he couldn't make it on such short notice."

"That's too bad, especially since this public howl was his idea," Taylor's father said.

"Aye, but it was our hard work that brought it to life," commented a deep voice from behind them.

They all turned to greet Gavin.

"I wasn't sure you were going to get here on time."

At Taylor's scolding, he gave her a peck on the cheek. "I wouldn't miss it. Not after all the effort we put into this."

The details for the howl actually had been worked out fairly quickly. Connor and Brad had set up a "howling area" about a quarter mile from Reunion, in a clearing in the woods, and Luke and the Camus clan had prepared flyers to post. Gavin had taken charge of contacting local resorts to let them know what they were planning. Then there was nothing left to do but wait.

Finally, one warm evening in June, they heard the wolves howling. The next day the posters were put up and anyone who'd agreed to advertise was notified.

Public Wolf Howl! the signs proclaimed, directing anyone who was interested to meet at Galloway Glen.

"Well, I'd say our work has paid off." Connor reached out to shake hands with Gavin.

"And so it should." Gavin grinned at them.

Connor's strong arm encircled Taylor's shoulders

again, and she leaned against him happily. "Well, looks as though we're going to be the stragglers," he said. Taylor followed his gaze to where the last few visitors were hurrying down the path.

"Let's go see if your friends will honor us with their presence." Gavin led the way.

They reached the clearing and joined the group crowded onto the log benches. Over fifty people listened with avid interest as Brad explained the history of wolves and their interaction with mankind. In the growing darkness, the slides of Sikis and his pack projected onto a large screen in front of the group almost seemed to come to life. Then Brad brought out a beautiful, light gray pelt. With sadness in his eyes and voice, he told Nokomis's story.

"There are those who consider wolves one of mankind's greatest enemies." Brad handed the pelt to a somber-faced woman. "I tend to think ignorance is far more dangerous. Nokomis was a creature of great beauty and grace, and her legacy will live on in her pups."

"What happened to them?" The woman brushed tears from her eyes.

Brad's smile was broad. "They're being raised by a biologist."

"Tell me they're not going to a zoo!" a man groaned from the back, and Brad joined the group's laughter. "Not at all. They'll be brought back here and reintro-duced to the pack next month. And with any luck, in a few years they'll be having pups of their own." Brad glanced at Connor. "Now it's time for what you've all been waiting for."

Connor came forward to explain how to imitate the wolves' howls. "Keep in mind that they change pitch several times in one howl, and they don't howl on the same note. If you want to sound like a wolf, forget everything you learned in choir." Chuckles met this instruction. "Discord is the name of the game. I'll start out. If the wolves respond, you're welcome to join in, a few at a time. Remember, there are quite a few of us here, so be sure to give everyone a chance."

A hush fell over the clearing as Connor turned to face Reunion, cupped his hands to his mouth, exhaled twice, then leaned back and howled. Whispers swept through the crowd, and a few young girls giggled in nervous excitement. Taylor felt a wave of joy as she watched Connor give a second howl, his voice lifting in a haunting imitation of Sikis and his pack.

Please, let them hear the wolves' song…the song you gave them.

Shivers raced up and down her spine when a lone wolf responded, lifting his voice in a rich and sonorous cry, filled with unutterable longing. Quick tears sprang to Taylor's eyes as a second wolf voice joined the first, and the wondrous music of nature filled the air around them.

Connor turned, his gaze seeking and finding her

even in the darkness. She moved forward to stand beside him, grinning as she watched Brad help a young boy with his enthusiastic howl. Others joined in—some cautious, some joyous—and Taylor was moved by the eagerness she saw in their faces.

The sounds rose and soared through the night, rising and falling, echoing over and over, incredibly wild. Incredibly beautiful.

"I think the whole pack is there," she whispered.

"They're playing our song." Connor pressed a gentle kiss to her lips.

"A song of reunion." Happiness filled her heart. "To celebrate their return to Wyoming."

"And your return to me." He reached out to tuck her against his side.

Taylor snuggled close, exhaling a long breath, and looking at her parents, who now stood beside her. When her gaze met her mother's, a warm glow of pure joy flowed through her.

"'I sought the Lord, and he answered me,'" Taylor whispered.

"'He delivered me from all my fears,'" her mother went on in a low voice, her eyes shining.

"'The angel of the Lord encamps around those who fear him, and he delivers them,'" her father added softly.

"'Taste and see that the Lord is good'"—they turned in surprise to stare at Connor, and his smile broadened as they finished together in quiet chorus—"'blessed is the man who takes refuge in him. Fear the Lord, you his saints, for those who fear him lack nothing.'"

"Amen," Taylor breathed. Then she turned her face to the sky and let the songs of the night and the wonder of Reunion wash over her.

Amen.

Dear Reader,

There's a lot I could say, about the wolves, about writing, about the wondrous adventure of faith. But first I want to thank you for sharing your time with me, and Taylor, and Connor, and the wolves. Writing this book was an adventure and a blessing. I hope reading it was as well.

Reunion is a microcosm of the loves in my life: animals, writing, the Lord, and my family. As a minister's daughter, I grew up in a household filled with laughter, nurture, and day-to-day examples of following Christ. And I found that it's okay to be an individual, to step outside of the molds and find out who God created you to be. Well, who He created me to be is someone who loves Him, who loves my family, and who loves animals. Wild, domesticated, big or small, it doesn't matter. There's something about animals that gets to me, deep inside. My parents, God bless them, nurtured that part of who I am with tolerance and wisdom. They endured years of me bringing home creeping, crawling, and slithering things to be nurtured and enjoyed. And then, when I decided I wanted to be a writer, they encouraged me in that insanity as well. Which is why this book is dedicated to them. I am who I am because of their love and nurture. So when the opportunity came for me to write a book, it only made sense to focus on animals and family and True Love.

If there's any message I'd like you to get from *Reunion*, it's that life is precious, love is a gift, and there's a world of delights around us every day. All we need to do is open ourselves to the wonders God has for us and find out who He made us to be.

Here's to you, then. May God delight you today.

Karen M. Ball

Write to Karen Ball:
c/o Palisades
Multnomah Publishers, Inc.
P.O. Box 1720
Sisters, OR 97759

Sara's terrified. She's falling in love with former
pro football player Adam Black—and it could
cost Sara her life. She's hiding from the man
who kidnapped her years ago, a man who's still
trying to find her and finish her off. Soon Sara
and Adam are caught in a web that brings Sara
face-to-face with terror—and with the knowledge
that only God can save her.

Available at a bookstore near you.
ISBN 1-57673-577-X

THE SUMMER STORM LIT UP THE NIGHT SKY IN A JAGGED DIS-play of energy, lightning bouncing, streaking, fragmenting between towering thunderheads. Sara Walsh ignored the storm as best she could, determined not to let it interrupt her train of thought. The desk lamp as well as the overhead light were on in her office as she tried to prevent any shadows from forming. What she was writing was disturbing enough.

The six-year-old boy had been found. Dead.

Writing longhand on a yellow legal pad of paper, she shaped the twenty-ninth chapter of her mystery novel. Despite the dark specificity of the scene, the flow of words never faltered.

The child had died within hours of his abduction. His family, the Oklahoma law enforcement community, even his kidnapper, did not realize it. Sara did not pull back from writing the scene even though she knew it would leave a bitter taste of defeat in the mind of the reader. The impact was necessary for the rest of the book.

She frowned, crossed out the last sentence, added a new detail, then went on with her description of the farmer who had found the boy.

Thunder cracked directly overhead. Sara flinched. Her office suite on the thirty-fourth floor put her close enough to the storm she could hear the air sizzle in the split second before the boom. She would like to be in the basement parking garage right now instead of her office.

She had been writing since eight that morning. A

glance at the clock on her desk showed it was almost eight in the evening. The push to finish a story always took over as she reached the final chapters. This tenth book was no exception.

Twelve hours. No wonder her back muscles were stiff. She had taken a brief break for lunch while she reviewed the mail Judy had prioritized for her. The rest of her day had been spent working on the book. She arched her back and rubbed at the knot.

This was the most difficult chapter in the book to write. It was better to get it done in one long, sustained effort. Death always squeezed her heart.

Had her brother been in town, he would have insisted she wrap it up and come home. Her life was restricted enough as it was. He refused to let her spend all her time at the office. He would come lean against the doorjamb of her office and give her that *look* along with his predictable lecture telling her all she should be doing: Putter around the house, cook, mess with the roses, do something other than sit behind that desk.

Sara smiled. She did so enjoy taking advantage of Dave's occasional absences.

Dave's flight back to Chicago from the FBI academy at Quantico had been delayed due to the storm front. When he had called her from the airport, he had cautioned her he might not be home until eleven.

It wasn't a problem, she had assured him, everything was fine. Code words. Spoken every day. So much a part of their language now that she spoke them instinctively. "Everything is fine"—all clear; "I'm fine"—I've got company; "I'm doing fine"—I'm in danger. She had lived the dance a long time. The tight security around her life was necessary. It was overpowering, obnoxious, annoying...and comforting.

Sara turned in the black leather chair and looked at the display of lightning. The rain ran down the panes of thick glass. The skyline of downtown Chicago glimmered back at her through the rain.

With every book, another fact, another detail, another intense emotion, broke through from her own past. She could literally feel the dry dirt under her hand, feel the oppressive darkness. Reliving what had happened to her twenty-five years ago was terrifying. Necessary, but terrifying.

She sat lost in thought for several minutes, idly walking her pen through her fingers. Her adversary was out there somewhere, still alive, still hunting her. Had he made the association to Chicago yet? After all these years, she was still constantly moving, still working to stay one step ahead of the threat. Her family knew only too well his threat was real.

The man would kill her. Had long ago killed her sister. The threat didn't get more basic than that. She had to trust others and ultimately God for her security. There were days her faith wavered under the intense weight of simply enduring that stress. She was learning, slowly, by necessity, how to roll with events, to trust God's ultimate sovereignty.

The notepad beside her was filled with doodled sketches of faces. One of these days her mind was finally going to stop blocking the one image she longed to sketch. She knew she had seen the man. Whatever the cost, whatever the consequences of trying to remember, they were worth paying in order to try to bring justice for her and her sister.

Sara let out a frustrated sigh. She couldn't force the image to appear no matter how much she longed to do so. She was the only one who still believed it was possible for her to remember it. The police, the FBI, the doctors, had given up hope years ago.

She fingered a worn photo of her sister Kim that sat by a white rose on her desk. She didn't care what the others thought. Until the killer was caught, she would never give up hope.

God was just. She held on to that knowledge and the hope that the day of justice would eventually arrive. Until it did, she carried a guilt inside that remained wrapped around her heart. In losing her twin she had literally lost part of herself.

Turning her attention back to her desk, she debated for a moment if she wanted to do any more work that night. She didn't.

When it had begun to rain, she had turned off her computer, not willing to risk possible damage from a building electrical surge should lightning hit a transformer or even the building itself; something that happened with some frequency during such severe storms.

As she put her folder away, the framed picture on the corner of her desk caught her attention; it evoked a smile. Her best friend was getting married. Sara was happy for her, but also envious. The need to break free of the security blanket rose and fell with time. She could feel the sense of rebellion rising again. Ellen had freedom and a life. She was getting married to a wonderful man. Sara longed to one day have that same choice. Without freedom, it wasn't possible, and that reality hurt. A dream was being sacrificed with every passing day.

As she stepped into the outer office, the room lights automatically turned on. Sara reached back and turned off the interior office lights.

Her suite was in the east tower of the business complex. Rising forty-five stories, the two recently built towers added to the already impressive downtown skyline. Sara liked the modern building and the shopping available on the ground floor. She struggled with the elevator ride to the thirty-fourth floor each day, for she did not like closed-in spaces, but she considered the view worth the price.

The elevator that responded tonight came from two floors below. There were two connecting walkways between the east and west towers, one on the sixth floor and another in the lobby. She chose the sixth floor concourse tonight, walking through it to the west tower with a confident but fast pace.

She was alone in the wide corridor. Travis sometimes accompanied her, but she had waved off his company tonight and told him to go get dinner. If she needed him, she would page him.

The click of her heels echoed off the marble floor. There was parking under each tower, but if she parked under the tower where she worked, she would be forced to pull out onto a one-way street no matter which exit she took. It was a pattern someone could observe and predict. Changing her route and time of day across one of the two corridors was a better compromise. She could hopefully see the danger coming.

Adam Black dropped the pen he held onto the white legal pad of paper and got up to walk over to the window, watching the lightning storm flare around the building. He felt like that inside. Storming, churning.

He had lost more than his dad—he had lost his confidant, his best friend. Trying to cope with the grief by drowning himself in work was only adding to the turmoil.

The passage in Mark chapter 4 of the storm-tossed sea and Jesus asleep in the boat crossed his mind and drew a smile. What had Jesus said? "Why are you afraid? Have you still no faith?" Appropriate for tonight.

He rubbed the back of his neck. All of his current exclusive commercial contracts expired in three months time. A feeding frenzy was forming—which ones would he be willing to renew, which new ones would he consider, what kind of money would it cost for people to get exclusive use of his name and image?

The tentative dollar figures being passed by his brother-in-law Jordan were astronomical in size.

The stack of proposals had been winnowed down, but the remaining pile still threatened to slide onto the floor.

All he needed to do was make a decision.

He couldn't remember needing God's guidance more than he did now.

Five years of his life. The decisions he made would set his schedule for the next five years of his life.

Was it that he didn't want to make a decision or that he didn't want to be tied down?

Adam knew the root of the problem had little to do with the work and everything to do with the state of his life. Grief marred his focus, certainly. It was hard to define what he wanted to accomplish. But he was also restless. He had been doing basically the same thing for three years: keeping his image in the public eye and building his business. It had become routine. He hated routine.

His dad would have laughed and told him when the work stopped being fun, it was time to find a new line of work.

They'd had eight days together between the first heart attack and his death. Eight good days despite the pain—Adam sitting at his dad's hospital bedside and talking about everything under the sun. They had both known that time was short.

"I'll be walking in glory soon, son," his dad would

quip as they ended each evening, never knowing if it would be the last visit. And Adam would squeeze his hand and reply, "When you get there, you can just save me a seat."

"I'll save two," his dad would reply with a twinkle in his eye that would make Adam laugh.

It was time to go home. Time to feed his dog, if not himself.

Sara decided to take the elevator down to the west tower parking garage rather than walk the six flights. She would have preferred the stairs, but she could grit her teeth for a few flights to save time. She pushed the button to go down and watched the four elevators to see which would respond first. The one to her left, coming down from the tenth floor.

When it stopped, she reached inside, pushed the garage-floor parking button, but did not step inside. Tonight she would take the second elevator.

Sara shifted her raincoat over her arm and moved her briefcase to her other hand. The elevator stopped and the doors slid open.

A man was in the elevator.

She froze.

He was leaning against the back of the elevator, looking like he had put in a long day at work, a briefcase in one hand and a sports magazine in the other, his blue eyes gazing back at her. She saw a brief look of admiration in his eyes.

Get in and take a risk, step back and take a risk.

She knew him. Adam Black. His face was as familiar as any sports figure in the country, even if he'd been out of the game of football for three years. His commercial endorsements and charity work had continued without pause.

Adam Black worked in this building? This was a nightmare come true. She saw photographs of him constantly in magazines, local newspapers, and occasionally on television. The last thing she needed was to be near someone who attracted media attention.

She hesitated, then stepped in, her hand tightening her hold on the briefcase handle. A glance at the board of lights showed he had already selected the parking garage.

"Working late tonight?" His voice was low, a trace of a northeastern accent still present, his smile a pleasant one.

Her answer was a noncommittal nod.

The elevator began to silently descend.

She had spent too much time in European finishing schools to slouch. Her posture was straight, her spine relaxed, even if she was nervous. She hated elevators. She should have taken the stairs.

"Quite a storm out there tonight."

The heels of her patent leather shoes sank into the

jade carpet as she shifted her weight from one foot to the other. "Yes."

Three more floors to go.

There was a slight flicker to the lights and then the elevator jolted to a halt.

"What?" Sara felt adrenaline flicker in her system like the lights.

He pushed away from the back wall. "A lightning hit must have blown a circuit."

The next second, the elevator went black.

Ten seconds clicked by. Twenty. Sara's adrenaline put her heart rate at close to two hundred. Pitch black. Closed space.

Lord, no. It's dark. Get me out of this box!

"How long before they fix it?" She did her best to keep her words level and steady. She had spent years learning control, but this was beyond something she could control.

"It may take a few minutes, but they will find the circuit breaker and the elevator will be moving again."

Sounds amplified in the closed space as he moved. He set down his briefcase? She couldn't remember if there was a phone in the elevator panel or not. How could she have ridden in these elevators for three months and not looked for something so simple?

"No phone, and what I think is the emergency pull button seems to have no effect."

Sara tried to slow down her heart rate by breathing deeply. Her cellular phone would not work inside this elevator, nor her signaling beeper.

"You're very quiet," he said eventually.

"I want out of here," she replied slowly so as to hide the fact her teeth were trying to chatter.

"There's nothing to be afraid of."

She wanted to reply, "You've never been locked in a pitch-black root cellar and left to die before," but the memories and the panic were already overwhelming her. Her coping skills were scattering to the four winds right when she needed them most. She could do this. Somehow. She had no choice. Her hand clenched in the darkness, nails digging into her palm. It was only darkness. It wasn't dangerous.

"Consider it from my viewpoint. I'm stuck in the dark with a beautiful woman. There could be worse fates."

She barely heard him. *Lord, why tonight? Please, not this.* The darkness was so bad she could feel the nausea building.

"Sorry, I didn't mean any offense with that remark."

She couldn't have answered if she wanted to. One thought held her focus fast: surviving. The memory verse she had taken such delight in that morning had scattered. Psalm 23 was a tangle. The moment she needed clarity, her mind was determined to retreat into the past instead. A cold sweat froze her hands. Not here. Not with someone else present. To suffer through a flashback when her brother was around was difficult enough. To do it with a stranger would be horrible.

Adam Black didn't understand the silence. The lady had apparently frozen in one position. "Listen, maybe it would help if we got introduced. I'm Adam Black. And you are...?"

Silence. Then a quiet, "Sara."

"Hi, Sara." He reached out a hand wondering why she was so tense. No nervous laughter, no chatter, just frozen stiffness. "Listen, since it looks like this might actually take some time, why don't we try sitting down." His hand touched hers.

She jerked back and he flinched. Her hand was like ice. This lady was not tense, she was terrified.

He instantly reviewed what he had with him. Nothing of much use. His sports coat was in his car, his team jacket still upstairs in his office. What had she been wearing when she stepped into the elevator? An elegant blue-and-white dress, that had caught his attention immediately, but there had been more...a taupe-colored coat over her arm.

First get her warm, then get her calm.

"Sara, it will be okay. Sit down, let's get you warm." He touched her hand again, grasping it in his so he could turn her toward him. Cold. Stiff.

"I'm...afraid of the dark."

No kidding.

He had to peel her fingers away from her briefcase handle. "You're safe, Sara. The elevator is not going to fall or anything like that. The lights will come back on soon."

"I know."

He could feel her fighting the hysteria. The tremors coming through her hands were growing stronger. He didn't have to be able to see her to know she was heading for deep shock. "You're safe. I'm not going anywhere. And I'm no threat to you," he added, already wondering what would make a grown woman petrified of the dark. The possibilities that came to mind all made him feel sick.

"I know that, too."

He carefully guided her down to sit with her back leaning against the elevator wall. He spread her coat out over her and was thankful when she took over and did most of it herself, tucking it up around her shoulders, burying her hands into the soft warmth of the fabric.

"Better?"

"Much."

He couldn't prevent a smile. "Don't have much practice lying, do you?"

"It sounds better than admitting I'm about to throw up across your shoes." There was almost the sound of an answering smile in her reply.

He sat down carefully, close enough so he could reach her if necessary but far enough away so she hopefully wouldn't feel any more cornered than she already did.

"Try leaning your head back and taking a few deep breaths."

"How long has it been?" she asked a few moments later.

"Maybe four, five minutes."

"That's all?"

Adam desperately wished for matches, a lighter, anything to break this blackness for her. "We'll pass the time talking about something and the time will go by in an instant, you'll see. What would you like to talk about first, do you have a preference?"

Silence.

"Sara. Come on, work with me here."

He was reaching out to shake her shoulder when she suddenly said through teeth that were obviously chattering, "Sports. Why did you retire?"

Adam didn't talk about the details of that decision with many people, but in the present circumstances, she could have asked him practically anything and he wouldn't have minded.

"Did you see the Super Bowl we won?"

"Of course. Half this town hated you for months afterward."

He didn't have to wonder if that was a smile.

"I liked the feeling of winning. But I was tired. Too tired to do it again. It wasn't just the physical exhaustion of those last games, but the emotional drain of carrying the expectations of so many people. So I decided it was time to let the next guy in line have a chance."

"You got tired."

"I got tired," he confirmed.

"I bet you were tired the season before when you

lost the Super Bowl to the Vikings."

"I was."

"Your retirement had nothing to do with being tired." She sounded quite certain about it. Her voice was also growing more steady. "You won that Super Bowl ring to prove you were capable of winning it; then you retired because the challenge was gone. You didn't play another season because you would have been bored, not tired."

"You sound quite certain about that theory."

"Maybe because I know I'm right. You're like your father. 'Do It Once—Right—Then Move On.' Wasn't that the motto he lived his life by?"

Adam's shoulder muscles tensed. "Where did you hear that?"

"You had it inscribed on his tombstone," was the gentle reply. "Sorry, I didn't mean to touch a nerve."

Adam didn't answer. When and why had this lady been to the cemetery where his father was buried? It was outside of the city quite a distance and it was an old cemetery where most plots had been bought ahead for several generations. That inscription had not been added until almost a month after the burial.

She was a reporter. The realization settled like a rock in his gut. She had executed this meeting perfectly. Setting up this "chance" encounter, paying off a building maintenance worker to throw a switch for her, giving him every reason to believe he was going to be playing

371

the hero, keeping her calm while the lights were out. He had been buying the entire scenario, hook, line, and sinker.

"I like the quote and the philosophy of life it contains."

"Sara, could we cut the facade? What do you want? You're a writer, aren't you?"

Silence met his anger.

"What kind of writer would you like me to admit to being?" The ice in her voice was unmistakable.

"Just signal for this elevator to start moving again and I'll consider not throttling you."

"You think I caused this?"

"Not going to try denying you're a writer?"

"I don't have much practice lying," she replied tersely, echoing his earlier words.

"Great. Then I would say we are at an impasse, wouldn't you?" He waited for a response but didn't get one. "When you get tired of sitting in the dark, just signal your cohorts that we are done talking and we'll go our separate ways. Until then, I have nothing else to say to you."

"That's fine with me."

And with that, there was nothing between them but a long, cold silence.

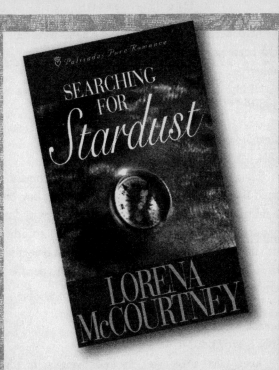

Jan and Mark, divorced years earlier, are thrown together in a quest to discover the truth about their son's death. As Jan and Mark search for a woman who may be carrying their grandchild, neither can deny that long-buried feelings of love between them are being rekindled. But can Jan believe that Mark's newfound faith has made him a new man?

♛ *Palisades Pure Romance*

Be sure not to miss these earlier releases!

Island Breeze, Lynn Bulock
ISBN 1-57673-398-X

Ex-cop Cody North has a full life as proprietor of Island Breeze condos and as father of a teenage boy. Bree Trehearn is on the run, needing to get as far away from rural Indiana as possible. It doesn't take long for Cody to wish that she had stayed in Indiana, but then Bree disappears. It takes all of Cody's police skills and his newfound faith to find her.

Summit, Karen Rispin
ISBN 1-57673-402-1

Julie Miller's a risk taker. She loves living on the edge, savoring the beauty and majesty—and the challenge—of God's creation. Nothing brings all of that together like rock climbing. Her career as a rock-climbing guide is ascending smoothly until David Hales, an internationally recognized rock climber, shows up and gets all her jobs. Which angers Julie almost as much as the fact she can't stop thinking about the man. Then Julie uncovers a sinister plot that puts both their lives in danger. Only by trusting each other—and God—will they survive the dangers that await them.

Hi Honey, I'm Home, Linda Windsor
ISBN 1-57673-556-7

Instead of finding her party guests at her front door, Kathryn Sinclair finds herself face-to-face with her supposedly deceased husband! An obsessive journalist who put his job before everything else, Nick Egan was reportedly killed in a terrorist attack over six years ago. But now he stands there, as impressive as ever, ready to take up where they left off. Well, Kathryn isn't interested! But Nick and their precocious boys have other ideas. They're determined to prove to Kate that God has truly changed Nick's heart—no matter what it takes.